Black Cyclists

SPORT AND SOCIETY

Series Editors
Aram Goudsouzian
Jaime Schultz

Founding Editors
Benjamin G. Rader
Randy Roberts

*For a list of books in the series, please see our website
at www.press.uillinois.edu.*

Black Cyclists

The Race for Inclusion

ROBERT J. TURPIN

© 2024 by the Board of Trustees
of the University of Illinois
All rights reserved
1 2 3 4 5 C P 5 4 3 2 1
♾ This book is printed on acid-free paper.

Library of Congress Cataloging-in-Publication Data
Names: Turpin, Robert J., author.
Title: Black cyclists : the race for inclusion / Robert J.
   Turpin.
Description: Urbana : University of Illinois Press,
   [2024] | Series: Sport and society | Includes
   bibliographical references and index.
Identifiers: LCCN 2023032830 (print) | LCCN
   2023032831 (ebook) | ISBN 9780252045752 (cloth :
   acid-free paper) | ISBN 9780252087851 (paperback :
   acid-free paper) | ISBN 9780252056611 (ebook)
Subjects: LCSH: African American cyclists—United
   States—Biography. | Cycling—United States—
   History. | Racism in sports—United States. |
   United States—Race relations—History.
Classification: LCC GV1051.A1 T87 2024 (print) | LCC
   GV1051.A1 (ebook) | DDC 796.6/20922 [B]—dc23/
   eng/20230819
LC record available at https://lccn.loc.gov/2023032830
LC ebook record available at https://lccn.loc.gov/
   2023032831

To all Black cyclists; past, present, and future.
And to my family.

Contents

Acknowledgments   ix

Introduction   1

1   From the Outset   11

2   The Mode of Liberation   22

3   Drawing the Color Line   39

4   In Response to the Color Line   60

5   The New Woman   77

6   Six Days in a Row   99

7   Going Abroad   120

8   Home Trainers and Vaudeville   138

9   Once Was Lost   157

Epilogue: Born Again   181

Notes   199

Index   225

Acknowledgments

With a project like this, one that takes several years to complete, it feels a little strange to have made it to the point where I get to reflect and acknowledge all the support and assistance I have received along the way. In the process of writing, researching, and preparing materials, I have never had to question how fortunate I am. I am forever thankful for my family who has been there at every step through this process. I am fortunate to have parents and a brother who have always encouraged and pushed me. Of course, with my brother, I mean that both literally and figuratively. My wife and two daughters have provided emotional support and shared in my excitement about various topics connected to this work. My wife is always my first sounding board. Beyond my immediate family, I was reminded of the love and encouragement from all my friends and family when I published my last book. I went back home to do a reading at the county library and family from hours away had made the drive, surprising me so much that I did not know how to thank them at the time. A couple friends that I have had since high school did the same. It is so beneficial to have people who are proud of you and always in your corner. I am lucky to have so many in mine.

This work was also buttressed by a good amount of academic and institutional support. I am lucky to work on the beautiful campus of Lees-McRae

Acknowledgments

College in Banner Elk, North Carolina, and I am fortunate to enjoy the encouragement and advocacy of my campus community. After a few conversations about this project, Todd Lidh encouraged me to apply for a fellowship from the Appalachian College Association. He even wrote a letter of support on my behalf. Evan Friss was also instrumental in strengthening my application materials. I am grateful that, with their help, I was able to secure that fellowship. It funded a one-year sabbatical, giving me time to write a draft of the majority of this book. I am fortunate that there is an organization like the Appalachian College Association out there who understands funding constraints at small, private, four-year liberal arts institutions. Alyson Gill has also been encouraging and always willing to help me find resources to bring this book to fruition. This project has benefitted from several Whalen grants and other professional development grants at Lees-McRae College.

The interest shown by colleagues and fellow academics, including Scott Huffard, Matthew Wimberley, Michael Vines, Jess Bellemer, Ken Craig, Abby Arnold-Patti, Megan Tewell, Katie Wahl, and Joe Spiker, added fuel to my fire. Michael Iauch has been excited about the project from the start, giving me potential avenues of exploration and even helping me edit some of the images. A former student, Liam Flanagan, cyclist extraordinaire, was of great assistance in translating French sources. Of course, there have been several librarians and archivists to help along the way. Jens Arneson at Eastern Kentucky University was invaluable in helping me access newspaper sources, especially the material from Louisville's *Courier-Journal*. Then there were all the others doing random and sometimes seemingly small but amazingly generous things to help. Matt Simpson and Rusty Sohm wandered around cemeteries trying to find and photograph headstones for me. My mother and father-in-law, Tom and Diane, have always been helpful in picking the kids up from school or watching them for a few hours when needed. They also provided some helpful prodding at times, when asking me about the progress of this project. They never seemed to ask when progress had been made, however, so they are probably just as surprised to see the final project as me.

I am thankful for the amazing educators at my daughters' elementary school. The first half of my sabbatical took place as COVID-19 was leading to the death of thousands of people. My mornings were spent listening to and assisting my daughters through virtual learning but because of their wonderful teachers, like Jaime Mains and Morgan Rankin, I could rest

Acknowledgments xi

assured that they were in extremely qualified hands. I was lucky to have "Aunt" Mary around for the second half of the day, as I locked myself in my room to write while she watched the girls. I think knowing I only had four hours a day to concentrate on writing was actually beneficial in some respects, and I was able to complete drafts of several chapters of this book during that year.

I am grateful for people like Oliver "Butch" Martin, Alex Harsley, Joanne Schumpert, Nelson Vails, and Rahsaan Bahati, who took the time to speak with me about subjects that are important to this book. Margaret Guroff and Deb Beckel both read early versions of chapter six and seven, offering valuable feedback and many great suggestions. Danny Nasset and the entire team at the University of Illinois Press have made the whole publication process a positive and pleasurable experience. David Herlihy and others at the International Cycling History Conference were enthusiastic and thoughtful when I presented research. Lorne Shields, who I met at that conference, assisted me by providing images from his amazing private collection of bicycle memorabilia. While I never got to meet Andrew Ritchie, we did exchange some emails and he was always helpful. He was instrumental in another way as well. At the suggestion of my former graduate advisor, Gerald Smith, I read and first learned about "Major" Taylor in the pages of Andrew Ritchie's biography. I was impressed by Taylor's determination but not exactly surprised by the pervasive racism he endured. If anything, I was more surprised by the fact that I had never heard of him. Before pursuing a PhD in history, I was a competitive cyclist who not only raced throughout the southeastern United States, but I was also a devoted fan of the sport. In all those hours spent watching television coverage of various races, reading cycling magazines, race reports, and books about the sport, as well as racing and riding my own bicycle, one thing stuck out—the overwhelming Whiteness of the sport. I became enthralled with the question of how the sport had such an astonishing lack of diversity if one of the most well-known stars of American cycling, in its infancy, was a Black man. This book, my answer to that question, is the culmination of more than ten years spent ruminating on the extraordinary emergence and seeming disappearance of the Black cyclist.

Introduction

In 1899, a twenty-one-year-old from Indianapolis named Marshall "Major" Taylor made history. His grandparents had endured the hardships of slavery and yet, on that day, he would become the first Black athlete from the United States to earn the designation of world champion in any sport and one of the first cyclists from the United States, of any race, to win a world championship. As such, Taylor soon became one of the United States' first international sports superstars, racing across Europe and Australia. He was the most successful and best-known Black cyclist in history. Due to restrictions based on race, however, he was technically the only professional Black cyclist in the United States at the time. He earned significant sums for his talents and retired around ten years after winning the world championship so that he could spend more time with his wife and daughter. Taylor had saved a lot of his winnings, purchased a large home in Worcester, Massachusetts, as well as other investment properties, and raced around the streets in his automobile—the first car in town. He would die a little over twenty years after retirement—in 1932. By that point, at the age of fifty-three, he was poor, alone, and forgotten. His body laid unclaimed, and he was eventually buried in an unmarked pauper's grave near Chicago. It was a tragic demise. Unfortunately, this was a common ending for the Black cyclists of the Progressive Era.

2 *Introduction*

Taylor began racing in the 1890s, when the bicycle was extremely popular, especially among the urban middle class. It was a machine that had been on a steady upward trajectory since the 1860s but its early history in the United States goes back to around 1819. It was in that year that American audiences were invited to see a version that was on public display. That early machine was called the draisine and it was a very crude version, which some historians would argue was technically not a bicycle. Karl von Drais, the German inventor of the machine, even called his creation a laufmaschine, which translates to running machine. Other than having two spoked wheels and the fact that the rider straddled the machine to ride and steer its front wheel, it was missing some of the key components associated with bicycles, like cranks, pedals, and a chain. The rider propelled the draisine by pushing off the ground with their feet. It worked much like the strider type of balance bicycle young children first learn to ride in the modern era, except it was much larger. The draisine was made almost entirely out of wood and iron, so it was relatively heavy, often weighing more than fifty pounds. Given the weight and crude materials, the instances in which the machine could attain significant speed occurred mostly when coasting downhill with both feet off the ground. Even then, the draisine was limited by the lack of brakes. The rider would have to drag their feet to stop it. Still, it held some promise. Enthusiasts went so far as to debate whether it would replace the horse. It would even come to be referred to as the hobbyhorse and the dandy-horse, since it was something of an amusement of the elite classes. The hobbyhorse, or draisine, never really caught on, however, because of its limitations, and therefore, bicycle development remained relatively dormant for around fifty years.

There were some attempts to create an improved machine in the meantime, but it was the mid-1860s before Americans would see and experience the velocipede, an early version of the bicycle that would surpass the draisine in popularity. The velocipede, introduced to Americans by Pierre Lallement, had the quintessential two spoked wheels in tandem but it incorporated cranks and pedals, which were attached to the front wheel. Now the rider could cover massive distances without ever touching the ground, once they learned to maintain their balance. Despite the relatively expensive price, which was around seven to fifteen weeks of wages for the average middle-class worker, the velocipede would soon enjoy a massive following. By 1869, due to demands, some of the more adept makers were producing

Introduction

3

up to fifteen bicycles per day.[1] The historian David Herlihy writes, "the American trade seemed poised to prosper from the seemingly insatiable demand." Clubs and rinks for riding began to pop up all over. Newspapers and magazines were full of articles about the new machine, and it quickly made an impact on other consumer goods. An Indiana newspaper made note of this, proclaiming, "everything new is called 'velocipede.' In walking about town, we notice in a shoe store the 'velocipede' boots for young ladies; at a music store, 'Velocipede' Gallop, and we suppose we shall soon have the 'velocipede' hat, the 'velocipede' necktie, etc., etc."[2] Other evidence of its popularity came from the size of the crowds that would gather to watch those who rode velocipedes. Some of the more popular cycling events in the Northeast experienced crowds as large as 5,000 in attendance at championship races held in larger rinks.[3] Indeed, the velocipede craze swept through many American cities, but it would be short-lived. One drawback came down to comfort. Due to the lack of pneumatic tires or any effective shock-absorbing embellishments, the velocipede became known as the "boneshaker." It was somewhat at home on the large wooden floors in most rinks, but its practicality out on the poorly maintained public roads was more open to debate. For this reason, many riders stuck to the smoother sidewalks, but that practice was soon made illegal in many cities, and so the velocipede was left looking like more of an amusement than a means of transportation.

Another thing holding the velocipede back was its lack of speed. Since the cranks were directly affixed to the front wheel, speed was determined by the revolutions of the cranks and the size of the front wheel. Taller individuals could ride machines with larger front wheels, but wheel diameters were still relatively limited. It would not be until after 1869 when newly invented wire-spoked wheels were popularized that wheels could be larger, stronger, and even lighter.[4] This was around the same time many velocipede rinks were closing in the United States, but the possibilities of larger wheels and therefore faster speeds would usher in the next version of bicycles, a version that would soon eclipse the velocipede. That design would be called the high wheeler and later, the ordinary, after the design became standardized. By the mid-1870s the high wheeler began to amass a considerable following. Often incorporating huge front wheels of around fifty inches or more, depending on the rider, it could maintain speeds of around eighteen miles per hour on flat ground. It was at this point that

4   *Introduction*

the bicycle really cemented itself in the popular imagination as a machine with real possibilities.

The 1870s were an opportune moment for new inventions like the high wheeler. This was a period that has been referred to as the Second Industrial Revolution, or the Technological Revolution. It was in this context then that the bicycle rolled into view as a promise of the future. It was a technological marvel in and of itself. To own and ride a bicycle demonstrated your own mastery over that new technology and from that, much more could be deduced. Riding a bicycle also said something about your social stature, health, gender, and taste. At first, cycling was an activity that was predominantly male, especially since it often included militaristic exercises. Men would wear suits and hats as they attended club events and rode around the streets. They often did drills out on the roads and were accompanied by a bugler who would signal for the choreographed maneuvers. Still, this paramilitary training and these overtly masculine uses of the bicycle had little impact on women's burgeoning interest in the new machine.

As more and more women came to cycling, particularly in the 1890s, they would use the bicycle to make a statement. Wearing their finest clothes and sometimes sporting controversial attire—due to the lack of coverage and figure-revealing cuts of bloomers—women took to the public streets and thoroughfares to be seen. The bicycle industry relished the bicycle's popularity among "society women" because it meant the bicycle was in vogue and sales were booming. Thus, the industry tried to capitalize on the fashionability of cycling by using society women in marketing. The assumption was that if society women rode bicycles, all other women would want to do the same—a concept which the economist Thorstein Veblen would call pecuniary emulation.[5] Women who took up the bicycle, however, were doing more than to simply say, look at my clothes, or lack thereof. They were demonstrating their own ideals of what it meant to be a woman. They showed their independence, endurance, appreciation of nature, and open embrace of the public sphere. The bicycle could be used in courtship, but it could also be used as an opportunity to socialize in the company of other women. The first women to mount the bicycle certainly experienced ridicule and were scorned by others but as it became normal, the women who rode bicycles felt empowered and autonomous.

It was also true that as a statement about gendered ideals, riding a bicycle could signal to others that you were a man, but a certain kind of man; a

Introduction

refined man who was healthy, plucky, and full of life. Riding a bicycle designated a certain financial status. Not only were the new machines relatively expensive, but you also had to have ample free time to participate. This was during an age when most of the working class labored long hours six days a week. Sunday was truly a day of needed rest and religious observance. Using free time to partake in a leisure activity, like cycling, was visible proclamation of financial security and therefore freedom and independence.

The bicycle existed in a fluid and sometimes contradictory state. It was a modern technology, but cycling was also seen as a cure to illnesses brought on by modernity. New diagnoses like that of neurasthenia—a general sense of nervousness exacerbated by the evils of industrialized urban living—could lead to a prescription for exercise out in nature. This was compounded by a distinct fear at the end of the nineteenth century that men were no longer men—especially those of the managerial and clerical classes. Their jobs, after all, necessitated sitting in a chair most of the day typing, writing, or doing other tasks that were not seen as physically taxing. Similarly, the managerial class was seen as a group who simply watched others work, rather than working themselves. These men were no longer doing hard manual labor, they were not felling trees, turning the soil, or hunting their food. They were not even experienced fighters, like the generation before them. Men who were perceived as having had their manhood tested in the Civil War and the generation before that against nature and Native Americans.[6] For the middle-class man of the 1890s, it was the bicycle, and sport in general, that stood as a surrogate for brute physicality. With it, cyclists could again test themselves against nature—riding out in the elements, cresting steep hills, covering themselves in dust and dirt as well as filling their lungs with the fresh air that could only be found outside of the city. The bicycle offered an escape from that city, and it got the cyclist back in touch with a more romantic world.

Charles Pratt, an attorney, writer, and early philosopher of the wheel, argued that cycling was "a gentlemanly recreation, a refined sport."[7] It was a sport for gentlemen because it did not use spurs or a whip and it was not brutal or depraved like boxing, billiards, or other sports that were popular in the 1880s. Cycling required balance and grace, not just muscular force or daring. Cycling granted one speed, mobility, and a consumeristic sense of pride in displaying access to an expensive modern machine. Men who rode bicycles then were demonstrative of a specific type of manhood. A middle-

6   *Introduction*

class version that was associated with Whiteness.[8] White men, however, were not exclusive proprietors of the wheel. Among cycling enthusiasts there were representatives of many races and creeds, including a significant number of Black men and women. The fact that Black men and women used bicycles to show they were perfectly capable of excelling at something considered refined and modern challenged predominant ideas at the time; ideas that stereotyped Black people as backward.[9] It should have changed more than a few minds on the question of race and various racial stereotypes. If that happened, however, there is little observable evidence. White cyclists, fans, and writers maintained that the Black cyclist was unequal, that he or she was inherently lazy, sexually promiscuous, conniving, childish, and merely attempting to imitate Whites. While the emergence of the Black cyclist did not put an immediate end to racism, the mere presence of Black cyclists shows that the sport was not always as White as it is assumed and that the bicycle was indeed a vehicle of liberation. Consequently, the Black cyclist represented a unique challenge to inequality and the racial hierarchy in the Progressive Era of American history. The most well-known Black cyclist of the era was Marshall "Major" Taylor but, as this work will show, he was far from alone. As it resurrects the stories of the Black cyclists to come before and after "Major" Taylor, this work argues that in spite of cycling's racist history in the United States, Black cyclists have been steadfast in their use of the bicycle as a means of affirming their freedom, masculinity, femininity, and equality.

"Major" Taylor wrote and published an autobiography in 1928 and there have been many subsequent biographies written about Taylor, beginning with Andrew Ritchie's, which first appeared in 1996. While these works have uncovered a great amount of detail about Taylor's life and career, there has been little effort to draw direct connections between the sport's past and its present. Taylor was far from the only Black cyclist to exist in the Progressive Era; however, the stories of all the other Black cyclists to come before and after him need to be told. There were many others who rose to considerable prominence in the United States. Some of them also became well-known throughout Europe. The time to broaden the discussion of the Black cyclist beyond Taylor is well overdue.

Some biographies of Taylor give credit to the benevolent White men who helped him along the way. While there were clearly benefits to having White allies, this book emphasizes that Taylor alone was responsible for

Introduction 7

his success. It goes further by showing that other Black cyclists, who did not have the same support network as Taylor, could also make significant achievements in the sport—albeit not without difficulties. It will stress their agency as well. Another shortfall of the numerous biographies of Taylor that exist is that they focus on him so singularly that they lead the reader to believe he was the only Black cyclist. This, perhaps unintentional, implication needs correction.

Contrary to other studies of Taylor, this work posits that "Major" Taylor did not actually "break the color line" in cycling. He was not the first Black cyclist and his success in the sport did not clear the path for other Black cyclists. If anything, Taylor's success against White men made things more difficult for other Black cyclists with aspirations of world championships. Even though there have been numerous Black cyclists in the United States over the past 150 years, the sport is still suffering from a distinct lack of diversity today. This has stifled the sport's popularity. Many presume cycling lacks broad appeal because it is expensive. The sport's failure to address issues of inclusivity and its own racist past, however, have been far more detrimental than the simple monetary cost of participation. Cycling was often heralded as having a democratizing effect, yet this book tracks how the sport grew increasingly exclusive, with regard to race. In spite of attempts at increasing cycling's exclusivity, Black cyclists were unwavering in their endeavors to get around each new barrier by finding alternative paths and using the bicycle as a vehicle of liberation. Kittie Knox, for instance, stands as a Black representative of the "new woman"—one who challenged racial and gender norms with her strength and agility. Her story is important because it shows that the Black cyclist was not just male and not confined to the world of competitive cycling since Knox embraced both the social and fashionable aspects of the bicycle. She stands out not only because she was a Black female cyclist, but also because she was perceived as both athletically gifted and beautiful during a period in which the two ideas were far from synonymous.

The bulk of the research to follow examines cycling's early history throughout the Progressive Era, from 1880–1920. A primary objective of this book is to unearth the stories of forgotten Black cyclists by providing biographical sketches of these individuals. This material is based largely on stories published in several different cycling magazines as well as various newspapers that reported on cycling, particularly those that catered to Black readers. The chapters are organized thematically with vignettes of a few Black cyclists per chapter incorporated to provide a narrative that highlights the hurdles they faced and the resilience they showed in navigating their way around racism and Jim Crow prohibitions. This is not, however, another feel-good story. It does not follow the traditional arc to which we have become so accustomed, especially in stories of sport for a general audience. It is not the story of Black people, or a singular Black individual, using sport to find fortune and fame and then living happily ever after. While there is certainly some triumph in the following pages, there is also tragedy. To be sure, the cyclists in this book overcame disadvantages and found their way around obstacles erected by racist Whites, but their victories were short-lived. Chapter nine shows that, like Taylor, many other Black cyclists of notable significance died tragically, with a few of them institutionalized in prisons or asylums after their racing careers were over. While many of the individuals to be discussed in this book succumbed to unceremonious endings, the way they used the bicycle while alive was a powerful challenge to the racist ideas of White society and a source of uplift for Black Americans. The courage of these Black cyclists and the in-roads they made must be remembered. Thus, the final chapter completes the biographical sketch of the early Black cyclists discussed by detailing their tragic endings and illuminating how their stories became lost.

The epilogue looks at the sport's history over the last 100 years. In 1984, Nelson Vails won the silver medal at the LA Olympics, becoming one of the first Black cyclists to make headlines since Taylor's death. More recently, Black athletes like Rahsaan Bahati, Justin Williams, Cory Williams, Nigel Sylvester, and Ayesha McGowan have made it a point to bring more diversity and inclusivity to the sport. Their social media presence, along with their countless supporters, and groups like BlackCycling, Pedal2thePeople, LA Sweat, Blackstone Bicycle Works, and the Level Up Cycling Movement, suggests that the monochromatic complexion of cycling is coming to an end. In 2021, one of the largest virtual cycling apps, Zwift, announced they would launch a Black Celebration Series and it would last throughout the entire year, not just Black History Month. Zwift has also spent considerable time incorporating a more inclusive variety of skin tones and hair textures as options for in-game avatars. This is a positive step but there is still much more that needs to happen.

Introduction 9

Even in Europe there have been only a small number of Black cyclists to compete in the Tour de France and none of those men have been American. The first to ever do so was the Caribbean rider Yohann Gene, in 2011. More recently, one of the most exciting and successful cyclo-cross racers has been the Dominican-born Dutchwoman Ceylin del Carmen Alvorado, who became world champion of the discipline in 2020. In 2023, Biniam Girmay, a Black cyclist from Eritrea, made history by becoming the first Black cyclist to ever lead a team at the Tour de France. Even still, cycling as a sport faces the stigma that it is only for middle-class Whites (predominantly male). It is also a sport that struggles to get any coverage by mainstream media outlets in the United States. If representation matters, then we not only need to see greater inclusivity, but we must also highlight the fact that the sport has not always been this way. Cycling's early history shows that, indeed, Black cyclists were a crucial part of the sport's success and appeal. Before cycling can fully regain its former status, it must exorcise its demons and pursue a policy of equity and inclusion. This book is not the final word on the subject. It is the opening of a broader discussion that needs to happen.

1
From the Outset

On April 10, 1869, the *New York Herald* made the brief and relatively restrained announcement, "Savannah, GA., has a colored velocipede club." The Herald was not the only paper to apprise the public of this fact. The same news appeared in *The Home Journal* of Winchester, Tennessee, the *Courier-Journal* of Louisville, Kentucky, and undoubtedly in other papers throughout the United States.[1] Had it just been an average velocipede club, one composed of White men, it is doubtful that the story would have circulated so widely. The report did not identify any of the members, nor did it specify how many people were in the club, but the very fact that it was a club formed by and for Black cyclists meant it was no average club. The Civil War had concluded just four years and one day prior. The Emancipation Proclamation was a mere six years past. With the South still under "Reconstruction," readers' reactions were likely to have ranged from feelings of pride, surprise, and even sheer outrage.

There were many other velocipede clubs, most were predominantly White, but the growth in the number of clubs illustrates the burgeoning popularity of the bicycle. By 1868, the United States was firmly entrenched in what could only be called a velocipede craze. The fact that a club had formed for Black cyclists was an early indication that this new machine's appeal ranged beyond the White middle class and that it was an activity with potentially deeper meanings than being a mere diversion. It is unlikely that earlier predecessors of the bicycle, like the draisine, would have had similar stories. While the draisine, or hobbyhorse, was a machine that marveled Americans in 1819, it was nowhere near as popular as the velocipede would prove to be. Excitement about the hobbyhorse was not only brief, but also somewhat contained regionally to cities like New York, Baltimore, and Philadelphia. It did not sweep the country in the same manner as the velocipede.

The velocipede distinguished itself from the draisine because it was much different than walking or running. With the rider straddling the draisine and walking or running to propel the machine, it offered some improvement over walking but had its limitations. The velocipede, however, with its pedals and the ability of riders to keep their feet off the ground while powering its front wheel, made the velocipedist's movement something different, something remarkable. The velocipede was also faster, particularly over flat ground. Better still was flat, smooth ground, and so the velocipede craze largely played out in and among velocipede rinks. These rinks not only attracted those who sought to tame and master the machine, but so remarkable was the machine that plenty more crowded in as spectators to watch others ride. People of all ages, classes, and races, got caught up in the excitement. One month before that announcement of the formation of a club of Black velocipede riders in Savannah, there was an advertisement in the pages of the *Charleston Daily News* for a performance by the Hanlon Brothers of New York. The Hanlon Brothers were an acrobatic troupe who began in England but were world renowned by the 1860s, especially for their trapeze acts. By 1868, thousands were lining up to see three of the brothers race velocipedes down an incline on stage. The spectacle proved particularly popular in southern cities like Savannah, Georgia, where the Hanlons "were followed everywhere by great crowds anxious to observe the proper method of managing" velocipedes.[2] They were undoubtedly successful in South Carolina as well. The performance advertised in the *Charleston Daily News* was promoted specifically as a performance of "two-wheeled velocipedes." These early cycling demonstrations by the Hanlon Brothers were exciting enough in 1869 for adults to pay a $1 admission fee for the performance. This was about half a day's wages for the average unskilled laborer at the time.[3] The crowds were apparently diverse as well, since the advertisement for the event pointed out that "colored seats" could be had for seventy-five cents and entry for children under ten years of age was only fifty cents.[4] Clearly, it was family friendly entertainment and the velocipede had captured the imagination of many different groups of people.

Crowds not only turned out for acrobatic performances on velocipedes, but there were also those who crowded into velocipede rinks to watch untrained individuals test their skill in balancing the machine, and soon people were filing into rinks to watch people race their velocipedes against one another. The rinks proved a more popular setting for velocipede riding because of the smoother rolling surfaces they provided. They were far smoother than what could be found out on any of the public streets. Often the rinks for velocipedes were merely repurposed ice skating or roller-skating rinks. As the craze intensified, velocipede rinks began to pop up all across the United States. Instructional schools for riding velocipedes and velocipede clubs were on the rise as well. By 1869 they could be found in most American cities. It was a somewhat hazardous activity after all, so the schools seemed prudent. The rinks also took precautions, generally by wrapping the supporting pillars rising up from their floors in padding, due to the inevitability of patrons crashing into them. Owners of these rinks were poised to profit handsomely from the craze. One owner claimed he was earning $30–$40 a day from the rental of five velocipedes. Some of the more exciting events attracted crowds of up to 5,000 spectators.[5] To be sure, Black Americans were among the crowds that turned out to watch the mystifying machine, but they were not merely passive consumers. Black Americans were also riding velocipedes and proving they could do it just as well, if not better, than their White counterparts.

Almost as soon as the numbers of velocipede riders began to rise, contests were created to see who could ride the best. Since this was a machine that was supposed to hasten human travel, many of these competitions were races. The most common format consisted of a handful of competitors racing around the rink simultaneously, completing multiple laps. If there were more than five riders, which was common, races would be held in heats. The faster riders attained speeds of somewhere around twelve miles per hour and they often won silver prizes.[6] In Lewiston, Maine, one such event at the Shaw and Hilton Rink "was crowded to its utmost capacity" as spectators watched a field of thirteen riders compete for a silver ice pitcher. All thirteen raced to complete seven laps around the rink, which equaled somewhere around 1,400 feet total, or a little more than a quarter mile. Four racers were disqualified for running afoul of the interior course

14   CHAPTER 1

markers. The winner among the nine remaining competitors was a young Black man named Jackson Lewis. He won by about a second with a time of one minute thirteen and a half seconds. The local newspaper reported that he was showered with "great applause," and in recognition of the spectators' hearty congratulations, Lewis took "off his hat, made a low bow and walked off triumphant with the pitcher under his arm."[7]

Jackson Lewis's exploit is evidence that Black people were not only early adopters of this technologically advanced form of mobility but that they were also extremely proficient. Whether this was a surprise is not commented on by the press. Further difficulties arise in obtaining statistics for just how many Black men and women partook in the velocipede craze; numbers of participants in general were seldom reported, at least not with any specifics. Still, there is enough evidence to show that they were in the stands and onboard velocipedes throughout the United States, from Maine to Georgia and parts in between. In Indianapolis, a "young colored man" riding a velocipede accidentally "knocked over a colonel."[8] The presence of Black Americans in and among velocipede events, however, did not seem to arouse the same fears or face the same level of backlash in cycling we would see by the 1890s. Part of this was because the velocipede was, ultimately, a passing novelty. The inability to really prove itself out in the real world, away from the wooden tracks and on the open road, meant that it simply was not taken very seriously. It was a vehicle but not one perceived as having the ability to take a person very far.

The shortfalls and limitations of the velocipede did not go unnoticed by bicycle designers and entrepreneurs. As a result of this, and as technologies advanced from 1869 to 1890, velocipedes would undergo significant alterations. Perhaps most notable in those advancements was the wire spoke that could be tensioned to allow for larger, lighter wheels. The larger wheels were necessary for greater speeds, since the bicycle had yet to incorporate chains or gears. As the wheels grew larger and began to incorporate rubber tires and rubber pedals, bicycles slowly transitioned away from velocipedes and toward a design that would come to be called the high wheeler, penny-farthing, or ordinary. The high wheel design was the most successful alternative to the velocipede. It was a design that made a strong impression on Americans at the Centennial International Exhibit of 1876 in Philadelphia. It was shortly after this exhibit that an enamored visitor and Civil War veteran of Massachusetts, Colonel Albert Pope, decided to start producing and selling the machine. As the name suggests, the high wheeler was marked by a noticeable difference in size between the two wheels. The front wheel was disproportionately large with a smaller wheel trailing behind. Like the older velocipedes, because the high wheeler incorporated pedals attached to the axle of the front wheel and it had no gears, the speed of the bicycle was dictated by the size of the front wheel, the length of the cranks, and the speed of their revolutions. This made larger front wheels more desirable. Since large front wheels were necessary for faster speeds, the high wheeler's geometry placed the rider far above the ground, and because the pedals driving the larger front wheel were attached to cranks that ran directly to the front axle, the rider's weight was positioned over the front of the bicycle. This made the machine prone to "headers," which occurred when the large front wheel struck an object that could stall momentum. Having a large front wheel meant this occurred less often than it would on a machine with smaller wheels, but still, it could happen. When it did indeed happen, the continuing forward motion of the rider often led to a quick ejection over the handlebars and down to the hard ground below. The danger of a taking a header, however, was not enough to dissuade many of the more adventurous individuals. It did not take long for the high wheeler to prove itself to the public, and soon there was a multitude of cyclists on American roads. The numbers of high wheelers seemed to dwarf those of the velocipedes of 1868–1869, especially since the high wheeler was more suitable for travel outside. It was not confined to rinks and schools like the velocipede. By 1881, newspapers like the *New York Herald* were commenting on the high wheel bicycle's growing appeal. The *Herald* told readers, "Persons who ride or drive above Fifty-Ninth Street cannot fail to note that within a year there has been a sudden and marked increase in the number of bicycles on the road, and residents on any well-paved road in the same part of the city can testify that 'the steel horse,' as the bicycle has come to be called in England, is often on the road as early in the morning as horses less tough of fiber."[9]

Part of the bicycle's appeal was that it arrived at an extremely opportune moment in which there were growing concerns about the nation's virility. One result of these concerns was a larger push for health and strenuous exercise in the outdoors.[10] The *New York Herald* alluded to this by pointing out, "The popularity which bicycling has suddenly reached in New York is as gratifying to many who never bestrode the ever-saddled courser as

Unidentified man in club uniform on a high-wheel bicycle circa 1886. Photo courtesy of the Cycling Photographica Collection of Lorne Shields, Toronto.

to the most earnest devotes of the new sport, for anything that will offer the young men of our city a new inducement to spend part of their time at vigorous exercise out of doors is of general benefit to the community."[11] As the *Herald* suggests, and because the high wheeler's design mandated it, the people who rode the high wheeler were often younger, daring, and athletic men. Due to its price, they also tended to be of considerable means. There were, however, second-hand machines available that reduced the typical prohibitive price tag of around $125.[12] At the same time, being seen on last year's model could have a deteriorative effect on your social standing—somewhat akin to using an outdated cellphone today.

Of course, there were also a few individuals with enough ingenuity to circumvent the high cost by creating their own machines, but they were somewhat uncommon. In fact, it was rare enough that when some enterprising novice did create their own bicycle, cycling magazines would run syndicated stories. This was the case for Charles Van Deever. Along with the article about a bicycle he created was a picture of Charles standing behind his high wheeler. With his legs crossed right over left and his right hand gently resting on the sloping backbone that connected the front and rear wheels, he stood proudly in his jacket and hat, exhibiting a calm demeanor, suggesting a mastery of the machine. While the reader's attention was drawn to the fact that this was "not a racing wheel," the story explained that the "home-made bicycle, designed and manufactured by a colored man" was, however, "an example of ingenuity and what can be done by a clever man, with limited means and appliances, it stands unexcelled."[13] The *Bicycling World and L.A.W. Bulletin* relayed Van Deever's account of how he came to build the high wheeler. Self-described as a "poor boy," he said he first acquired the old wagon wheel that he mounted to the front of his machine from a man who was not using it anymore and who did not believe Van Deever could actually make a bicycle with it. Van Deever then made the forks from a piece of hickory he found "behind the barn" and he got the "backbone" from a blacksmith. In all, he only had an axe, draw knife, and some bits for boring. The *Hartford Times* ran the story about Van Deever first. Their article provided a long description of the machine, writing that the rear wheel was "a round disk 18 inches in diameter cut out of an oak plank an inch thick, bored full of holes to make it lighter." There was also an iron handlebar and pedals that were "not exactly ball bearing, but square blocks of wood with small holes for oiling." The entire machine weighed close to 100 pounds. That was considerably more than the average high wheeler but that did not seem to deter Van Deever. He claimed to have ridden his homemade bicycle around 4,000 miles by the time of the interview.[14]

Van Deever was not the only young man going to such great lengths to will himself into a cyclist. John Pash, another young Black man, this time from Bardstown, Kentucky, would also make it into the pages of The *Bicycling World and L.A.W. Bulletin* for the "remarkable bicycle . . . he made

"Not a Racing Wheel," Charles Van Deever and his handmade bicycle. *Bicycling World and L.A.W. Bulletin*, October 11, 1889, 642.

with his own hands, every part and piece of it, not out of pieces of old bicycles, but out of raw materials...."[15] Pash's and Van Deever's exploits show that this new machine was not entirely limited to those with discretionary income but at the same time, the fact that they went to such lengths to obtain their own bicycles and that it was rare enough for a newspaper and cycling magazine to pick up the story, shows that this was an extraordinary occurrence. It also shows that even before the bicycle boom of the 1890s, the bicycle already had an appeal that cut through lines of class and race even though it seemed most accessible to White middle-class males. Further evidence of the high wheeler's broad appeal comes from men like Robert Crutcher of Auburn, New York. Crutcher was allegedly "the only colored bicyclist in the city." He was apparently not very skilled. In what must have been an exaggeration, it reportedly took him four hours to ride a mile "including headers" on his "elegant English nickel-plated bicycle."[16]

While it was true that a majority of those mounting the high wheeler were White and middle class, the bicycle had captivated the attention of men and women, Black, and White, indeed all complexions of people.

The danger inherent in the high wheeler, with its penchant for "headers," was undoubtedly attractive to some of the younger, more athletic men, but it also effectively deterred others from taking up cycling. Most obviously, the high wheeler all but excluded women. That is not because they were not athletic or brave enough to ride them. Rather, it was the social mores of the time that made some deem it inappropriate. Not only would the woman be straddling a machine, fairly high above the ground, she was also expected to wear a dress, which could become entangled in the spokes. It was hard enough for men to pedal and turn the large front wheel simultaneously, it would have been even more difficult if one tried to do so while wearing a long dress. The high wheeler's design also deterred older men who were afraid of injury. The alternative solution for both of these groups during the height of the high wheeler's popularity was the tricycle. Tricycles were larger, heavier, more expensive, and, to a degree, slower than high wheelers. Due to this, most racing men would choose high wheelers over tricycles, but the tricycle did develop something of a following on its own. It was especially popular among wealthier individuals, society women in particular.[17] There were even men who raced the tricycle, like the Black cyclist John Williams, who was first to conquer Corey Hill on a tricycle and whom the *Springfield Republican* referred to as the "colored champion tricycle road rider."[18] Williams was also referred to as the "colored flyer" and held the records for the 6-mile, 7-mile, 8-mile, 9-mile, 10-mile, 25-mile, and 50-mile road races.[19] Those records were all measured against other tricycles, however, not high wheelers. In general, the tricycle, while more physically accessible to men and women of all ages, had drawbacks due to its cost, weight, and overall sluggishness.

The fact that Williams and Van Deever both lived in the Boston area is not mere coincidence. Boston was, in fact, a hotbed of early cycling. *Harper's Weekly* described the city as "indisputably the home and head-centre of cycling in America."[20] It was perhaps unsurprising then, that the League of American Wheelmen (LAW), the most important and primary organizing body of American cyclists, would hold their seventh annual meet in the city. Of the various business and activities the league conducted during its three-day sojourn to Boston in the late spring of 1886, the event that captured the bulk of the public's attention was the Corey Hill climbing contest. The hill was named after Timothy Corey, the man who was first to conquer and tame the topographical feature in the 1760s by clearing it for pasture. His children would go on to build houses and live there in what would become known as the Corey Hill neighborhood, which is situated at a high enough elevation to boast the "best views the greater Boston area has to offer."[21] Over one hundred years after Timothy Corey's initial conquest of the hill, several of the area's strongest cyclists took on the rise of 199 feet in elevation spanning nearly half a mile. They, like Corey, were intent on conquering Mother Nature and the mound she placed before them. On the morning of the contest, spectators crowded both sides of the road. Men looking on, in their jackets and top hats, various officials, and ladies with parasols observed the challengers, at least one of whom wore a shirt tight enough to see every muscle on his upper body, as they flexed and contorted their bodies over their machines in an effort to turn the pedals and drive their bicycles ever upward. The wheels on their high-wheel bicycles rose one foot for every 11.41 feet they traveled and while personal bests and a record for the day were set, previous records were not broken.[22] One of those records still holding firm was that of John Williams, a Black cyclist whose family had migrated to Boston from the South.[23] More impressive than climbing Corey Hill on a high wheeler, Williams set the record time for an attempt by a tricyclist a year earlier, in October 1885. A week after his feat, The *Bicycling World* reported, "this is the first tricycle that has ever been up the hill, under the conditions laid down in the rules for the contests."[24] Of course, there were plenty of men who attempted the climb on various models of high-wheeled bicycles as well. The fastest time on a high wheeler would have certainly been faster than any tricycle, but the two machines were on a more even keel when vying for consumer's favor. Even though the high wheeler was generally faster, the tricycle was seen as safer and more practical due to its adaptability for utilitarian functions.

This was an interesting developmental moment for the bicycle. No one design held the dominance that the diamond-shaped safety bicycle would hold by the late 1890s and thereafter. It is no mere coincidence that these changes and improvements to come about during the 1870s and 1880s were occurring at the same moment the world was witnessing revolutionary changes in broader technologies. It was a period of competing bicycle designs, with velocipedes, high wheelers, and tricycles all having their moment among different groups at certain times. At each step of the way, the Black cyclist was present. More than just a passive audience member in the stands, Black Americans attended cycling events but they also took to the wheel and quickly proved themselves as capable cyclists, knowledgeable and affluent consumers of new technology, and still others showed they were ingenious craftsmen who could create their own machines. All of these individuals took up cycling before there was a "Major" Taylor and some of them may have even caused White cyclists to wonder, "what does it mean if they are better?" Taylor does not mention it in his autobiography, but it also raises the question of whether he may have seen a Black cyclist or two out on the roads near his boyhood home of Indianapolis and if so, what was the impact?

The fact that Black Americans took to cycling at such an early stage was a statement in and of itself. After all, velocipedes and high wheelers were considered technological marvels in their day. They were also relatively expensive machines and once the high wheeler appeared on the scene, bicycles were proving themselves as serious forms of mobility. In a time period in which Black Americans were expected to "know their place" by racist whites, the bicycle provided the opportunity to move between places, to ride among White people, and to even show off the fact that their skills were sometimes greater than average. Because the bicycle stood as a representation of class, masculinity, health, and a forward-thinking embrace of technology, those who rode showed the world their status and values. For Black Americans to demonstrate these traits would have flown in the face of many stereotypes. Whether they were conscious of it or not, the Black cyclists of the 1870s and 1880s made waves when they mounted their wheels. By the late 1880s it would become clearer that some Black Americans were conscious of this, and so they used their bicycles as a part of a broader struggle for equality.

2

The Mode of Liberation

"The colored people [can] only get just and fair treatment by the wise and judicious use of the ballot," said James Monroe Trotter, as he stood to accept his appointment as the temporary chair of the Conference of the Colored Men of New England.[1] The men sitting there, on September 14, 1886, inside the Charles Street Church located on Boston's Beacon Hill, had been called together by the prominent Black journalist, J. Gordon Street. It was a fitting venue for such a meeting. As a former host to celebrated speakers like Frederick Douglass, Harriet Tubman, William Lloyd Garrison, and Sojourner Truth, the spirit of liberation had left an indelible mark on the building and its sanctuary. To that same end, the conference, which had convened on that Tuesday afternoon, was intent on issuing "a strong protest against discrimination."[2] The men gathered there, highly respected Black men of New England, needed little time to single out Trotter as their obvious choice for leadership.

James Monroe Trotter was a veteran of the Civil War, serving in Massachusetts' Fifty-Fifth Regiment. He not only served but distinguished himself by leading a boycott against the War Department. A boycott that would not end until Black soldiers' pay was equal to that of their White counterparts. That meant doubling their pay. With that victory under his belt, as his tenure in the military came to a close, Trotter continued his fight against racial discrimination. In that fight, he would ultimately be

The Mode of Liberation

compelled to resign from what was clearly a financially comfortable position at the Boston Post Office, after eighteen years of service. Trotter's resignation was widely publicized, especially among the Black press. He minced few words in announcing that he was motivated by the "discrimination against Negroes in promotion." He pushed further, however, highlighting how the problem was bigger than the post office; it was a problem that could be traced to the Republican Party. This was after the Republican Party, to which he owed his appointment, began to draw the color line. This seeming about-face of the Republicans was a painful betrayal for Trotter, who would disavow his allegiance to the party completely just two years later, in 1884, declaring himself a Democrat. He was open and vocal in his charge that the Republican Party had abandoned Black people.[3] In the process, he proved himself a valuable ally of the Democratic Party, and for his support in Grover Cleveland's successful bid for the presidency, Trotter reaped his reward. He earned a presidential appointment as the Recorder of Deeds, a remarkable distinction he would share with a few other important Black leaders such as his predecessor Frederick Douglass and his successor Blanche K. Bruce.[4] As a man who was described in a biographical sketch as having "the kind of abolitionist spirit which seemed to be a particular mark of the Boston Negro," Trotter was just as apropos a leader for the Conference of the Colored Men of New England as was their choice of venue.

Among the group of distinguished Black men gathered with James Trotter and J. Gordon Street at that initial meeting was a Black cyclist in his late twenties named David Drummond. Sitting among those men in the Charles Street Church on that day, Drummond did more than passively listen. He heeded the call. The group resolved that "discrimination was not only practiced against the colored people by merchants, store-keepers and others, but it was also done by political parties." They would begin monitoring these acts and David Drummond agreed to serve as assistant secretary. The group also observed that even though they perceived a "general change" regarding discrimination in the country, it was still prevalent, and the results were "galling and depressing." Part of Drummond's responsibility as assistant secretary of the Conference would be to "look up and note cases of discrimination."[5]

The following year, 1887, David Drummond was listed among the names of another group of august gentlemen to attend a banquet in honor of

James Monroe Trotter. Drummond was even called to say a few words on Trotter's behalf at the closing of the banquet.[6] Drummond may have felt a little bit out of place, sitting at the banquet table with the likes of lawyers, pastors, newspaper men, and politicians. Like Trotter and other Black men of Boston with that "abolitionist spirit," Drummond was clearly a man who abhorred the racial discrimination he experienced in daily life. To some, he was merely a carpenter and amateur cyclist but clearly, he was more than that. Not only was he politically active, but David Drummond would also use his bicycle to mobilize against the system of racial discrimination he and so many other Americans encountered in daily life.

America's Reconstruction after the Civil War was a moment of great promise for Black Americans and racial equality. The South experienced record numbers of Black political representation; numbers the United States would not see again until the end of the twentieth century. In the North, there was also hope that full equality could soon be an actuality. One northern city in particular stood forth as a beacon of that emancipatory promise for Black Americans. "Boston was," as the historian Kerri Greenidge writes, "considered the 'mecca of the Negro,' a city in which property-holding black men had been voting since the 1780s, where the public schools were desegregated in 1855, and where a highly literate, politically savvy, and inherently activist colored community led free black resistance to slavery."[7] The idea of freedom would experience significant revisions in the nineteenth century, particularly among Black Americans and women who called not only for freedom from bondage, but for full economic autonomy and political participation. Going hand-in-hand with the demands for freedom and equality were physical demonstrations of equal talents and capabilities by those whom White people considered physiologically inferior. At the same time, the bicycle was emerging as the technological embodiment of these ideals of freedom and independence. Therefore, it is no coincidence that both women and Black Americans were drawn to the bicycle as a means of exercising their demands. This was occurring several decades before "the Great Migration"—when Black southern farmers moved to the North. In fact, a great number abandoned the South almost as soon as the Civil War had ended. Some were escaping the terror of violent racism and the Ku Klux Klan as well as the horrors of violent racism and the Black Codes. Others were drawn north by greater opportunities. Records show that of the growing number of people settling in Boston, many had recently emigrated from North Carolina and Virginia.[8]

Six of those newcomers were the Black laborer John Drummond, his wife Susan, and their four sons, Cornelius, David, John, and George. Both John and Susan were born in Virginia, just like their parents before them. Despite being well rooted in the state, that was not enough to keep them planted there after the war ended. By 1870, the family of Virginians had moved to Cambridge, Massachusetts. It was there that they would start a new life, enrolling their sons in a desegregated school and buying a home. They would spend the rest of their lives there. The country was a much different place when Susan and John Drummond first married. Marred by the approaching fury of the Civil War, its dramatic conclusion, and amid a flurry of technological advancements that were quickly altering daily life, Virginia had certainly changed during their first thirteen years of marriage, from 1857 to 1870. Many would assume those changes were mostly positive for Black people. For the Drummonds, however, even after the war, Virginia did not promise the opportunities they believed their family deserved—the opportunities available to them in a place like Boston.

This powerful period of drastic change for the concept of freedom and scientific inquiry in which they lived would send shockwaves through society and culture. Of course, there have been other periods of technological change throughout history, but the changes were so great from the 1870s to the 1910s that it has become known as the Technological Revolution. Many individuals who lived through these changes, like David Drummond, would find themselves attracted to one new technology in particular, the bicycle. Countless other Black men found the bicycle's potential compelling, just as women on the move for their own liberation would do the same. Along with Drummond, other Black men, like those discussed in the previous chapter, would prove themselves notable figures in the early days of Boston's cycling craze. They were all predecessors to the most well-known Black cyclist to ever live, Marshall "Major" Taylor, by nearly ten years. In spite of their proximity in time and somewhat overlapping histories, in terms of the pace of technological advancement during this period, there were significant gaps between these men. Drummond, for instance, was born in 1859, and therefore had approximately twenty years on Taylor. He inhabited a period in which the bicycle experienced momentous improvements. Because of this, Drummond's and Taylor's experiences with the bicycle would be radically different.

David Drummond is another example of the fact that the bicycle was not only ridden by the White middle class, that some Black men were very serious and talented cyclists, even during the bicycle's infancy. Furthermore, he shows that some Black cyclists consciously used their bicycles as a tool of their activism. Drummond moved north to Massachusetts from Virginia and came of age as the high-wheeler craze entered full swing. The fact that he happened to settle in Cambridge, just outside Boston, is of course, also significant. David Herlihy argues that it was "increasingly clear as 1877 unfolded [that] if there was to be an American bicycle renaissance, Boston would lead the way."[9] Drummond, who was fifteen in 1877, was clearly swept up in the high-wheeling exploits. As early as 1885, he was already a well-known cyclist and pacer in the Boston area. He was even occasionally mentioned in the pages of *The Bicycling World* for the pace-making work he did for long-distance and record-setting efforts on the road. Drummond and nine other riders, for instance, took turns pacing Louis "Birdie" Munger as he completed a long-distance ride over the course of twenty-four hours on November 20 and 21, 1885.[10] Munger is a significant figure in bicycle history because of his skills on a bicycle, but also because of his friendship with, and tutelage of, the future world champion cyclist Marshall "Major" Taylor. Munger was a full-time professional high-wheel cyclist racing throughout the Midwest and Northeast. He was well known for his racing exploits and record breaking, particularly on the high wheeler.[11] The fact that Munger, who was something of a legend in racing circles, would enlist the help of Drummond in one of his record attempts shows his trust in Drummond's abilities as well as Drummond's apparent reputation and notoriety. Of course, helping Munger would have raised Drummond's status and credibility among other cyclists even more.

Munger was attempting to beat the twenty-four-hour record held by A.A. McCurdy, a prominent cyclist from Lynn, Massachusetts. McCurdy had even been paid $150 by the builders of the Star bicycle to specifically target the twenty-four-hour record. He achieved that objective, but his record was soon broken, so the makers of Star offered him $250 to take it once more.[12] What is perhaps surprising is that while Munger and McCurdy both competed for the twenty-four-hour record, their relationship did not seem at all adversarial. Around the same time Munger was going for

The Mode of Liberation 27

the twenty-four-hour record in November, he and Drummond both were directly assisting McCurdy in his attempt to capture the 100-mile record. Munger paced McCurdy for the first fifty miles before Drummond joined in to pace McCurdy over the last fifty miles.[13] While it may have been a bit of a coincidence that McCurdy would choose Drummond as a pace-maker, since they both lived in the Boston area and the record attempts were made in Boston, it is perhaps more telling that Munger, who was from Detroit, would also ask for Drummond's help. At the very least, it appears that Drummond was thought of as one of the most talented riders in the area, which is saying a lot since, as Herlihy points out, it was ground zero for the cycling renaissance in the United States. Drummond was clearly a talented high-wheel rider in his own right, however, as he did more on the bicycle than to simply help others set records. Race reports from the time show that he was capable of winning contests for himself.

David Drummond entered the Boston 100-mile race in the fall of 1886. This time he raced against A.A. McCurdy, instead of pacing him. On that occasion, he was unsuccessful. He apparently ended up lost with several other riders as they inadvertently deviated from the complex course.[14] Drummond was not only a long-distance specialist, however, he also participated and found success in races over much shorter distances. By 1888, he was winning some of the most important races in the Boston area, namely, the annual Fourth of July races held on Boston Common. The Fourth of July was a particularly poignant occasion for a Black man from the South, like Drummond, since the day was often used as a moment for Black Americans to demonstrate their patriotism and citizenship after emancipation. Drummond participated in bicycle races on that same holiday in 1887 and riding before thousands of spectators, he won the consolation race—a race for those who failed to win one of the other races throughout the day.[15] The *New York Freeman* took care to mention that Drummond was "lustily cheered by both white and colored people when the judges awarded him the medal."[16] Such success and the treatment he received brought him back in 1888. Of the five big races held on that day, David Drummond won two—the only two he entered—thereby earning two gold medals before a crowd of over 7,000 spectators.[17]

Despite his success, there is some evidence that he was not as highly respected as his White counterparts. The names of the men he competed against were listed in the *Boston Daily Journal*, but Drummond's is the

28   CHAPTER 2

only one whose first name was given. Other riders, like P.J. Berlo and H.L. Caldwell Jr., were listed by their first and middle initials and full last name, as was customary for the time. *The Bicycling World* did not find it necessary to use his first name at all, nor did it find it worth explaining who he was, or where he was from. Even the specification that he was a "colored rider," so often present in news articles that mentioned Black cyclists, was generally excluded.[18] Either he was extremely well known throughout the Northeast, or the cycling press preferred to use as little ink as possible on him by ignoring his significance. In contrast, when announcing that he was elected to join the Cambridgeport Bicycle Club, the *New York Freeman*, a paper targeting an African American audience, called him "Mr. Drummond" and referred to him as "the champion bicycle rider."[19] All of this suggests that even though he was successful and "lustily cheered by white" spectators, he did not always receive the same level of respect as the White cyclists whom he competed against. Many may have recognized his athletic ability on the bicycle, but that did not necessarily equate to respecting him as a man. This was before ideas of masculinity and athleticism were so intertwined and during a period in which White men did not see interracial competition as a threat.[20] That would soon change. After sport became a measure of manliness, there would develop a whole host of reasons to explain Black athletic success. Most of those explanations "rested on whites' beliefs that blacks lacked civilization."[21] Thus, racist stereotypes, like the idea that Black boxers could excel in the sport because they had thicker skulls, served to dampen White men's insecurities when they lost.

In spite of these editorial slights, David Drummond continued to prove himself as an experienced and clever racer. The report for the Fourth of July Day race of 1888 in Boston mentions how he often held back, following in second wheel, and rarely riding at the front so he could benefit from the other rider's draft. In the fourth race of the day, the three-mile race for amateurs, Drummond also demonstrated his heads-up maneuvering abilities within the group. Circling the track, approximately the same length as a standard 400-meter running track today, it took four laps on the sod and gravel surface to complete a mile. To be sure, that surface would have been more unpredictable than the wooden tracks constructed in the 1890s, especially since it was noted that there was a soft spot on one of the upper turns, "which brought three riders to grief."[22] Two of those fell in the fourth race. The first-place rider, Caldwell, apparently hit that soft spot and took

The Mode of Liberation

a "disastrous header" flying over the handlebars high above the large front wheel to the sod below. Drummond, ever watchful and agile, was able to avoid running into him. P.J. Berlo, however, was not so fortunate. He "was riding, as [was] his custom, with his head down, and failed to see the accident."[23] The race concluded with Caldwell and Berlo taking a trip to the first-aid station while Drummond easily bested his White competitors and took the victory.

The following year, in 1889, there was some disagreement between Berlo and Drummond. *The Bicycling World* described it as a "little jealousy" that existed between the two riders, which became more pronounced by Berlo's refusal to allow Drummond to race the final heat of the quarter-mile safety race at the Fourth of July races on the Boston Common. There is no real explanation of Berlo's objections to Drummond's participation, but by the time of the final heat Drummond was a "fresh man."[24] If Drummond made it to the final heat without having to expend effort in the preliminary heats, Berlo may have seen that as an unfair advantage. Simply put, Berlo did not want to risk the chance of being beaten by Drummond once again and looked for any chance to have Drummond disqualified. If there was any sense of comradery between the two, Berlo's objections would have assumedly created a rift. If it did, however, that rift did not exist very long, or at least it was not something for which Drummond was unwilling to forgive him. The next year, both David Drummond and Peter Berlo had apparently patched things up enough to become club mates as they both pledged membership to the recently organized Tri-Mountain Athletic Club of South Boston. The club intended to have a presence at nearly every race in the Boston area, like the open races of the Harvard University Cycling Club. Of Tri-Mountain's members, only two racers of note were listed, Drummond and Berlo. Berlo was referred to as the "South Boston Flyer" while Drummond was described as "an equally fast rider," which may have meant he was actually faster.[25] Other members were no doubt cycling enthusiasts who rode often, but they were not "racers."

Drummond's involvement in Boston's cycling craze is notable not only because he was a Black cyclist, but also because of the fact that it predated the introduction of the safety bicycle, and he made the transition to that new machine successfully. Because of the dangerous perception of the high wheeler and the flaws of tricycles, innovators continued to pursue safer and faster bicycle designs. This culminated in what came to be known as

30 CHAPTER 2

"safety" bicycles, which were given the nickname precisely because of how much safer those models seemed in contrast to the high wheeler. At first there were many different versions of safety bicycles, but the eventual winner in the court of public opinion was the rover-styled safety bicycle. This model came to adopt equally sized wheels, at about thirty inches each. It was propelled by the rear wheel, which was turned by a chain and sprocket. Soon the "safety" incorporated a diamond-shaped frame, making the bicycle of the 1890s look very much like today's modern bicycle. The diamond-shaped frame was developed with the intent of smoothing the ride, but what helped even more was the development of pneumatic tires. Once these air-filled bicycle tires were around long enough to be improved so that they were cheaper and more dependable, they became standard on all safety bicycles. Pneumatic tires brought a vast improvement in the ride quality of the machine, which led to a dramatic rise in the number of cyclists. Over time, the safety was proven faster than the high wheeler. The safety could be geared to the equivalent of a high wheeler with a sixty-inch front wheel, or much smaller—depending on the size and strength of the rider. Men and women both flocked to the new design and ultimately, even people who believed the safety would never be as fast and efficient as the high wheeler were forced to admit that the safety was superior. Once safeties with pneumatic tires began toppling all the previous records set on high wheelers, the evidence of their superior speed was irrefutable.[26] As the 1889 articles in The Bicycling World and the Worcester Daily Spy point out, as early as 1889 and 1890, Drummond had made the switch to racing safeties.[27] This reflects the larger trends that were happening in cycling. In the 1870s and 1880s, the ordinary or high wheeler was the most popular model of bicycle for racers. By the 1890s, however, the safety would supersede all other designs and usher in the bicycle boom, but Drummond's interest in and contributions to the sport began before this period. He was a Black cyclist clearly at the forefront of this developing new craze, and he was a leading figure in Boston's cycling renaissance.

Drummond was, of course, not the only one to take up the safety bicycle. Staggering numbers of Americans caught the cycling bug. In 1891, because of the commercial popularity of the safety, around 150,000 were sold. This effectively doubled the number of cyclists in the United States.[28] Bicycle production in the United States was on the rise. In 1888, it is estimated that around 16,750 bicycles were produced. By 1890, that number was up

The Mode of Liberation

to 29,890 and it more than doubled two years later, growing to 60,700 bicycles produced in the United States alone.[29] The numbers continued to grow from there, reaching a peak in 1898 and 1899 at around one million bicycles produced per year. Production would fall drastically after that, but it is clear that the 1890s represented an all-out boom for American cycling.

This rise in manufacturing is not the only indication that the bicycle's popularity was growing by leaps and bounds. The sheer numbers in estimates of attendance at cycling events also demonstrate cycling's meteoric rise in American society. By the mid-1890s, cities like Long Branch, New Jersey, hosted "a parade of ten thousand cyclers [who] rolled their decorated machines through the streets, while an estimated seventy-five thousand spectators watched."[30] Not to be outdone, the *New York Herald* estimated 100,000 people crowded the sidewalks of Riverside Drive and Western Boulevard in New York City to watch a parade of 12,000 cyclists roll past in 1896. Of course, since this was a parade sponsored by the *Herald*, there is good reason to suspect the numbers were fudged.[31] Membership in the League of American Wheelmen, the national organization and sanctioning body for cycling events, also saw steady growth during this period. In 1880, the year the League was founded, there were 527 members. That number had more than tripled by the following year and was up to 2,131 in 1883. From there, it would nearly double to 4,250 in 1884 and do so again by 1886 with total membership at 8,463.[32] By the time cycling was on the verge of a full-blown explosion in 1893, there were approximately 40,000 members in the League of American Wheelmen.[33] In 1897, amid the golden age for cycling in the United States, it is estimated that there were around five million active cyclists on American streets. This was at a time when there were only seventy million people total in the United States and the population in urban areas, where cycling was most prominent, was closer to thirty million.[34]

Clearly connected to the growth in the number of cyclists, there was also a precipitous surge in membership and participation in regional cycling clubs and organized cycling events. In Boston alone, there were countless cycling clubs—aside from Drummond's Tri-Mountain Athletic Club. The same was true of New York, Chicago, and many other larger cities. The *Chicago Tribune* calculated that Chicago was home to forty-eight cycling clubs in the year 1892 with a total membership at around 6,000 individuals. There was obviously some consolidation shortly thereafter because three years later, the number of clubs had shrunk to thirty-three, but the total membership had grown closer to 10,000.[35] Many of the clubs focused primarily on socialization through the bicycle. A lot of the events they organized were club outings, or group rides, that were more about the comradery than the competition. Of course, there were often members of the club who were more interested in the competitive aspects.

The clubs that existed also spanned socioeconomic levels. The Tri-Mountain Athletic Club, for instance, was affiliated with the YMCA and used their facilities as a locker room with showers and storage.[36] Other clubs, such as the Massachusetts Bicycle Club, enjoyed much more ostentatious locales. Their club occupied a beautiful three-story house festooned with the name of the club on the third floor, high above the large bay window located on the second floor. The house was complete with an area for bicycle washing and storage on the first floor and showers and locker rooms on the second floor. After cleaning off the residue of the day's ride, the members could make their way to the parlor to chat, drink, and smoke with fellow members. There were separate parlors for male and female members. The men's parlor "was finished in cherry with floors of polished oak. It feature[d] a large rug and grand fireplace. . . . The furniture included a piano, mahogany table, and russet-colored leather chairs. The central chandelier sported gilded bicycle wheels with hubs of colored stone. . . . The adjacent 'ladies' parlor' featured a library, devoted mainly to cycling. The third floor included a gymnasium and meeting room. The basement housed a furnace, bowling alley, and tables for billiards and pool."[37] Similarly, among the other clubs that built their own clubhouses, if they could afford to do so, was the Old Park Cycling Club of Chicago, which constructed a clubhouse for its members that cost fifty thousand dollars.[38] Clubs also spent their often-ample funds on cycling-related venue renovations. In 1886, the Meriden Wheel Club of Connecticut was halfway to their goal of raising $1,500 to construct a one-third-mile track at a nearby park for horses.[39] Clubs that desired and could afford such amenities were obviously populated by people of a certain class and means since much of the funding for such projects came from club members.

Individual club members also represented a somewhat imperceptible range of socioeconomic backgrounds, but there would undoubtedly have been more variation from one club to the next. Even then, it would not have been a very wide range, middle class to upper class for instance. For the most part, new bicycles were beyond the financial reach of the lower classes. There would have been a second-hand market that may have filled some of the consumer demands among the lower classes, but as the historian Carlton Reid points out, many of the photos of bicycle clubs from the era capture images of members who were middle to upper class. It was not until the late 1890s that photos of clubs with members "who appear to be from the skilled working class" began to appear and even then, those photos are somewhat rare.[40] Still, cycling proponents of the 1880s and 1890s certainly argued that the bicycle had an ability to level social classes, and some of them may have even believed it. The bicycle was commonly heralded as a vehicle for democratization. The historian Evan Friss emphasizes this point with various quotes from print media in 1896. Articles chockful of these platitudes were hard to avoid with statements such as: "The Bicycle is the most democratic of machines"; "Old and young, rich and poor, men and women, boys and girls—all caught the 'bicycle fever'"; "As a social leveler the bicycle has been unequaled"; and "Its use is confined to no class."[41] While these remarks employed a certain amount of exaggeration, there was some truth to the praises. There were indeed male and female cyclists, young and old, as well as a range of socioeconomic classes and racial categories. Most cycling historians agree, however, that the majority of cyclists were middle-class White adults. Still, it is also clear that the number of minority cyclists was not insignificant and many of them came from the working classes.

Simply because they were all adherents to the church of the wheel did not necessarily mean all were seen as equal. The fact that clubs were often segregated by class and race suggests as much. There was a club for Chinese cyclists, for instance, aptly named the First Chinese Bicycling Club of Philadelphia. There was also a club for Japanese cyclists called the Rising Sun Cycle Club. There were even clubs for socialists and one for "fat men," in which membership regulations required that you weigh at least 250 lbs.[42] Of course, there were also clubs for African Americans. There were, however, also integrated clubs in the late 1880s and early 1890s. In Milwaukee, for instance, one "Mr. Dorsey [was] the only gentleman of color belonging to [a] club" but the "white members of the club [were] proud of him" and his bicycle, which was one of the finest machines in the club.[43] A Mr. Andrew Braggs of a Cleveland club also made it into the pages of *Cleveland Gazette* for being "the only colored member" to take a trip to Toledo and Michigan

34   CHAPTER 2

via bicycle. He "report[ed] splendid treatment and a most enjoyable time [though] [h]e was the only colored 'cyclist' at the Toledo meeting."[44] While the story made the news because he was the only Black member, it was just important for readers to learn that he was not mistreated—a fact that may have been the most surprising aspect of the story. Similarly, David Drummond was also in one such integrated club. His club, however, clearly served a slightly different class of people than the Massachusetts Bicycle Club and their purposes seemed to vary as well. Drummond's Tri-Mountain Club, with their home base at the YMCA, would have done the majority of their socializing while out on the bicycle. The Massachusetts club, on the other hand, had lavish accommodations for socializing well after the riding was over. There were also clubs that were more focused on racing and competitive cycling while others merely sought leisure and diversion as they paraded their expensive machines and riding outfits about the city with like-minded members. While there was indeed some segregation based on class, race, and gender among the clubs, it is also true that outside the confines of their respective clubhouses, the club members would have often mingled out on the open roads. They also encountered each other at race meets and larger cycling events open to all clubs. This, then, is how David Drummond and other Black cyclists came to rub elbows with, and make impressions on, people well outside their own social sphere. This is also one reason why they embraced the opportunity to use their bicycles to make a statement about race.

For David Drummond and others, the bicycle could also bring social mobility. In the pages of the Cambridge city directory, Drummond was listed as a "spar maker" from 1882 to 1890. As a specialized carpenter who helped fabricate spars, masts, and cargo booms for sailing ships, he likely made two and a half dollars per day.[45] At the same time, a base model Columbia bicycle produced by the Pope Manufacturing Company would have cost around $150. That was more than two months' wages for Drummond. By 1893, however, Pope had reduced those prices to $125 per bicycle.[46] That would have still been a significant financial undertaking, not just for Drummond, but for all among his income bracket, which was average for the period. Despite the cost, it is unlikely that Drummond's bike was a base model or anything that would have been sneered at, due to his prowess on the racing circuit. Many racers received sponsorships from bicycle manufacturers, such as the Pope Manufacturing Company. Similar to today, a

The Mode of Liberation

certain status would have been conferred on the rider based on the make and model of their machine. Those who rode the most expensive models would have been assumed a serious cyclist who was either wealthy or fast enough to receive a bike at a significant discount, if not free. Drummond was given a bicycle by a manufacturer as early as 1886 when the Stoddard Lovering & Company, "a bicycle concern . . . presented . . . [him] a handsome machine worth $140."[47] He may have really liked that particular bicycle and kept it, but it is also very possible that he immediately sold it—using the proceeds for another bicycle, or parts. Whatever model he settled on, Drummond's bicycle, undoubtedly lighter and faster than the average carpenter's, allowed him to navigate social circles beyond that of a carpenter as well. It is little surprise then, that Drummond soon earned himself more comfortable employment. By 1891, the Cambridge directory listed him as a clerk. This may have been at a bicycle shop since his occupation would be listed as "bicycle repairer" and even "bicycle maker" over the next few years. By then, he would have even greater access to high-end models and extra time to maintain his own bicycle. While the pay, around $12.00 per week for the average clerk in 1896, may not have been much more than a spar maker, as a well-known and respected cyclist, working in a bicycle shop would have more psychological rewards and fringe benefits than carpentry work in the shipyards.[48]

David Drummond was clearly a well-known and popular fixture in the Boston cycling scene, but his stature and the respect other members in the community had for him extended beyond cycling circles. Aside from being a young Black athlete who turned heads on the racetrack, Drummond was also an educated young man who could read and write. He used those skills to exercise his rights of civic engagement. Further evidence of Drummond's connections, status, and activism comes from his membership and leading role in the Order of the Knights of Pythias, a fraternal organization in which he was elected the "keeper of records and seals" in the summer of 1887.[49] While the Knights of Pythias were integrated, at least in 1887, there was some controversy over the subject as "the white Supreme Chancellor of Massachusetts, Mr. Douglass [charged] that the colored Pythians were bogus members of the order."[50] The Knights of Pythias focused on friendship, charity, and benevolence in their work. Drummond's membership in a fraternal order like this would have necessitated a certain status in his community. He was obviously a well-respected and notable figure in

Boston's Black community, but he also showed his equality with Whites in terms of civic contributions. In these circles, Drummond had established a strong friendship with the Black journalist J. Gordon Street, who was always willing and able to share Drummond's exploits on the wheel with the readers of the *New York Freeman* and other Black newspapers to which he was a regular contributor. For instance, in a section on the happenings in Boston, the *New York Freeman*, which catered to an African American audience, let readers know "Mr. David Drummond of Cambridgeport, the champion bicycle rider was recently elected a member of the Cambridgeport Bicycle Club."[51] Working together, Drummond, Street, and James Monroe Trotter offer a strong example of the coordinated attack against racial discrimination that was being waged by the men of New England.

For all of these men, the fact that a Black man was equal to that of a White man was unquestionable. While Trotter proved this through his high positions in the military and civil service, David Drummond and other Black cyclists proved their equality on the bicycle. They, too, were proud to be members of their race and considered it a virtue to have the "manliness to say" so. While Drummond's friend and ally James Monroe Trotter was described as "a man who had honored colored Americans by his manhood, his courage, his honesty and unsullied character; a man of intense race pride and devotion to his people," it appears that David Drummond embodied many of those same virtues. He undoubtedly carried his belief about racial equality aboard his bicycle as he rode among and against his White peers. He was not supportive of the idea expressed by Booker T. Washington in his "Atlanta Compromise," that "in all things that are purely social we can be as separate as the fingers." With his bicycle, beside and often out in front of the bicycles of White men, he could show, rather than tell, the world that he was far from inferior to White men. He undoubtedly inspired others. In fact, James Trotter's son, William, would go on to be one of the early adapters of the bicycle on Harvard's campus and one of the most vocal opponents of Washington's accommodationist stance on issues of race.[52] It was likely that Drummond and William knew each other well as they were little more than ten years apart in age and both were frequently wheeling around Boston.

Just as first-wave feminists like Frances Willard, Susan B. Anthony, and Elizabeth Cady Stanton were all vociferous proponents of the wheel, it is not surprising that African Americans who also saw the 1880s and '90s as

The Mode of Liberation

a critical moment to be active in the fight for their own civil rights were seduced by the wheel. First-wave feminism and the roots of the Civil Rights Movement were both firmly established during this period, and many of those activists saw bicycles as yet one more way to liberate themselves from oppression. The mere presence of Black cyclists, let alone their accomplishments with the wheel, was held up as a sign of progress for the race. A section of the *Indianapolis Freeman* focusing on "political, social, and business achievements of the colored people" highlighted the fact that in 1888, "Chicago ha[d] a colored bicycle club." It was somewhat small at first, with a president, Robert Ellinger, and eight other members.[53] Regardless of size, the mere creation of such a club said something significant—that there were enough Black men with the same affluent interests in a sporting and leisure activity to create a club. Together, they would go for group rides where they would exert their right to public space and the open road.

From the beginning, and as bicycles grew in importance to American society, Black Americans were there to enjoy and employ the bicycle toward their own idealistic pursuits. In the 1880s and 1890s, the bicycle represented a new and exciting technology. Simply riding a bicycle was a way to signal one's embrace of modernity. Most clearly, in the 1880s it was a signifier of class, but it also allowed people to express their own ideals of gender and race. David Drummond and many other Black cyclists used this new technology to exert their masculinity and proclaim their equality. It was one thing to outwork another man, or to prove you were stronger, but the bicycle allowed you to do that while also demonstrating your mastery of new technology that was still too expensive for the masses. Drummond and others also used the bicycle to demonstrate their class mobility and to achieve a sense of muscular assimilation. Riding a bicycle was demonstrative of their financial means, and racing against, often beating, White men in cycling competitions would then demonstrate that the color of their skin did not denote physical inferiority. The fact that cycling, unlike boxing, was heralded as a refined sport that suited middle-class ideals of masculinity by men like Charles Pratt, a leader of the League of American Wheelmen, meant that Black cyclists were making a powerful statement about classist ideals and respectability when they mounted their machines.[54]

For the Black cyclists who were members of cycling clubs, the bicycle also afforded them opportunities to socialize with prominent men in their communities. Many of these men were also politically active. The League of

American Wheelmen certainly had a pronounced political agenda. In fact, it was largely a political body in and of itself, but for the most part, it was a single-issue constituency. That single issue was good roads. It was a very powerful voting block, however, so much so that politicians like William Henry Harrison played nice with the league. Carlton Reid argues, "Cyclists weren't influential in the 1890s merely because there were lots of them. They were influential because many prominent individuals—from business, high society, politics, and more—were keen cyclists. The 'freemasonry of the wheel' was real. Politicians who weren't cyclists knew not to cross them."[55] These circles that Black cyclists were able to maneuver about during the 1880s and early 1890s would, however, soon begin to draw closed. Even in Boston, Black men and women would find new barriers erected that would serve to curtail social and political activities. Much like the potential and promise of radical reconstruction in the South, this period would stand as something of a great moment of optimism for the Black cyclist. Moving forward, their story would be one of struggles against increasing racial discrimination in the world of cycling.

3
Drawing the Color Line

Just after lunch on Tuesday, February 20, 1894, Colonel William Wagner Watts of Kentucky took the floor in parlor B of the Galt House Hotel in Louisville, Kentucky—his hometown. Standing there, before the 178 delegates in attendance at the National Assembly of the League of American Wheelmen, Watts endeavored to put the finishing touch on a goal that seemed his sole objective for more than a year. He was there to ask the League of American Wheelmen (LAW) to add one simple word to their constitution. That one word was "white." It was to be added to a critical passage. If adopted, the LAW constitution would read, any "amateur white wheelman" is eligible for membership, instead of the less restrictive "amateur wheelman" that was stated in the constitution already. Most delegates sat quietly. Some may have dragged lightly on cigars, paying more attention to their tobacco than to Watts. After all, this was not the first time they had sat through such an appeal from the dark-haired and thickly mustached thirty-four-year-old Kentucky lawyer and editor of the *Southern Wheelman*. Just one year prior, during a thirty-minute soliloquy at the National Assembly of the LAW in Philadelphia, Watts cried out, "I demand in the name of the South . . . that the word 'white' be inserted" into the constitution. Reverberating throughout the hall, Watts declared, "Wipe out the nigger and we will give you many white members in his place."[1] More specifically, he claimed this addendum to the constitution would help draw in as many as 5,000 additional members, mostly in the South. For an organization with around 37,000 members and annual dues set at around one dollar and fifty cents per member, that would have meant about 13.5 percent growth in membership and $7,500 more in their operating budget. In 1894, however, the delegates gathered in Louisville would not see him going through the same oratorical efforts he used one year earlier in Philadelphia.

William Watts's failure to get the amendment through in 1893 had impressed upon him that votes were to be secured well in advance of putting the question to the floor. He kept his point brief in Louisville, spending a majority of his time reading a letter from the "colored" Union Cycle Club of Kentucky. Written by their president, Frederick J. Scott, and signed by twenty-five members, the letter was presented as evidence that even Black cyclists were supportive of inserting the word "white" into the league's constitution.[2] As president of the Black Union Cycle Club, Scott allegedly told the league's secretary, Thomas Dorsey, upon handing him the letter, "We believe in the objects of the league, and we want to aid the league in carrying them out as far as we possibly can. We do not want to belong to an organization where we are not wanted, because we are gentlemen and men of sense, and understand these things."[3] With the point made, Watts then notified the members in attendance that he needed to leave the meeting early to be at home with his sick daughter. Before yielding the floor, however, he added, "I want to say that the whisky which Mr. Bassett mentioned to you will be delivered to you by Colonel Johnson of Kentucky. I hope that each man will see that he receives his package. There is enough for everybody. The Kentucky members take pleasure in giving it to you as a souvenir, because they know it is good. Take it home and keep it there."[4] The room erupted in applause. Watts savored the sound until it faded and then asked that the vote be taken without discussion. He said goodbye and departed.[5]

Curiously, the *Indianapolis Journal* reported that the question of inserting the word "white" was then momentarily tabled while the league moved on to the question of where to hold the annual meeting in July. That meeting would potentially host several thousand in attendance since it was a meeting for all members of the league, not just the leaders who were present at the assembly. As a result, this seemingly innocuous decision was actually quite contentious. Three locations were up for consideration: Boston, Asbury Park, and Denver. However, the Boston supporters decided

Drawing the Color Line

to remove their city from consideration just before the national assembly at the Galt House and to abstain from voting on the issue. They apparently saw Asbury Park in New Jersey as the more popular choice among the North and East. Splitting the votes of those regions between Boston and Asbury Park would have certainly aided in Denver's bid to host the meet. The Colorado city had the votes of all territories west of Missouri secured and even a few eastern delegates had agreed to vote for Denver. With the predictions of a close contest in mind, the men campaigning for Asbury Park, including champion cyclist Arthur Zimmerman, brought thousands of cigars to distribute with wrappers that read "Asbury Park for '94: We want the meet and nothing more."[6] Some of the men also wore badges that read, "Asbury Park for '94."

Eastern constituents were perhaps a little surprised when the vote, taken by ballot, resulted in a 93 to 70 decision in favor of Denver over Asbury Park. With the location of next year's meeting decided, the league then came back to the amendment that would effectively draw a color line for the organization. As Watts requested, there was no discussion and the issue went straight to a vote resulting in 127 affirming and fifty-four voting against adding the word white to the constitution.[7] Needing two-thirds of the votes to carry, the motion won by a mere seven votes. There were eighteen more total votes on the amendment than there were on the relatively more mundane question of where the next annual meeting would be held, but that could be explained by the abstention of the Massachusetts delegates. Both decisions were made by ballot vote, but the issue of where to hold the next meeting garnered a "long discussion" whereas the question of amending the constitution was not discussed at all.[8] Reporting on the upcoming assembly the day before it began, Louisville's *Courier-Journal* seemed to think the decision to hold the 1894 meeting at Asbury Park and the adoption of the color line were as good as decided.[9] That was not to be the case with regard to Asbury Park. Reports on the assembly make it clear that there was a lot of caucusing prior to voting. That caucusing began long before the delegates even arrived in Louisville. With deals negotiated, certain members may have wanted to see how the vote for location of the annual meeting shook out before voting on the constitutional amendment. If it was favorable for Denver, western members might have pledged their support to the South on the question of the color line. The fact that Watts assured members they would get the "Belle of Nelson" whisky promised to them also makes it clear that the South took extra steps to secure a favorable vote for the color line.[10] Upon hearing the results of the vote on the color line, Colonel G. Edward Johnson, the man who was to deliver that whisky, stood to thank the assembly "on behalf of Kentucky and the Southern states for drawing the color line." Then he assured the body that membership would grow.[11]

An advertisement for Belle of Nelson whisky from 1892 shows that it was owned by the Bartley, Johnson & Co. of Louisville, Kentucky. Col. Edward Johnson was obviously well connected. He was employed as the circulation manager for the *Courier-Journal* and *Louisville Times* as well as the "private secretary" of the legendary booster of the "New South," Col. Henry Watterson.[12] Not only did Johnson reportedly know Watterson "more intimately than any other Louisvillian," he also served as the "private secretary" of General William Birch Haldeman for a number of years.[13] Aside from the office of Adjutant General of Kentucky, Haldeman declined many nominations for public office but still he was known as a powerhouse in the Democratic Party. He was also elected Commander-in-Chief of the United Confederate Veterans at a reunion in 1923. He was a continual presence at the erection of confederate monuments around the state of Kentucky and extremely influential in horse-racing circles.[14] Of course, William Watts ran in many of those very same circles. Both Ed Johnson and William Watts would be buried at the beautiful, and somewhat exclusive, grounds of Cave Hill Cemetery in Louisville. Johnson would get there first, but even then, Watts served as a pallbearer at Johnson's funeral in 1921, along with the well-known Louisville cyclist Howard Jeffries.[15] William Watts, Ed Johnson, and Henry Watterson were all "Colonels," which was an honorific handed out by Kentucky governors of that era—often as favors to men of wealth and means. By no means did it denote military service. It does appear, however, that Watts's father, William O. Watts from Kentucky, served as quartermaster for the 37th Kentucky Infantry for the Union Army in the Civil War.[16] The fact that the father participated in what some would see as an effort to end slavery and yet the son stood before the LAW to ask that those very same people, and their descendants, be barred from membership, teases out some of the complexities of racial sentiments in the 1890s. It is likely that Watts did not see himself as racist or the color line as a bad thing for Black people, since Black cyclists were free to form their own league. As the historian Chandra Manning argues, Union troops supported

Drawing the Color Line   43

the Thirteenth Amendment but after that, they believed their obligation to African Americans was met. To put it in the words of John English of the Union Army, he believed the Thirteenth Amendment made "the Negro . . . free forever in this country, as every other race and nation, and on an equality before the law," but that equality did not necessarily apply "in a social point of view."[17] In short, William Wagner Watts's role in drawing the color line is not at odds with the service of his father, nor were his sentiments unique to the South at the time.

Another pivotal factor affecting the question of adding the word white to the constitution came a day earlier, on the first day of the National Assembly, when Charles H. Luscomb of New York was elected president of the league. His sole challenger was Thomas F. Sheridan of Chicago. Sheridan was chief consul of the Illinois Division of the league. More importantly, he was the first vice president of the LAW, but in spite of those prominent positions of leadership, Sheridan sealed his fate during the election early in 1893, when Watts first presented his amendment. Whereas Luscomb would be the obvious choice of the divisions from New England, the North, and the East, Sheridan could expect to have the support of the western divisions. The only way Sheridan could have overcome the East's powerful numbers, in comparison to membership in the West, was to win the support of the South. In a clever display of diplomacy, the South would not vote as a solid unit for one candidate over the other. Instead, they traded votes with members of the West for support of the constitutional amendment to add the word white. They only traded some of their votes, however, reserving the rest for Luscomb. Enough to ensure his victory.[18] The South's desire to see Luscomb of New York take the helm over Sheridan of Chicago dated back to the 1893 National Assembly of the LAW that took place in Philadelphia.

To say the previous assembly, the one of 1893, got off to a disorganized start is an understatement. League members were unsure of exactly where in Philadelphia the meeting would be held at first. Once that issue was settled, the meeting was eventually called to order by President Burdette, who was so disheveled he was forced to use a bottle of salt in lieu of a proper gavel. To understand the debates and eventual vote to insert the word white at the 1894 assembly, one has to start with the National Assembly of 1893. This is true for a few reasons. First, it was at that National Assembly in 1893 that it was decided there would no longer need to be Constitutional

44 CHAPTER 3

Conventions to amend the constitution. First Vice President Sheridan offered instead that the constitution could be amended simply by publicizing
the proposed amendment in the printed organ of the LAW at least thirty
days in advance and it had to receive two-thirds of the votes. Sheridan's
proposal stated further that league divisions would then have the chance
to ratify the amendments individually, but that part was removed. The rest
was adopted unanimously.[19] The National Assembly of 1893 also broached
the topic of amateurism within the league and whether they should create
a separate class (class B) of riders thereby becoming more lenient on members who earned monetary rewards for racing. The elites who led the LAW,
for the most part, embraced the ideals of amateurism and believed that
cycling should be done for the pure enjoyment. Racing, therefore, should be
done solely for the sport, not for the potential to earn money. They found,
however, that a strict sanctioning of members who did profit from racing
led to a significant and time-consuming headache for the league, as well as
a loss of membership due to the expulsion of members. Records presented
showed that 566 sanctions were granted and 139 members, "racing men"
specifically, were either suspended or expelled for violations.[20] The league
found itself inundated by the sanctioning and governance of a rapidly growing number of bicycle races, and in 1893 there were already hints that some
members wanted to put an end to the league's role as a sanctioning body
for bicycle racing all together. After a long discussion, the amendment for
a class B was withdrawn, but the debate was far from over.

On Tuesday, February 21, the second day of the 1893 Assembly, Vice
President Sheridan called the meeting to order at 9:20 a.m. It was there that
William Watts first presented his amendment to exclude non-Whites. *The
Referee & Cycle Trade Journal* says his speech was brief and to the point, but
other sources reported that he talked for nearly thirty minutes. *The Bearings*
magazine described it as "two hours of red hot and at times almost rancor-
ous debate . . . heaped upon the wooly head of the colored men."[21] After
Watts finished the main thrust of his argument, the secretary for the league
had raised the point that there were "only six or seven colored members"
total in the entire league. Watts did not dispute the paltry figure but instead
rebuffed that if those six or seven were gone, the league would have 5,000
White members in their place. The assembly then heard arguments for and
against the amendment. It was during this debate that the bearded man
from Chicago with a high part in his hair, Vice President Thomas Sheridan,

Drawing the Color Line

rose to the floor to oppose "Watts' amendment" and object to Watts "using the word 'nigger' in general."[22] When cornered, Sheridan himself would not say that "he actually desired the admission of negroes." Instead, he danced around that question, explaining that "the league could not afford to oppose itself to the principles adopted by the United States."[23] More specifically, Sheridan and the Illinois Division worried that explicitly barring Black cyclists would be a political liability that may cause them to lose government support for their "good roads" initiative.[24] Good roads were tantamount to the league's, and bicycles' in general, success. Because of these concerns, instead of adding the word white to the constitution, Sheridan supported other means of keeping Black cyclists out of the league, such as the voucher system that was already in use among many divisions. This would require any new member to obtain written vouchers from two standing members before they could join.[25] The southerners, however, could not stomach the idea of vouchers, fearing the thought of a White man even being asked to vouch for a Black man. They preferred an outright ban. As one writer in the *Wheelman's Gazette* would point out, the intricacies of racism in the North versus those in the South were not lost on league members. He wrote, "If they [the South] don't want negroes, they have their remedy. Let their local divisions settle the difficulty. Here in the North where prejudice is not so pronounced, or at least, where it is better concealed, we can handle the matter to our own satisfaction."[26]

The league's president ex officio, Charles Luscomb of New York, took the floor after Sheridan. Described as a lawyer and orator, he began his rebuttal of Sheridan by relaying a "suppositious case." He said, suppose "I meet a friend who sees my league button and says, 'Ah, what is that?' 'That,' I say, 'is my LAW button.' 'Oh, yes,' says my friend, 'my colored coachman wears the same button.'"[27] Implying that the prospect of more Black members sullied the prestige of the league, it soon became quite clear that Luscomb was opposed to extending membership to anyone who was not White. Though he was from New York, his rationale sounded much like that of his southern brethren in the league. Simply belonging to the same club as non-Whites, let alone associating with them, was absolutely objectionable on its face. He was cheered on by other members, including those of the South, when he said, "We only want those in the league whom we are willing to associate with. If we don't want the negro we should have manhood enough to stand up and say so."[28] This cut to the core in the disagreement between the

46   CHAPTER 3

North and the South on the issue. For Luscomb and others, neither faction wanted Black members, on that they were the same. It was the matter of how they should enact their exclusion that was at issue.

Sterling Elliott from Massachusetts was then given the floor to explain that he believed the league should allow membership of non-Whites because, "the best way to educate an ignorant man is to encourage him by showing him that he may, in due course, attain the positions held by his *superiors* [emphasis mine]."[29] Even Elliot, who seemed to be one of the biggest allies of Black members, was not casting doubt on the idea of White supremacy. He ascribed more to the sort of thinking pronounced in Rudyard Kipling's "White Man's Burden" that White men were called to uplift all other races of the world. Elliott had gone on record with considerable vehemence in the pages of *The Bicycling World and L.A.W. Bulletin* just months before the 1893 Assembly. He wrote, "There seems to be a considerable number of the League brethren who are willing to go on record as advocates only of a League of 'White trash' for the white trash, and who would debar our sable relative from the advantages of membership in an organization which already contains the salt of the earth (yes, and much of the pepper and mustard)."[30] Elliott believed the more members there were in the league the better, and that class and décor were more important than the members' complexion. Complicating his views on race, Elliott argued that the league was, at its heart, a "great political party" and its main objective was to see the building and improvement of good roads. Since that was the case, he wrote, "We want every member and every dollar and every vote that is to be had. A black gentleman is infinitely superior to a White hoodlum. Let us size up the applicant by his behavior, not by his color."[31] Thus, the members in attendance knew Elliott's position long before he rose to the floor, but this time he played to member's racial paternalism, rather than political pragmatism.

Isaac Potter of New York and W. H. Pontius of Indiana then followed Elliott on the floor and added their support for keeping membership open regardless of race, but the speech that was remarked on most was that of the ex-President Kirkpatrick of Ohio. Kirkpatrick lamented that he was bound to vote for the color line by order of his division, but he stated that his personal opinion was against such a restriction. Offering more of a patriotic perspective, he said, "If we are to go down, by all means let us go down with our colors flying and loyal to the principles of our nation."[32] He saw a color

Drawing the Color Line

line in the league as a contradiction of his nation's principles. Kirkpatrick's speech was considered the finest of the day, maybe even the best in league history. *The Bearings* offered the opinion, "Voters in the Assembly seemed to be singularly influenced by the eloquence of Mr. Thomas J. Kirkpatrick. I believe his remarks decided the negro question. . . ."[33] It was Watts who closed the debate, however, "spreading wide his arms he cried: 'Relieve us in the South from this embarrassment; don't force us to associate with the negro.'"[34] Sterling Elliott then asked for clarification if Watts meant to "exclude all men having a trace of negro blood." When Watts answered in the affirmative, Elliott asked Watts if he knew that two of the highest officers in the league had "traces of negro blood." *The Bearings* reported that a "subdued sensation" followed this accusation and that Elliott was allowed to take the floor later that day to explain that he did not mean to make any specific accusations, he was just trying to illustrate a point. A proxy vote held after the long debate ended resulted in 108 votes in favor of inserting the word white and 101 against. Since it was a constitutional amendment, it needed 138 votes to carry.[35] Watts had failed. Due to his leadership on the issue, the amendment to insert the word white would become referred to as the Watts amendment.

Watts and his fellow Kentuckians certainly earned credit for the idea. It was one year prior, in July of 1892, that the Kentucky Division of the LAW decided to draw the color line in its own constitution. That idea reportedly "took so well that there was at once a demand for a national constitutional amendment shutting out the negro."[36] It was William Watts, of course, who took the initiative to propose such an amendment, but Ed Johnson was no doubt working with him. Johnson's employer, the Louisville *Courier-Journal* seemed to support the color line for the national LAW by reporting, "all of the Southern, most of the Western and some of the Northern States supported the proposed amendment. Massachusetts, Connecticut, Indiana and two or three other States with large memberships fought it, however, and prevented its adoption."[37] The *Courier-Journal* was not wrong, but even though there was a simple majority in favor, the amendment was a few votes shy of ratification. After the loss, Watts mounted the platform and graciously said, "To those who voted with us we extend our thanks and to those who voted against us we extend the right hand of good fellowship."[38]

While it was not entirely clear what the immediate effects of the amendment's failure would be, many forecasted a "falling off" of membership in

48   CHAPTER 3

the South and the West but that "no perceptible difference" would result in the North and East.[39] There was also speculation about the potential effects of increasing Black membership in the league. A. S. Hardin took to the pages of *The Bearings* to offer a decidedly different perspective than that of Sterling Elliott. Directly addressing the arguments of political pragmatism and corruption, he wrote, "One of the chief arguments used by those favoring the admission of the negro to League membership is that the League is about to become an important political body. Now it is a well-known fact that where money is not used in elections, the negro almost universally votes for republican candidates, and when votes are being purchased, his vote is generally for sale to the highest bidder. If we are to go into politics, we want no one in our ranks who can be bribed. Therefore, from a political standpoint the League has no use for the negro, because he is not reliable. Again, the admission of negroes to membership will deter a great many cyclists we do want from joining and we cannot afford to lose desirable White members for the sake of a few negroes."[40] Hardin then went on to paint a picture of what the future would hold for an integrated league. He surmised, "The first thing they [Black cyclists] would probably do would be to demand accommodation at League hotels, and the LAW would be compelled to sustain them in the demand. Everyone can see at once what a storm that would bring about our ears. No sensible hotel keeper catering to the White trade would take a League contract that might require him to give to a negro the same accommodation he would a White man. They would always be out in full force at race meets and on all occasions of note, and at such times negroes are always loud, overbearing and boisterous, and on account of their noisy, officious and demonstrative activity, would seem three or four times as numerous as they really are."[41] For Hardin, and many others insisting on the color line, it was convenient to blame the racism of others. Here, it was the hotel owners and operators who would be the problem, not league members. He does not merely hide behind that excuse, however. He brings his own racist presumptions into the hypothetical. Though, to be clear, it was not just Hardin who felt this way. After all, 108 of the total 209 votes in 1893 were in favor of the color line. In 1894 there were even more.

For the time being, those in support of barring Black men from membership consoled themselves with the fact that it "[would] not be an easy matter for a negro to get in anywhere." This was an allusion to the unspoken racial discrimination and voucher system already in place, which required applications be endorsed by two LAW members. The difficulty Black riders would have had in finding two such men to vouch for them is not hard to imagine.[42] A further obstruction was a plan to publish the addresses of applicants, thereby verifying their identity, or allowing members to do so. Members could object to any new application and it would be denied, granted the reason for objection was seen as legitimate. It was made clear that an objection based solely on the perceived race of the applicant was enough.[43] Even still, the supporters of an outright color line saw signs of progress. They believed the league was coming around to their perspective by proclaiming, "we were knocked out this time, [in 1893] but are certain of victory next year. One year ago the Assembly would not even consider the question. This year a majority of the members favored a white limit."[44] Indeed, their predictions of the amendment's eventual success were correct. Colonel William Watts and his supporters seemed to will the color line into existence.

The mobilization around barring Black cyclists from joining the LAW in the early years of the 1890s is not out of context with larger historic trends. Most obvious, or perhaps the climax of the growing outward expression of racism directed at African Americans, was the codification of segregation that came in 1896 with the Supreme Court's decision to endorse the concept of "separate but equal" in the case of *Plessy v. Ferguson*. Racial violence was also on the rise. In his study of Kentucky, George C. Wright, pulled together statistics from the NAACP and various newspapers to highlight the uptick in reports of racial violence in the 1890s. The number of lynchings of Black people in Kentucky reported per decade from 1860 to 1940 peaked at sixty-six between 1890 and1899.[45] December of 1896 seemed to be particularly brutal in Kentucky. The *Courier-Journal* ran reports from fourteen different newspapers that spoke of a "lynching wave" during the last week of December. Wright highlights how out-of-state journals commented on the events in a sometimes mocking and sarcastic tones. One paper reported, "In Kentucky this Christmas the favorite decoration of trees is strangled negroes." Another paper wrote, "It was a Merry Christmas week in Kentucky—six lynchings within six days. But while this may be a joyous way of celebrating in Kentucky, we cannot regard it with unmixed feelings of

50   CHAPTER 3

satisfaction from the standpoint of the country at large."[46] Kentucky had a reputation for racial violence that men in the LAW were certainly aware of before traveling to Louisville. One report on the upcoming 1894 Assembly in Louisville pointed out that Kentucky had "a reputation for good whiskey, bluegrass, and negro haters."[47] That reputation was not entirely baseless. A little over three months after the eventual decision to ban Black cyclists from the league in 1894, Ed Johnson's close friend Henry Watterson, editor of the Louisville *Courier-Journal*, penned an editorial that took issue with Ida B. Wells and the British Press for their condemnation of racial violence in Kentucky. He contended that Wells, the "negro woman from Memphis is still stirring up the British over the barbarism of the Southern people in lynching negroes." He argued that the British, as well as other outsiders, should not cast aspersions simply "because the Southern whites protect their women by killing their ravishers."[48] Ida Wells would become famous for investigating the claims of sexual misconduct against Black men and proving an overwhelming majority false. Several years later, Watterson would take a much less defensive tone when discussing lynchings, even going so far as to call for their end. Similarly, *The Bearings* took issue with the British, this time for their comments on the league's decision to bar Black riders. Without quoting directly, a small paragraph said, "It is somewhat amusing to read in the cycling papers of England, the country that did its best to keep the American negro in bondage by aiding the Southern cause, paragraphs condemning the movement to keep the colored man out of the LAW."[49] While Watts' 1893 attempt at the amendment failed in Philadelphia, it was clearly on much more favorable terms by the time it was proposed again, the following year in Louisville.

Soon after Watts failed at the Philadelphia meeting of 1893, there were reports that several cities, not in the South, began enacting their own restrictions against Black cyclists. Chicago, St. Louis, and Denver were all taking action to enforce segregation in cycling a little over a month after the Philadelphia assembly. At that assembly, A.C. Davis of St. Louis was said to have become a "prominent figure" among wheelmen "on account of his strong opposition to the negro."[50] The attempts at enacting restrictions extended beyond exclusion from club membership, however. There were also efforts to bar Black cyclists from bicycle racing. On April 17, upon spotting "two colored wheelmen," members of the Denver Wheelmen began to question whether those two men would be allowed to enter the upcoming road race. Even though they were both described as "intelligent, well-behaved young men [who] ride high grade wheels" the final assessment was that they would not be allowed to race because "their skin [was] too dark."[51] This suggests that Sterling Elliott's emphasis on the class and décor of a person being more important that the color of their skin was certainly not a belief held by all members of the cycling community.

It seemed even more surprising that in Chicago, where Thomas Sheridan would be appointed as the referee for the Pullman Road Race, the color line was also drawn. On September 9, 1892, the *Plaindealer* of Detroit called attention to a vote among the members of the Associated Cycling Clubs of Chicago of 80 to 20 against admitting the Chicago Colored Cycling Club into their association. As the short announcement pointed out, it would be safe to infer that the Associated Cycling Clubs was also "opposed to the admission of colored cyclists to the League of American Wheelman."[52] The *Cleveland Gazette* followed up on the story a little over eight months later pointing out that Associated Cycling Clubs of Chicago had also decided to bar Black cyclists from specific events, like the Pullman Road Race. The *Gazette* described the consternation that decision was causing since Black cyclists were indeed allowed membership in the LAW and had been participating in numerous cycling events with no signs of discrimination.[53] It was perhaps surprising that the precedent for barring Black cyclists from sanctioned events was set in Chicago, rather than other cities around the United States more openly hostile to African Americans. Chicago does, however, have its own its own troubling history on issues of race. In the Chicago Associated Cycling Clubs' April 12th decision to bar Black cyclists, it was reported that only two delegates voted to allow Black cyclists to enter the race. The *Bearings* explained, "no one seemed anxious to speak on the subject, and when the question was put only Gardiner . . . and Root . . . voted for the *Africans* [emphasis mine]."[54] It is safe to assume Thomas Sheridan was at that meeting and even though he took the floor to argue against adding white to the constitution in Philadelphia, on this occasion, little over a month later, he was noticeably silent. The *Courier-Journal* took note of the inconsistencies reporting that "Illinois voted for the negro in Philadelphia and against him in Chicago."[55] This seemed to fit well with the assumption among many southerners that the people supporting the inclu-

52   CHAPTER 3

sion of Black cyclists in the LAW did not actually want them as members, they were just not "man enough" to face the political ramifications, or they were outright Janus-faced hypocrites.

Southern members in the league had reacted to the decision against Watts' amendment in a familiar manner; one that was not lost on northern members. Ex-chief consul of Tennessee, T.J. Deupree, said, failing to exclude Black cyclists in Philadelphia "has certainly caused a great deal of dissatisfaction in Tennessee, and I have no doubt in other parts of the South." He believed there was a real chance that a "number of Memphis wheelmen" would withdraw from the LAW. Even though he believed it "would be foolish." Deupree also said he could "understand" the possibility of such a reaction explaining, "The feeling against the negro is very strong down there, and as there are as many colored men in Memphis as there are whites, the disagreeable qualities of the son of Ham are more in evidence than you can imagine."[56] Clear proof that the decision to vote down the Watts amendment in 1893 hurt membership seemed to be contradicted, however, by a report in early 1894 stating that the LAW had a total of 36,950 members with an increase of 2,646 in total membership and a drop in female membership from 1,162 to 915.[57] Of course, these statistics do not specify where those new members were from, but it is somewhat surprising that the decline of female membership was not somehow fictitiously linked to the failure to ratify the Watts amendment.

The question of whether individual members would leave was one thing, but there were also rumors that a broader secessionist effort was afoot, which began spreading immediately after the vote in 1893. One week after the vote, Chief Consul Holm of St. Louis denied that there was any movement to secede from the LAW, especially as far as Missouri was concerned. Just before the Philadelphia meeting, however, *The Bearings* wrote that it received a report, which it considered dubious, from Illinois Cycle Company President, H.J. Winn. He said that he had spoken with Chief Consul Holm, who told him that "negotiations had been going on for some time between the leaders of several divisions, including Missouri and the southern states," and if demands that divisions be given the right to exclude Black cyclists were not given, "secession should take place."[58] In denying the content of this reported conversation, Holm said of the idea, "We tried it once in 1884 and were glad to get back into the fold."[59] Regardless, that did not put an end to the rumors of secession. In April, the Captain of the Capital City

Cycling Club of Nashville claimed to know eighty-three LAW members who were in agreement with him that there "be either a white LAW or a blank southern membership"[60] In May, *The Bearings* was still reporting on the developments writing, "the efforts of would-be secessionists to form an association in the south antagonistic to the LAW are laughable." The magazine determined that those promoting such action were "not versed in cycling matters" pointing out that they even had to pull in a northern consultant and prominent cyclist, Arthur Augustus Zimmerman, to create a mock race schedule for such an organization. The brief article about the prospect of secession in May concluded, "A charming prospect. But honestly, Secesh, what is the good of it all? Suppose you do organize. You will have accomplished nothing practical and your chances at the next National Assembly will be lessened."[61] In short, if they would just remain patient, the color line would come to pass.

By September, the turmoil had yet to subside as some continued to advocate for the South's secession from the LAW and for forming their own league. This was contingent upon the LAW failing to draw the color line in the near future. Southern cyclists who advocated for their own league argued that "by forming a separate league they would keep much money in the south that is sent north in the shape of dues and initiation fees and that they would be able to hold their own authorized championships."[62] George K. Barrett, editor of *The Bearings*, wrote, if the decision to form a southern league were based on finances or to have its own recognized southern championships, then "we can have some little sympathy with the movement." If the move were based solely on the desire to "keep the negro out of the LAW . . . then we can have no sympathy whatever with it." He then described such motivations as akin to a "child who 'won't play' unless he can have things all his own way."[63] Barrett called on "Southern Knights of the Wheel" to make their fight "bravely" and not to make threats they did not intend to carry through and not to carry through on those threats just because they could not have their way.[64] His remarks were met with some disdain from southern members, or at least one in particular. Under the pseudonym of "Dock" one such supposed southerner went so far as to accuse northern members of waiving the "Bloody Shirt," which had its roots in the aftermath of the Civil War and Southern feelings that the North put the blame solely on the South for all the death and destruction of the war itself.

54 CHAPTER 3

It was Barrett himself who drew attention to the reception his comments received. Writing in December of 1893, a little over three months after his initial editorial, Barrett took to the pages of *The Bearings* again to summarize his previous points and to lay out "Dock's" response, which Barrett claimed had made "the rounds of the obscure country papers in the south" and had circulated back to *The Bearings* "on average of twice a week for months."[65] Writing to a Mr. Charles Thacker of Cleburne, Texas, in reaction to Barrett's editorial, "Dock" listed his grievances: "Heretofore I have taken little interest in the proposed southern league; but Charley, when the 'Bloody Shirt' is brought in the league politics, it makes my blood boil, and I am with you heart and hand. I had hoped that the negro element would amount to nothing, but Charley, they throw it in our teeth that they will receive the negro as a brother. Like you, I say if they want to inhale these 'pungent perfumes' and fraternize with the so-called Afro-American, no true southerner can regard them with any feelings except repugnance."[66] In response, Barrett's first question was, "who is 'Dock'?" but he also seemed a little lost on who exactly Charles Thacker was and why he was the one spearheading the effort to begin a new league for cycling in the South. He was apparently not a well-known figure in the larger LAW and Barrett mused that no one had really heard of Thacker outside of "the narrow confines of the little Texas hamlet" he was from. Writing about the fact that the LAW technically extended membership to Black cyclists as a violation of southern rights, Dock's letter went on to say, "We 'southern knights of the wheel will make our fight bravely,' and we will show these negro-loving people that we have rights, and that we can defend them."[67] Even just the mention of the "bloody shirt" revealed the lingering antagonism between the two regions, but Dock was even more explicit. His letter described "fires in the southern hearts [that] have never been extinguished, and now, as they tread over their smoldering ashes, the breezes from the "Bloody Shirt" may start a flame which all hell itself can't put down."[68] This was a call to arms. Dock wanted to "show these people that the southern wheelmen at least don't need their assistance, nor their beloved brothers, the dusky sons of African soil." He closed with a proposal for action that all southern members could take if they wanted to get directly involved, writing, "I am red hot, and think I shall write the league to scratch my number out."[69] Thus, the appropriate course of action in response to such an insult against the South on behalf of the LAW would be for southern members to effectively boycott the national league and create their own southern version.

Tennessee seemed quick to jump on board with the idea. Just two weeks later, *The Bearings* reported that in a recent annual election, the division only saw a total of six votes cast out of the total of 150 members in the state. A correspondent from *The Bearings* was told that "the lack of interest in League affairs is due entirely to the negro question and this is the case all through the south." One "prominent Tennessee rider" stated directly, "We do not care to belong to any institution that has negroes in its membership and that's the whole reason of it.... If the League had seen fit to legislate against the negro, then you would have seen the League boomed out of sight in the south; but as it is, the members are one by one dropping out and I very much doubt if we shall have many more than six members in the division another season."[70] The rider went on to explain that they desperately needed an organization like the league in the South and expressed feelings that he would be unsurprised if a southern version of the league was created. He did specify that he was not saying anything of the sort was contemplated, only that it may be.[71] This seemed a little confusing since there had certainly been rumors, speculation, even alleged ringleaders of such an organization. Several months earlier, *The Bearings* had reported that as a result of "a few League members in the South . . . feel[ing] affronted because the color line was not drawn at Philadelphia. . . . A few of those young hotspurs" who believe "they have been deeply wronged" called a meeting for May 20, at Brunswick, Georgia. There, the plan was to make a decision to "withdraw from the LAW and form an association of their own."[72] Due to the fact that the potential for southern secession from the LAW was still being discussed as a possibility by December, it is clear that the May 20 meeting either did not result in the desired outcome, or it did not happen at all.

While it was apparent that there were at least some southern members of the LAW who were extremely upset by the vote against the Watts' amendment to bar non-White cyclists, objections to Black cyclists were much more extensive. The fact that Chicago, Missouri, and Colorado took individual steps to deter Black cyclists' participation was one indication. There were also members of the bicycle industry who openly voiced their opposition. The Premier Cycle Company of New York for instance, in an article published to discourage women from wearing "abbreviated skirts" while riding, also took a moment to note the detrimental effects of diversifying participation

56   CHAPTER 3

in the sport. Premier wrote, "We regret to be compelled to mention . . . we feel it our duty to warn retail cycle dealers against supplying or in any way encouraging negroes to cycle. We are strong Northerners and Abolishionists [sic], and firm friends of the colored race, but the fact cannot be ignored that a strong prejudice exists at the present day, and that nothing can be more fatal to the adoption of the wheel by ladies than its use by colored women."[73] Leaders in the bicycle industry operated under the assumption that consumer demands spread from the top down and therefore, in their view, women would be encouraged to ride bicycles if they saw wealthy "society women" participating, but they would be discouraged by the sight of someone presumed to be socially inferior on a bicycle.[74] In both scenarios, Southerners arguing that allowing Black cyclists to be members of the LAW would be a detriment to league membership in the South; and similarly that Black women on bicycles would drive away White women from participation; the objection to Black cyclists did not appear outright. Rather, both arguments allowed the individual to circumvent taking a stand directly and to instead say that *others* would object. This was very similar to A. S. Hardin's point. It was a common theme and a convenient way for individuals to often mask their own racism.

In the fall of 1893, events that occurred during a group ride organized out of St. Louis suggested that Missouri cyclists not only supported Watts' initiative, but that they instituted their own de facto color line and were willing to terrorize Black riders to see it enforced.[75] On October 8, out of the 204 riders in participation, five were ladies and at least one was a Black man. In the ride to Creve Coeur Lake, which was described as a "great success," there was "quite a rumpus . . . caused by a negro rider taking a position in line." When riders asked that the man be removed from the ride, they were told that "the roads were free and the negro could not be kept off." Apparently unsatisfied with that response, several riders concocted a plan to "duck the darky and the worthy Missouri chief consul in the lake" but they were unable to find the "darky" once they arrived at the lake.[76] Such episodes made it clear that the issue of the color line was not settled with the vote against the Watts amendment.

League delegates from Massachusetts were certain the question would come up at the 1894 meeting as there were reports that they pledged to take a stand on the issue and vote in favor of admitting non-Whites, providing they were not illiterate.[77] *The Bearings* certainly assumed the question was

Drawing the Color Line 57

coming back around as well, writing of the upcoming 1894 meeting, "The principal matter for discussion will doubtless be the negro question. The southerners have never given up the fight and vow that they will win the next time the matter is brought up."[78] The writer, likely George Barrett, went on to say that *The Bearings* had never given "much space to the discussion of the question" and while there were not a great number of editorials devoted to it, there were indeed a lot of articles relaying LAW discussions and votes on the question. In this particular article, written nearly two months before the 1894 National Assembly in Louisville, *The Bearings* urged readers to "bar the negro."[79] The rationale for taking such action was a dispassionate argument that there were not many Black cyclists in the LAW and there never would be many. Conversely, even though southerners agreed, they were "opposed to the negro on principle. The very fact that a negro can become a member of the same organization with them is enough to make their blood boil."[80] *The Bearings* said that the North opposed the color line solely on principle too and that both sides were stubborn so the only logical thing to do was to vote "the way that will benefit the League the most; in other words, vote for the exclusion of the negro."[81] It went on to explain further that this was the best way to ensure continued growth in membership since allowing even a few Black cyclists membership would drive away southern members, but drawing the color line would not drive any White cyclists away. "In short," it argued, "the League has much to gain by barring the African and nothing to lose."[82] That opinion, *The Bearings* alleged, was well received among members of the LAW and not just those of the South. The journal claimed to have received "nearly a hundred letters from prominent members of the League" all commending the stance taken.[83]

Emboldened by those letters, in the same issue, racist cartoons appeared. Some of those racist depictions of African Americans were accompanied by a poem entitled "Ephraham Jones' Prediction." Caricatures of dark faces with large white lips appeared scowling at White men, one holding a razor up to check that it was sharp and many more at the bottom smiling with mouths agape, missing teeth and immodestly showing off their finest clothes. The poem, written in a stereotypical dialect read, in part, "Dars a powful ag'tation in de culled cycle club, Yo' ken heah de trouble brewin' f'm NewAwhns to de Hub; Dars a tempest comin' honey, an' as sho' as yo's a coon, Dars gwine to be some carvin' done an't can't be done too soon. De white trash thinks dey run de league but, say, yo' heah me shout? Dars gwine

58 CHAPTER 3

to be some carvin' Ef Dey Don't Look Out!"[84] A week earlier a warning had appeared in the pages of *The Bearings*. The writer told northern delegates traveling to Louisville, "I have it on the very best of authority that there is a darkey waiter in one of the hotels of Colonel Watts' bailiwick, the pride of whose heart lies in three large, competent, and healthy razors. . . . I would advise my northern friends to insist on a secret ballot when it comes to a vote on the negro question. I have always found it best never to disturb a colored brother's razor when it isn't looking for trouble."[85]

There were a considerable number of perspectives offered that suggested those in the North who did not support adding the word white would have a different opinion if they were to walk in the shoes of southern Whites. Chief Consul Harris of the Alabama division of the LAW articulated this rationale saying, "We don't want any negroes in ours and neither would you northern men if you were in our place. They are a dirty lot and not fit to rub against the white men. We have about one hundred riders of color in this city and I want you to take notice of them. You people in the north only see the colored men who have sense enough to leave this country of ease and plenty, and work their way up in the world instead of living off someone else. We have no negroes here who are good enough to travel in the same car with us on a railway train. They are a dirty lot and not as clean as the swine in the gutter yonder."[86] When this point was put to northerners, like a leader of the Illinois wheelmen, F.W. Gerould, he agreed that there was a difference of the "class of the colored men in the south" and those in the North. Gerould did not see that as a problem, however, because he observed a class exclusivity built within the LAW that would serve to keep that "class of colored men in the south" out by default.[87] Harris, of Alabama, believed that if the assembly were to be held in the South, south of Baltimore specifically, the northern members would see "what we have to put up with down here, and appreciate our position on the subject."[88] While not quite as far south as Atlanta, Birmingham, or Charlotte, the next scheduled meeting to be held in Louisville may have satisfied Harris's hopes.

While the 1880s offers multiple examples of Black cyclists taking to their wheels in integrated settings, by the early 1890s there was clearly a movement to put an end to that. There were undoubtedly even more Black cyclists by 1890 and this would be one of the reasons for more vocal objections by White cyclists. If the Black cyclists had been completely devoid of skills or the fitness required to ride bicycles, they would have merely been lampooned and treated as a joke. The fact that White cyclists objected to Black cyclists shows that Black cyclists were a serious threat. The Assembly of 1894 in Louisville made it clear that the opportunities for the Black cyclist were drawing closed, even in the North. The opinions expressed in the debates carried throughout 1893 show the severity of the prejudice Black cyclists faced and the trajectory of the conversation suggested that the situation was on a deteriorative course. This, then, is the backdrop for the Black cyclist and the prejudice they would encounter in the 1890s and thereafter.

4

In Response to the Color Line

Immediately after the League of American Wheelmen's passage of the Watts Amendment at the Assembly of 1894, the Sunday edition of the *New York Daily Tribune* ran an article, buried among the morning news section, which said, "Wheelmen generally must look with some disfavor upon the outcome of the convention of the League of American Wheelmen at Louisville."[1] Specifically, the paper cited the league's approval of drawing the color line and the move to create two amateur classes as decisions that only served to discredit the association and its delegates. The feeling was that having two separate classes of amateur riders, either "A" or "B," would loosen the league's restrictions against those who had earned financial gain through cycling competitions. This was controversial because some considered it to be antithetical to the ideals of amateurism embraced by the league and sporting men of the day. The *Tribune* suggested, "the class A, class B idiocy will certainly keep the cycling world in hot water."[2] This was undoubtedly due to the perception that the rule blurred the lines further between amateur and professional. As to the color line, the *Tribune* believed "fair-minded men will condemn the exclusion of colored men from all race meets. . . ."[3] If that was the case, the condemnation of the color line certainly did not make for a significant proportion of the cycling news for the weeks and months following the decision, at the Assembly of February 1894 in Louisville.

Clearly, not everyone agreed with the decision to draw the color line, but the attitude that "all protests quickly die down" seemed to prevail. George Barrett, the editor of *The Bearings*, believed it was "a question that would soon be forgotten, except on the occasional observation of the League's growth in the South."[4] *The Bearings* did find it important to point out that even with the "white amendment" added to the constitution, Black members of the league would remain members, "so long as they pay their renewal fees *promptly* [emphasis mine]."[5] While Black cyclists could technically remain members of the league, any new applications from Black cyclists would be denied. There were indeed at least a few who condemned the Watts' amendment, which instituted this color line. Rather than penning a letter, some members of the League voiced their disapproval simply by resigning from the organization. It is unclear how many, but a little over a week after the assembly, *The Bearings* reported that the league's secretary had "received several resignations on the ground that they do not wish to belong to anything that draws the color line."[6] For the most part, the discussion of the reaction to the amendment held that protests against it came from "the stiffest of the northern men."[7] Perhaps unsurprising, yet still difficult to ignore, however, was the manner in which league elites seemed to exclude Black voices even from the debates over the color line. Of course, Black Americans did not all feel the same about the LAW decision. Their opinions ranged from indifference, or even acceptance, as something they could not control to those who attacked the LAW publicly and sought punitive measures against the organization. As far as the cycling press was concerned, the opinions of those who accepted the decision and moved on, possibly even attempting to form their own league, received the most coverage and respect. The only voice of outright dissent that was publicized was thoroughly lambasted. Overall, the number of reports on the opinions of Black cyclists was scant at best.

The most prominent among those individual Black voices that were heard were the racer Marshall "Major" Taylor, the leader of the Black cyclist club in Louisville (Fred Scott), and Robert Teamoh—a member of the Massachusetts House of Representatives. When Black opinions were considered, such as with Scott of Louisville, or an unnamed Black Pullman porter on the B&O railroad, there was a common theme in which White writers implied that most Black cyclists did not care about the color line and would simply

62 CHAPTER 4

form their own club if they were excluded from the LAW. The story of the Pullman Porter included in *The Bearings* just after the failure of the Watts Amendment in 1893 would go so far as to actually offer support for the color line due to the racist nature in which the porter was portrayed.

Described as having a portentous manner and a new uniform that would have made an African king envious, the Black porter was quoted at length in a stereotypical dialect. He allegedly put on a performance for all aboard the car, explaining, I am "a putty sma't man on ma feet, but time de bisickel fe speed, I tull you."[8] This was one week after Watts' failed attempt in 1893, so he was asked his opinion about the "Philadelphia squabble on the color line." *The Bearings* recounted his response at length. He said, "'I haven' give that subjick much consideration. Don' affeck me neither way. Got some cullud men in now, but I don' s'pose I could, really 'n hones'ly, git in 'thout lyin'. Ise a p'fessional. Y'see I got t' be kind of a racing man 'n I made a little stuff on d' side.' His chest swelled perceptibly here. 'I don' see why a cullud man should be kep' out th' League. 'Course we might form a 'sociation of our own, only they ain't 'nough of us."[9] He explained how he had not only been a bicycle riding instructor in the past but that he had also helped organize the Calumet Club in New York and the "fuhst cullud club in 'th country" the National Bicycle Club of Washington—possibly the Hannibal Athletic Club of Washington, DC.[10] Because of his experiences, he claimed the color line made no difference to him. *The Bearings* described him as a braggadocious nuisance, and said that once the electric call-bell sounded, "the oracle became your humble servant once more" and after he "shambled off," some sighed and others looked out the windows in "oppressive silence." Had a "test vote on the color line [been] taken at that moment," *The Bearings* reported, the result "would have been unanimously favorable to the insertion of the word white."[11] With the porter supposedly serving as a representative for all Black cyclists, the story was intent on pointing out that not only was it silly to vote against the color line when Black cyclists did not care. They would continue to ride. They would even form their own clubs. In depicting the porter as arrogant and uncultured, it emphasized why respectable White cyclists would want to keep their distance from such characters. The fact that he raced for prizes, like a professional, only served to make him seem even more unsavory. The allegory of the passengers in the Pullman car would have left readers considering how they might have

In Response to the Color Line

to endure similar encounters if the number of Black cyclists in the league was permitted to grow. Even worse, the Black cyclist would ride among White cyclists for extended periods of time, as an equal member of a social club. At least in the case of the Pullman porter, he operated as a servant, someone who would eventually be forced back to his work.

Others noticed the implications. Some readers may have even accused *The Bearings* of being one-sided on the issue. Several months later, just before the successful vote on the amendment in 1894, in touting their own lack of bias, *The Bearings* stated that it "is always ready to give both sides of a story" and even though it was in favor of the color line it was "willing to give the colored man a chance to air his views."[12] To that end, it reprinted a letter to the editor from a young phenom from Indianapolis, the Black cyclist Marshall "Major" Taylor. He was fifteen years old at the time. Taylor immediately pointed out the lack of Black cyclists' voices in the debate over the color line. He also made some allusions to the flaws of political liberalism arguing that politicians courted Black voters and "that it's not the 'coon' they want, neither is it their dollar—but their big black vote is the coveted prize."[13] On that point, he seemed to echo the sentiments of James Monroe Trotter. Taylor went on to draw connections to cycling by explaining that all Black cyclists with "horse sense" knew that there were no members of the league who truly wanted him and his "colored friends" as a club mate. For him, the LAW seemed unnecessary to his enjoyment of bicycles. He spoke more in terms of self-determination writing, "let us think of our own troubles" and alluded to the possibility of a separate league for Black cyclists. In Taylor's opinion, the number of African Americans who wanted to "mix with white men" had been exaggerated in the White mind. Like many of his contemporaries, Taylor subscribed to the idea of race as biologically determined and meaningful. He argued that in spite of the elevated status African Americans had received from the United States government, "we are still a race as different from others as God first made us."[14] The passive phrasing he used to describe emancipation also shows that he was, by no means, adopting a radical view on race relations. His main point was that Black cyclists did not want "membership in any white man's league of wheelmen" but he did not proclaim to speak for all Black cyclists and expressed a keen interest in hearing "from the colored cyclists as a body."[15] This was an astute point since he was relatively new on the scene,

64   CHAPTER 4

but it also highlighted the lack of publicizing Black voices on the matter, as well as the fact that in spite of White people assumed, Black cyclists did not all think and feel the same.

One month after the color line was drawn, the opinion of Fred J. Scott, the President of the Black cyclists' Union Cycling Club of Louisville was published. Scott grew up approximately ninety miles southeast of Louisville in a small enclave of African Americans named Shelby City. The 1870 census shows he was "at school" around age 11, having been born in 1859. His mother was listed as a housekeeper and the 1900 census would list Scott as a sleeping car porter who could read and write. He rented a house in Louisville, where he lived with his wife Lanora and daughter Helen. *The Bearings* described Scott as a "pleasant and intelligent man" who was "born and raised in the South and knows of the race prejudice" in that region. He was also described as "one of the few who do not care to force themselves where they are not wanted."[16] This seemed to verify "Major" Taylor's point that intelligent Black cyclists did not want to be a part of White clubs that did not want them as well as the common misconception among Whites that they did. *The Bearings* said Scott was "one of the few" but Taylor would have categorized Scott as one of many. To prove the point that Scott was indeed in the minority, *The Bearings* reported that "for having the courage to express his opinion," Scott had been "very strongly condemned by Negroes."[17] The most extreme reactions among those writing him letters and questioning his motivations were those who went so far as to claim Scott was paid off. The one specific example given was the inclusion of a reproduction of a letter from the Riverside Cycle Club of Boston, which merely expressed some incredulity and asked for an explanation why he would seemingly support the color line.[18] A separate article first published in the *Louisville Times* and then reprinted in *The Referee & Cycle Trade Journal* also lauded Fred Scott. There he was described as "a gentlemanly fellow, quiet and modest, and he regrets the fame he has attained. He was the first colored wheelman in Louisville, and he gained the good-will of all the old riders through his courtesy and the fact that he knew his place and kept it. He never intruded on white parties, and never 'chipped in' a conversation unless invited to. Were all colored riders like Scott, there would have been no call for the color line."[19] Even though Scott could read and write, the real barometer for Black intelligence among the White elite cyclists, was that the person "know their place" regardless of their education or economic class. Of course, if the Black cyclists "knew their place" then there would be no need for the color line in the first place because they would not even try to join the league.

For the most part, Scott was only well-known as a Black cyclist in the Louisville area. Even "Major" Taylor was still more of a regional figure in 1894, being described as a Black cyclist of Indianapolis. He had yet to achieve the international level of stardom that would come with his world championship success. Of those few Black voices that were printed, perhaps the one with the most influence was the thirty-four-year-old State Representative of Massachusetts, Robert Thomas Teamoh. Prior to that position, he worked as a "newspaperman" according to marriage records. This was a profession he obviously returned to after his political career since his 1912 death certificate lists his occupation as newspaper editor. Early in his career, he worked as a reporter for the *Boston Globe,* where he clearly distinguished himself. He earned the distinction of being the "first colored man elected to an incorporated white man's club in Boston" when he became a member of the Boston Press Club.[20] Robert Teamoh and J. Gordon Street were both considered "of the colored writers employed by white journals [to be] perhaps the most representative and widely known."[21] Unlike Scott and Taylor, it was not clear that Teamoh was a cyclist and where Scott and Taylor's opinions might be characterized as complacent, or accommodating, Teamoh was much more openly outraged by the LAW decision to draw the color line and thus the articles reporting on Teamoh's reaction were of a decidedly different tone.[22]

As state representative, Teamoh introduced a resolution of censure against the LAW in the Massachusetts House of Representatives. Even though Teamoh was one of many who were upset with the league's decision, he was treated as the ringleader in the pages of *The Bearings.* There, he was described as a "young colored politician with more push and nerve than brilliance."[23] His seeming inability to "know his place" clearly factored into the assessment of his intelligence . In announcing, "Negroes are Indignant" *The Bearings* informed readers that the "colored LAW members" of Boston, along "with a few of their leaders in the legal fraternity and their representative in the house are trying to create a public opinion on the subject and they have not yet succeeded except with their own race."[24] *The Bearings* did not believe their efforts for censure would ultimately be successful, however, because the league was "not in the protection or under

66   CHAPTER 4

the obligation of the state at all."[25] This was due to the fact that the LAW did not own property and was not incorporated.

Prior to the publication of the report about Teamoh, "the colored cyclists of Boston" held a meeting in which the secretary present read letters from "various other colored members of the League of American Wheelmen, all of whom expressed extreme indignation at the LAW" The club also "commended" Robert Teamoh for his resolution of censure as well as showing favor for the Massachusetts delegates vote against the color line.[26] The members present at the meeting also expressed some incredulity over the authenticity of the letter from Fred Scott. One unnamed attendant at the meeting reportedly laid out his opinion of the chain of events for the pages of *The Bearings* saying, "I'll tell you how I think it was. I think that Mr. Watts went to one of these men who, perhaps, had no authority to act at all for his club as a body, and placed a matter before him and asked him if he did not agree with him and dropped some silver into his hand and the colored man agreed with him and Mr. Watts wrote the letter and then read it in the convention as coming from the colored club and representing the sentiment of all its members."[27] The Black man suggesting this scenario was reminded that Mr. Watts was an honorable gentleman, but he insisted in his belief that Watts wrote the letter himself. He even went so far as to write to the Black cycling club of Louisville demanding an explanation. It is clear then, that at least in Boston, there were numerous Black cyclists who openly condemned the league's adoption of the Watts Amendment to insert the word white into their constitution.

The Bearings then went on to talk about Representative Teamoh and the politics of Boston. It described delegates seeking political support in Boston as being "held in the eye of the colored population" which represented approximately 10,000 votes total.[28] Their leader, as the paper surmised, was a "newspaper man and when one considers his professional nerve is augmented by the position in which he finds himself placed, one can consider how he is making the colored members of the city of Boston toe the mark of his own drawing."[29] Here too, the passive construction of their words robbed both individual Black Americans in Boston of agency as well as Teamoh, who was portrayed as being given a position in the House through surreptitious maneuvering. Accordingly, he did not earn his position and his resolution of censure would "never pass either the house or the senate."[30] The resolution had been referred to the committee on rules and the assumption was that there would be its final resting place. The following week the "negro question" was reportedly "still bubbling and simmering, but all interest in the matter has died out."[31] By that point, Teamoh's resolution was described as "stuck at the second reading." To emphasize the point that the efforts in Boston and the vote in general were relatively inconsequential, Secretary Bassett of the LAW was asked if there had been any resignations in reaction to the vote to adopt the Watts Amendment. This question was apparently asked in person because Bassett responded by taking out a "tin box" and showing the reporter "all of fifteen resignations which have come in from all over the land since that vote was passed by the Assembly." He was also asked about Teamoh's resolution for censure and allegedly scoffed at the idea of the Massachusetts legislature passing such a measure.[32]

Just two weeks later, both Bassett and *The Bearings* would be forced to eat their words. *The Bearings* did so with noticeable contempt. It reported, "That resolution of Mr. Teamoh's has gone through after all and it is said that the governor has signed it. What if he has? It can't have any effect on the LAW, as the state has no power over the organization any more than any other social organization. What use this will be put to by the colored cyclers of Boston and the North is hard to say. The passage of a censorious resolution by the legislature might have some effect if the people cared anything at all about this question, but they do not in the least. Outside the colored inhabitants of the city but very few people know that there has been any such resolution introduced or passed."[33] With that, it then moved onto other matters of general interest to the LAW and the Good Roads campaign.

Robert Teamoh was not treated any more favorably in the pages of *The Referee & Cycle Trade Journal*. It also reported on the success of Teamoh's resolution and added that in a "printed interview [Teamoh] charged the Massachusetts delegation to the assembly with selling out for the second vice-presidency, the secretaryship, the national meet for 1895 and a member of the racing board of the present year."[34] It went on to explain that by these claims, "the colored member of the Massachusetts legislature" had "show[n] his ignorance."[35] It then echoed comments found in *The Bearings* that even though Teamoh's resolution had passed, it really evoked no response except among "the colored men." In "his published interview, however," it proclaimed he had "over-reached like a horse."[36] The article continued by laying out the errors in Teamoh's contention that the Massachusetts del-

68   CHAPTER 4

egation had sold out. The author of the article, who identified himself as a member of the Massachusetts delegation to the National Assembly said they were unpledged on all questions except the agreement to abstain on the question of the national meet but that there was a general understanding that they would vote against the color line. To his recollection they did just that and cast a solid vote against the amendment. After explaining a few more details, he concluded the article by writing, "Come, Mr. Teamoh, find something else upon which to talk."[37] Similarly, *The Bearings* returned to the subject a few weeks later writing, "our friend Mr. Teamoh has been talking through his hat again . . . [making] some remarkable statements which did not hold water, and . . . revealed his painful ignorance in general, and in League matters in particular."[38] It pointed out that he was also "adequately called down" by Arthur K. Peck in the Boston *Post*, who "told [Teamoh] some things that will do him lots of good to know and remember."[39] Peck quoted some of Teamoh's points including, "For has Massachusetts not received more than her share? She has Perkins, Bassett and Robinson in the best offices and a cinch on the meet for '95."[40] Peck, a member of the Massachusetts delegation, then went on to say that Teamoh "does not know so much of what he is talking about as he thinks he does." After explaining how each of those results could and did occur without the need to sell votes, Peck then wrote, "You see, Mr. Teamoh, your conclusions are a little out of order, as much so, in fact, as if without knowing you we were to accuse you of acting in this matter for selfish political purposes."[41] For Peck and many others, Teamoh was simply carrying out an act of political grandstanding to ingratiate himself to what was assumed to be the base that got him elected in the first place. It did not seem that Teamoh was completely off base for making the accusations about the Massachusetts delegates, however, since he echoed points made by other sources. Still, the attacks on his intelligence illuminate a vehement opposition to Teamoh from a few White journalists that seem to belie his professional accomplishments, some of which necessitated a certain amount of respect and trust among his peers and colleagues.

Whether or not Massachusetts cast a solid vote against the color line, however, would prove impossible to determine because the vote was taken by secret ballot. Although, it is clear that Robert Teamoh was not the first to raise the idea that the delegates of his state had sold their votes. A month before Teamoh's allegations made headlines, in its report on the results of the National Assembly, *The Referee* pointed out, "We have Mr. Perkins' word for it, and are glad to record it, that, to the best of his belief, Massachusetts cast its entire vote against the exclusion of the negro. We mention this especially, because it has been charged that Perkins had pledged himself to vote against the negro to secure for himself a place on the executive committee."[42] Perkins ran unopposed for the position of second vice president so the charge that he sold his vote for the position seems curious but it was an appointed position and there was indeed some backroom dealing in regard to the election of officers, particularly the position of president. *The Referee* described the outcome of the presidential election as a "surprise" to "many" because of a discrepancy in the number of votes pledged for one candidate and the final tally he actually received.[43] Clearly, some delegates either changed their votes or did not honor their pledge regarding the presidential election. Similarly, there may have been some clandestine maneuvers that ensured Perkins would have no opposition for the vice-presidency, provided he pledge to vote for the Watts Amendment, but that is not something that could easily be discoverable. Other accounts identified Perkins as being a part of the Luscomb ticket, rather than running unopposed.[44] Most likely, if political favors were negotiated, they were done in private and with great care that they remain that way, but some members even speculated that the adoption of the "class B" resolution was done under a veil of corruption. In a letter to the editor, J. W. Overstreet of Little Hickman, KY, explained he was "opposed to the 'nigger' in the LAW, but prefer him to the class B gentry." He asked, "Was class B adopted and the convention run by the delegates in their senses, or under the influence of 125 bottles of bourbon whisky, prize, coon, dog and cock fights? Was the secret ballot adopted through cowardice or want of conviction that the voters were wrong? Did the south sell out to Denver? Did the Denverites sell out to the south?"[45] Clearly it was not just Teamoh and Black cyclists that were left scratching their heads about the results of the 1894 assembly, and for good reason.

Other decisions that were made at the 1894 assembly were not without their own surprises. First was the election of the president. *The Referee* reported that on the Sunday night before the assembly began, the "western caucus . . . found that seventy-eight votes were pledged to Sheridan for the presidency. The [final] vote was: Luscomb, 126; Sheridan, 55. The ballot was a secret one, more's the pity, so that it will never be known who the men

70 CHAPTER 4

were who proved treacherous. A very shrewd guess might be made, however. They may pride themselves, however, on having accomplished one of the most despicable pieces of treachery in the league's history." The same report revealed potential maneuvering regarding the full meet of 1894, scheduled for that summer. This is when Boston withdrew as a candidate, leaving only Denver and Asbury Park. Not only was Boston withdrawn, but the Massachusetts delegates pledged not to vote on the question. This apparently "caused great satisfaction among the Denver men, whose chances were greatly increased thereby." The assumption was that Boston would have voted for the New Jersey location since it was closer to home and the regions (Northeast, West, and South) tended to vote in blocks. As a partial concession for bowing out of the contest for the 1894 meet, Boston was given the 1895 meet. With that decided, the assembly was ready to take up the question but was then "headed off by an invitation extended by the Colorado men to the assembly to participate in an entertainment during the evening, at which stereopticon views of Denver and its surroundings would be shown." After that display, the meeting was adjourned with plans to reconvene the next morning, Tuesday, at 9:30.[46]

As for the points the man from Little Hickman, Kentucky alluded to above, however, there was reason to question the men's actions that Tuesday morning. The delegates came stumbling in late and the meeting was not reconvened until 10:05, but at that point, only "seven members, including the President and Secretary," were present.[47] The night before, after watching Denver's stereopticon and the meeting was adjourned, the delegates were treated to a night out on the town, led by William Watts. A "majority of them were regaled by the spectacle of a 'cocking main' and the edifying sight of a bulldog tearing the life out of an inoffensive coon." There were illustrations in other journals of the bulldog and the raccoon but they were more vague on why they were included. *The Bearings* referenced the night with the small headline "Investigating the Three-Dollar Coon." Close to that short and vague blurb was an account of how William Watts spoke to the police chief of Louisville before taking the men out on the town and they were given the all clear to essentially go wild.[48] *The Bicycling World and L.A.W. Bulletin* included the drawings of the bulldog and raccoon with the caption "that there dog never lets go nothing' till it's dead!" and "'This yer coon cost three dollars!'" Given the propensity of the league and cycling journals of the era to refer to Black cyclists as "coons" it begs the question of whether

In Response to the Color Line

the dog and "coon" fight the members attended on Monday night, arranged by William Watts, had any metaphorical connections to the league's own thoughts on race and the upcoming vote on the Watts Amendment to bar Black cyclists from the league. There was also a small drawing of a bottle of Belle of Nelson whiskey with a tag reading "Kentucky Hospitality."[49] *The Referee*'s account filled in some of the gaps informing the readers, "a large number of members of the assembly attended a cock fight and a dog and coon fight under 'special protection'."[50] Insinuating that the night out had been an extremely drunken affair, it explained that the men were so hung over the next morning they found it "necessary to take full advantage of the 'bracers' tendered them before breakfast."[51] Once they had their "hair of the dog" and breakfast, the men finally made it to the meeting and after a morning of excitement in which a proxy vote was requested for the decision of who would host the 1894 meet, Denver won with a total of ninety-three votes. There were seventy for Asbury Park. It was immediately after this vote that the delegates turned their attention to William Watts' question of drawing the color line.

Withdrawing Boston from the running for the 1894 meet could certainly be seen as a favor to the western delegates and the western delegates were assumed to be voting with the South on the question of inserting the word white into the constitution. Concerns with Massachusetts' vote on the racial issue were apparent a few weeks before the vote at the National Assembly. This became clear after there was some indication that the state's delegates may have had a change of heart on the question and were now more in favor of racial exclusion in league applications. *The Bearings* magazine asked, "what has caused the sudden apathy on the part of Massachusetts on the negro question. [*sic*]"[52] In answering that question, it first pointed to "Mr. Perkins going on the Luscomb ticket, and it is whispered that Mr. Luscomb doesn't love the colored man at all."[53] The rest of the article was devoted to a sort of parable that sought to explain why Luscomb felt that way.

The story opened with a dance held at the city hall in Springfield, Massachusetts, in celebration of the autumn meet of the cycling divisions in that state. This was described as a brilliant ball, surpassing those of the Yale-Harvard assembly, with an orchestra and all the finest of decorations. After the first dance, a generic racer named "Johnnie Rapid," during a quiet conversation with a female attendant, commiserated on "how anyone in his sane senses could vote against the dear colored brother."[54] Not only did he explain that he had met some who were very intelligent, but he also claimed that if only he were a delegate, "he would vote for the negro every time." He believed men like him could "show the solid south that they were trying to revive the war spirit." The expression of these philosophical views endeared him to his female companion who also "thought that men were just too horrid for anything to vote against the negro." She was described as a "deep thinker" who believed in racial equality, like Johnnie. That was, until the ballroom lights were dimmed and she turned to see "a negro girl with a white satin dress cut low—very low—and trimmed with orange watered silk ribbon half-a-yard wide. It was gorgeous" and with that sight, she "gasped and escaped." The "colored girl was escorted by a colored man with a dress suit on." He was also described as wearing the finest clothes. The two "danced every dance that evening and they were in it till the lights were turned out, and now Johnnie Rapid just wishes he was a delegate to the National Assembly so he could vote against the negro who doesn't know enough to keep his place in society events." The young lady he had been speaking too also had a change of heart. Johnnie's opinion "was much strengthened when [he] went to Cottage City in July and found half-a-dozen colored couples on the floor dancing with reckless abandon and enthusiasm." Thus, the article was titled "Two Little Ballroom Scenes the Cause" because "those two dances settled the fate of the negro so far as Massachusetts' fighting for him goes."[55] For both Johnnie and the young lady, the question of whether Black people were their equals seemed at least a potential yes, but both were also apparently unaccustomed to actually having first-hand experience in sharing their social sphere with a different race. They obviously perceived that sphere as somewhat exclusive. This was where they both drew the line. This parable bolstered southern arguments that northerners were all for equality until they came to the South, or until they experienced firsthand the perceived challenges to the social privileges they held, based on their inherited position in society.

The story about why some northerners may have had a change of heart on the question of the color line along with all the potential ways in which votes could have been traded in order to ensure a victory for the Watts Amendment in 1894 lends support to Robert Teamoh's belief that the vote was corrupt. Watts clearly treated the men to a night of debauchery just before the vote was to take place. That undoubtedly resulted in some growing comradery, and it gave the southerners more of an opportunity to bring the other delegates around to their point of view. It is also curious how the cycling magazines of the era, like *The Bearings* and *The Referee*, were aware of all these details, even reporting on them haphazardly, yet they both still treated Teamoh and others who questioned the legitimacy of the vote as absurd. Not only did they dismiss his complaints, they attacked him personally as a man by describing him as outspoken but not very intelligent. In treating him as the ringleader, it was also made clear that there were others, besides Teamoh, to demur.

Other, less prominent, Black cyclists expressed their disapproval of the league's decision to draw the color line by attempting to form their own organization. A letter to the editor published in the Richmond *Planet* expressed a collective "desire to have every colored wheel rider to give us their assistance and co-operation in trying to organize a league for the benefit of the colored wheelmen of America." It continued by saying, "we have the material and the talent as well as our white brother, and which also needs greater development. This matter should be considered thoroughly by all who take interest in such things, and we would like to know the opinion of those in regards to the proposed league, and also to know at what place would be suitable for a convention should we be successful in effecting a decision."[56] The letter was undoubtedly submitted to multiple newspapers as it came by order of the Eureka Wheel Club of Cleveland, Ohio and all correspondence on the matter was to be addressed to F.J. Isaac, the "Corresponding-Secretary" of Cleveland as well. Unsurprisingly, *The Bearings* supported the idea. Shortly after the letter to the editor was distributed, it ran its own report saying the "colored wheelmen of Cleveland" were "freely sympathized with and seconded by all dark-complexioned riders in this section" presumably Chicago. *The Bearings* continued, if the separate league was formed, it would be "freely patronized by members of that race throughout this country." It then proposed potential leadership for the club asking, "How would President of the L.A.B. sound as a handle to Mr. Backus, Zimmerman's 'Dark Secret'?"[57]

Arthur Augustus Zimmerman was one of the most recognizable names among competitive cyclists in the United States at the time. His success on the track gave him a great deal of influence among league members. John Backus, who was Black, from Philadelphia, and approximately sixteen years old, was Zimmerman's trainer for an extended period, although he was often referred to as Zimmerman's "mascot," "good luck charm," and "dark

74 CHAPTER 4

secret" at various times. Backus was often the target of jokes and pranks perpetrated by White men in the United States bicycle racing circuit. He was described as "occasionally quite witty" but also as "shouting and smiling as only an African can." *The Referee* felt it was worth reporting on what it saw as a humorous, yet demeaning, occurrence at the zoo in Rockville, Connecticut. As John Backus, Zimmerman, and other cyclists stood before the monkey cage, Backus' presence reportedly disturbed the monkeys to the point of them holding a "council war." *The Referee* jokingly chalked it up as evidence that "monkeys are greater 'nigger haters' than even the southerners."[58] Regardless of the overt racism, Backus was also seen as instrumental to Arthur Zimmerman's success on the track. So much so, that others even played pranks on Zimmerman to make him fret over the absence of Backus in his corner at a race. When Zimmerman traveled to race in England, leaving Backus at home, a correspondent for *The Referee* "knowing that without Mascot John Backus, Arthur would be at a disadvantage" mocked Zimmerman by presenting to him a "cute Chinese doll . . . [that was to] be carried to all race tracks abroad, and on no account should Zimmie start in a race unless the baby was there."[59] After two years, the relationship seemed to be coming to an end, just after Backus had traveled to Paris in support of Zimmerman. He landed on his feet, however, and soon had a job working for M. Watson, a high-ranking member of the Dunlop Company. Even this news was reported with the characteristic backhanded racist scorn commonly found in the pages of *The Bearings*. It reported, "John Backus, Esq., very colored, ex-grand massager and utility mascot to A. A. Zimmerman, has struck a job. With his self-assurance the wonder is that he needed a job at all, but he's got one, and it is one that ought to make darkest Africa envious."[60] Even though he was clearly important to Zimmerman, it is hard to tell whether *The Bearings* was sincerely recommending Backus as a potential leader of the proposed league for Black cyclists or whether it was merely a sarcastic joke.

There was, at least, a committee formed to explore the possibility of creating a league for Black cyclists. It expected to call a National Convention in June or July and the subject of a separate league was "being generally agitated in all parts of the United States." *The Bearings* went on record to say that "when the new League is launched, it will be a credit to the negro and a monument to the improvement and progress of civilization."[61] It apparently did not come to fruition, however, as the discussion of forming such a league was still ongoing two years later. In 1896, members of the Hannibal Athletic Club (a club for Black cyclists) "proposed a complete boycott of the League [of American Wheelmen] and the formation of a parallel black League."[62] It seemed that proposal also failed. While much of this took place well before the historic Supreme Court decision handed down in *Plessy v. Ferguson*, the rationale and sentiments expressed in the league's decision to draw the color line and the support White cyclists seemed to give to the idea of a separate league for Black cyclists certainly forecasted what Homer Plessy would hear in that decision in 1896.

The Black response to the Watts Amendment to exclude Black cyclists from the League of American Wheelmen demonstrated a broad spectrum of opinions even in spite of the fact that very few of those opinions actually made it into print. Fred Scott's reaction, if honestly reported, represented the most accommodating stance. He was described as believing that integration was bad for the growth of league membership and therefore it was best for the league, and for all cyclists regardless of race or ethnicity (due to the political power of the league) to pursue a policy of segregation. There were plenty more like Taylor and the porter who were unwilling to vocalize objections to the color line, taking the stance that they did not want to be members of an organization that did not want them. Some of those went further by agitating to create an organization of their own. Robert Teamoh and other unnamed men in Boston represented the most vocal and outright objection to the Watts Amendment by publicly condemning the decision and seeking censure against the league in Massachusetts. Their allegations that the color line was obtained through clandestine maneuvers, though disregarded by the press, certainly seemed plausible. In 1895, refusing to give up on the issue, Teamoh even traveled to the league meet, along with Boston delegates, to request that he be given an opportunity to speak to all delegates present about the color line. He explained that "the discrimination against his race raised a question of principle with him, and he thinks he can convince the delegates that the negro ought to have an equal chance in the league with the white man."[63] While there were apparently no objections to his doing so, not even by William Watts, his points were ineffective as the color line remained in place for more than 100 years.

The question of racial exclusivity in the league would continue to be a controversial issue, at least throughout 1897, but by then, the league was on the verge of handing the governance of bicycle racing over to another

76 CHAPTER 4

organization. By that time, cycling in general was on the precipice of a steady decline. The bottom would drop out for the industry in terms of bicycle production by 1900 and league membership hit its high-water mark in 1898 with 103,000 members.[64] Therefore, the period in which the bicycle was most popular in the United States was a time that was clouded by racial discrimination; presaging the Jim Crow Era of American history. Regardless of the diversity of opinions among Black cyclists about the racist policy, all intimated that they would continue to ride and enjoy their bicycles no matter what the league or White cyclists thought. To be sure, there were a number of Black cyclists who would simply not accept the color line. Rather than speaking out against the policy, as did Robert Teamoh, "Major" Taylor and others proved the irrationality of the color ban through their actions on and off the bicycle. To varying degrees, those other Black cyclists, to be discussed in following chapters, such as Kittie Knox, Woody Hedspeth, Melvin Dove, William Ivy, Hardy Jackson, Ulysses Scott, Ike Lindsay, and many others, would continue to push back against the scourge of racism.

5

The New Woman

In a large leghorn hat and a beautiful ensemble of pink and black, Kittie Knox entered the ballroom in Asbury Park and immediately caught the eye of the 600 other guests in attendance. Many stood transfixed. Some, White women in particular, looked at Knox scornfully, believing she should not be there. Others were undoubtedly made to feel embarrassed by Ms. Knox. She had outclassed many of them, something they, as White women, thought non-White women were incapable of doing. Her appearance eclipsed that of the majority of other women in attendance. They had shown up without hats and in "light garb"—looking as if they were prepared to go riding, rather than donning the formal attire organizers of the ball expected.[1] To add insult to injury, not only was Kittie Knox present and claiming her space with a large hat and stylish attire, but she also had the nerve to be the first out onto the dance floor—waltzing her way around the room in the embrace of a White man. It did not take long before many of the women in attendance had decided they had seen enough. In disgust, they began making premature departures from the evening's festivities. That was just fine by Ms. Knox. She was not there to make friends as much as she was there to make a point.

The ball in question was hosted by none other than the League of American Wheelmen, the organization that had decided to draw the color line one year prior, in 1894. In early 1895, Knox's compatriot from Boston, Rob-

78   CHAPTER 5

ert Teamoh, had made his way to Asbury Park to ask league delegates to reconsider their racist stance. Even a White delegate from Illinois, Louis Jacquish, was rumored to be clamoring to propose an amendment to remove the word white from the league's constitution. Teamoh's leadership in seeking a resolution of censure against the league, as well as his travels to Asbury Park to directly address league delegates, were endorsed by the Riverside Cycling Club of Boston. Riverside was a club for Black cyclists, and it just so happened to be the club of which Kittie Knox was a member. It was the very same club that had vowed to send one of their members to a meeting in Worcester, Massachusetts, in protest of the Watts Amendment, which drew the color line. To be sure, Knox went to the League of American Wheelmen meet, including their ball at Asbury Park in July of 1895, with a certain sense of purpose.

Kittie Knox carried dual burdens. This was especially true regarding her cycling pursuits. She was not White, and she was a woman. If coverage of the opinions and accomplishments of Black men on bicycles were scant, the stories about Black women who rode bicycles were even more rare. In fact, they hardly existed at all. Still, there were certainly Black women who did ride bikes and clearly some who did it with great skill and only through much perseverance in the face of rejection by others. While Black men encountered barriers to cycling based on their race, Black women had to overcome both racist and sexist objections to their participation. Before the invention of the safety bicycle, women were often discouraged from cycling. They faced considerable scorn if they were brave enough to attempt to ride the high wheeler. There were a few reasons for this. First was the fact that the high wheeler was seen as dangerous due to its propensity to throw riders into in a forward summersault over the handlebars and to the ground. This was known as a "header." Another reason cycling was discouraged among women was the sheer difficulty involved in riding the high wheeler while wearing a dress, due to the fact that the rider was positioned over the large front wheel. A woman's dress could easily become tangled in the spokes. Even if the dress stayed clear of the spinning wheel, the height of the woman's position, more than a few feet off the ground, would give some the opportunity to see up into the woman's undergarments. These impediments, however, did not keep women off bicycles, but for a while, many seemed to prefer tricycles—a safer, albeit heavier and slower, machine. Soon, however, the safety bicycle came along and revolutionized

Anna Morrison in San Diego, California, circa 1898. Photo courtesy of the Cycling Photographica Collection of Lorne Shields, Toronto.

cycling. With its triangular frame, congruent wheels, and chain powering the rear wheel, the safety was exactly that, much safer than high wheelers and much more efficient than tricycles.

As the safety became increasingly popular, production grew by leaps and bounds. More and more, women took to cycling for a variety of reasons. The safety centered their weight, reducing the chance of headers. Soon it also had pneumatic tires—making cycling more comfortable—and it could even be equipped with a dress guard over the rear wheel. Some women rode

80 CHAPTER 5

in dresses, long and short, some donned knickerbocker uniforms, but by the mid-1890s, an increasing number were wearing bloomers. As women became increasingly active in cycling, each step along the way was met with resistance.

At first, conservative ideas regarding gender norms suggested women should not ride a bicycle at all. After women refused to accept that restriction it was then argued that if they were going to ride, they should ride tricycles. After the safety bicycle was invented, female cyclists became more widely accepted but even then, they were discouraged from riding too fast or too far. Women disobeyed those attempted limitations as well, often riding more than 100 miles, or in the case of Annie Kapchovsky, even attempting to "ride around the world." Women also rode competitively, racing their bicycles, formally and informally. It is likely that some of those women who were daring enough to mount the high wheeler were not White, but evidence for that remains elusive. There is evidence, however, that by the time the safety bicycle had become popular, there were indeed women of color to join in on the fun and liberating feeling of pedaling a bicycle out into the countryside. Black women in the South were certainly taking to the bicycle. There were evidently enough Black women cyclists in the small town of Brunswick, Georgia to call for the creation of their own cycling club.[2] Doing so signified their status as "new women." As Patricia Marks points out in her book, *Bicycles Bangs and Bloomers: The New Woman in the Popular Press*, bicycles were appealing to the new woman because they gave the new woman the autonomy to go where she wanted, when she wanted, with or without a male companion. Breaking free from domesticity, she was no longer confined and could "actively seek new experiences" with the intention of "hav[ing] some impact on the world around her."[3]

The new woman included well-known figures such as Elizabeth Cady Stanton, Susan B. Anthony, and Frances Willard. Not coincidentally, all three were vocal in their love of the bicycle. Willard even went so far as to write the book, *How I Learned to Ride the Bicycle*. It was not the bicycle that made these women famous though, they were better known for their efforts to advocate for women's rights. The act of helping organize the Seneca Falls Convention, and/or direct involvement in the suffrage movement was clearly a way to make their voices heard, but the bicycle's role in helping women make a statement should not be underestimated. Women who rode

The New Woman

81

bicycles not only exerted their independence, but they also defied societal norms and medical opinions that argued their place was at home. Medical opinions went so far as to offer dire warnings that cycling, and strenuous exercise in general, could cause permanent damage to women's reproductive organs. Cartoons lampooned the seeming and much feared reversal of gender roles with images of men staying home watching the children while women were out cycling, derelict in their obligations to motherhood.[4] The fact that women were doing this and some were even going so far as to reject traditional clothing and adopt bloomers instead, a controversial item of clothing invented around 1850 but in revival in the 1890s due to its perfect suitability for cycling, was a step too far for some authority figures. One such female cyclist, a Ms. Hoey of Little Rock, was arrested for "indecent apparel" when she had the courage to appear in bloomers on her bicycle in 1895.[5] All female cyclists had to navigate these obstacles. Female cyclists who were Black, however, faced these obstacles and more.

Early evidence of Black women riding bicycles would suggest they, and Black cyclists as a whole, were unruly and dangerous when they mounted the wheel. In a series of lithographs by the Currier and Ives printing company of New York called the "Darktown Comics" there were a few depictions of not just Black men, but also Black women on bicycles. Even though they were merely comics, they seemed to be based on popular perceptions. In a set of drawings from 1892 titled "The Darktown Bicycle Club" the first drawing shows the club (composed of four members, two Black men and two Black women) on parade while the people of the town stand outside and hang from windows to watch the cyclists pass. The man in front rolls with his feet off of the pedals saying, "don't she glide lubly" in reference to his "rumatic" tires. The tires were clearly improvised and the use of "rumatic" instead of pneumatic was based on stereotypes and an attempt to poke fun at the assumed ignorance of the cyclist. The drawing that follows shows the four Black cyclists amid a crash after a goat freed itself from the hands of a young man standing near the parade. In the background are countless other Black men and women reacting to the commotion caused by the Black cyclists. The caption reads, "Dar! I knowed dem odd fellers was breeding mischief."[6] In a similar scene but different set of lithographs from the same "Darktown" series, four Black cyclists, again, two males and two females, race behind a black cat. They are all hunched over the handlebars

"The Darktown Bicycle Club—On Parade." Currier and Ives, 1892: Library of Congress Prints and Photographs Division.

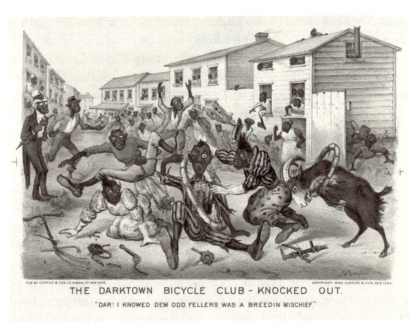

"The Darktown Bicycle Club—Knocked Out." Currier and Ives, 1892: Library of Congress Prints and Photographs Division.

"The Darktown Bicycle Race—The Start." Currier and Ives, 1895: Library of Congress Prints and Photographs Division.

"The Darktown Bicycle Race—A Sudden Halt." Currier and Ives, 1895: Library of Congress Prints and Photographs Division.

in the "scorcher" position, depicted with gaps in their teeth and in their finest cycling attire. Again, the men's tires appear to be a type of improvised cushioned or pneumatic tire that is tied up in sections with strings. The series had a constant theme of emasculating the men by depicting them as childlike but this one went further by showing one of the women just behind the man in the lead and beating the other man in the scene. The second image in that set shows the two leaders, man and woman, after crashing into a pile of lime in the middle of the road. It was apparently left there by Black construction workers who were building a brick structure. Another theme in this series is the idea that the members of the "darktown" cyclists were too proud of themselves in their fancy clothes and modern conveniences. Due to their childlike ignorance and pride, they often encountered problems. In the bicycle race series the caption says, "I knowd we'd have busted de record if it hadn't bin for dis misforchin."[7]

Another set of satirical drawings from the Darktown series shows two Black cyclists, a man and much larger woman dressed in their cycling costumes, bloomers and gaiters for the lady. They are mounted atop bicycles that appear to be home-made and out of wood. As they ride beneath a pear tree in which another Black man has climbed to apparently steal a pear, he falls and crashes on top of the pair of cyclists. There is a sign on the tree forbidding trespassers and another Black man is peaking over a rock fence. The first image is titled "Darktown Bicycling—A Tender Pair" and there is a caption that reads, "I'se gwine to git dat pear or bust sumfin."[8] The next drawing depicts the result of the pear poacher's actions. Both he and the woman's companion are shown tumbling atop her. All are entangled, Wooden bicycle parts are strewn across the road and all around. The woman is prostrate, in her cycling bloomers, clutching broken bits of wood in both hands, with her head busting through the spokes of a wheel. The caption reads "sumpins busted" continuing the racist stereotype and supposed vernacular of the subjects depicted.[9]

The idea that Black cyclists were a danger to themselves and others was pervasive in the 1890s. Many of the accounts of Black cyclists in popular periodicals during the era report on the accidents they allegedly caused while, of course, making sure to point out the race of the offending cyclists. Historians Evan Friss and Nathan Cardon both discuss this phenomenon with Cardon arguing that such stories were published not only to single out Black cyclists, but to also call their ability to "control and tame bicycle

The New Woman   85

technology" into question."[10] One such article in the New York *Sun* had the headline "Negro Cyclist Kills Woman." The story explained that it was an elderly woman, Mrs. Frances von de Linden, who was a local business owner that was "run down and killed . . . by a negro on a bicycle." A crowd apparently gathered just after and were on the verge of lynching the cyclist before he was whisked away to the local police station. Further down in the detailed account it becomes clear that the woman stepped from the sidewalk into the road directly in front of the cyclist, James Harris.[11] There are many newspaper reports of a similar nature throughout the 1890s and early 1900s.[12] Each time, the fact that the cyclist was Black and the person injured was White is always made clear. This helped to perpetuate that stereotype that all Black cyclists, including women, were dangerous and irresponsible.

Of the Black women who rode bicycles at the turn of the century, the most notorious was the young woman from Boston mentioned earlier, Katherine Knox. Born in 1874, her mother was a White Mainer and her father was a Black Philadelphian. He was a tailor but died at an early age and young Katherine, more commonly referred to as Kittie, grew up with her mother and brother on the west end of Boston. Following in the footsteps of her father, Kittie worked as a seamstress and dress maker.[13] How she came to cycling is unclear, but as a young lady of the Black middle class living in a city where cycling was extremely popular, it is little surprise that she was excited by and interested in bicycles. While she may have identified with the "new woman" how she identified racially is more difficult to discern. Many of the reports on her activities seemed to employ the one drop rule and referred to her simply as "colored" but others refereed to her as "a mulatto."

Since bicycles were at the forefront of modernity and they had a distinct appeal for the leisure class, as well as those who envisioned themselves as socially mobile, Kittie Knox would have ridden her bicycle with many like-minded individuals. As a member of the Riverside Cycling Club for Black cyclists, there were at least two other Black females and companions to Knox. Their names were Viola Wheaton and Benzina Reese.[14] Knox was also in the more unique position of being a Black member of the League of American Wheelmen in 1895. She secured her membership in April of 1893; just after the vote that nearly succeeded in drawing the color line in February of that year and before the successful vote on that same issue

"Kitty Knox the Colored League Member." Photo taken at Asbury Park, NJ, in 1895. *Referee & Cycle Trade Journal*, July 18, 1895.

in February of 1894.[15] She may have been the only Black woman to be a member since there were reportedly only around a dozen Black members total, at most, in the national association at the time the color line was drawn. While Wheaton and Reese may have very well been members of a local cycling club, they were probably not members of the national association (LAW). Various reports about Knox state that in 1895 she had already been a member of the LAW for five to six years.[16] This seems highly unlikely since she would have only been twenty-one years old in 1895 and the LAW by-laws stipulated members must be at least eighteen years of age—meaning the earliest she could have joined the league would have been in 1892.[17] Even though there was some disagreement on when she became a member, the sources do agree that she was indeed a member of the LAW. As such, she would have recognized that an overwhelming majority of her compatriots were White. While those members may have agreed on the joys and benefits of the wheel, when it came to issues of gender and race, their opinions were free to diverge. Since this was the case, most of the reports on Knox's activities focus on the controversies which centered around her.

Of course, Kittie Knox did more than simply elicit controversy and it certainly does not seem like that was her sole objective, in spite of what some cycling magazines of the era seemed to insinuate, but she also surely knew it was an inevitable repercussion of claiming her space. As a cyclist, Knox clearly rode her bicycle well and she rode it a lot. She completed a century ride (100 miles in a single day) during rainy conditions in the summer of 1895—a feat which was impressive for even the most experienced cyclist. She was reportedly the only woman to finish that particular century. She outlasted many men as well.[18] On another occasion, while on a club run during the national meet of the League of American Wheelmen, of the more than 150 riders taking part, Knox set herself apart. It was reported that on the return trip back to Asbury Park "someone started a grind which was increased slowly but surely into a veritable road race, until less than a dozen of the entire party remained. Miss Kittie Knox, the colored girl who has been so discussed, was one of the stayers, and when the Park was finally reached about noon by the survivors, riding at a better than three-minute clip, Miss Knox was less than 200 yards behind."[19] That such an exploit made it into the news demonstrates her remarkable strength.

In other articles, Knox's skill and grace on the bicycle were also noted. Upon her arrival in Asbury Park with the Boston delegation she reportedly "did a few fancy cuts in front of the clubhouse" on the first afternoon and "was requested to desist." There was apparently some fear that her demonstration may "result in temporarily opening the color line question" which had just been "settled" by the league one year earlier and they were anxious to put it behind them. It was also widely believed that things could turn worse, with the officials of the Asbury Park Wheelmen possibly going so far as to "protest against permitting Miss Knox to remain a member of the League."[20] Even in the comments about her skills and grace, the focus seemed to veer toward the potential controversy her presence might evoke.

88 CHAPTER 5

More often than commenting on her poise, cycling magazines and popular newspapers chose to focus on her appearance.

It was her face and figure that seemed to be the real source of controversy. Perhaps that was because she did not fit the ideals of White gentility and femininity. In part, it was her confidence and clothing that ruffled feathers, but a more important factor than that was the color of her skin. Nearly every report about her made note of her complexion. Many were more descriptive than simply referring to her as "colored" or "mulatto." The *New York Times* called her a "pretty young colored girl" while the *Red Lodge Picket* of Montana described her as a "light mulatto" who was "handsome and very graceful."[21] The *New Haven Journal Courier* referred to her as a "comely colored girl" while the *San Francisco Call* went a little farther saying she was an "extremely comely colored girl."[22] The cycling trade journal, *The Wheel*, said of her, "Aside from 'the livery of the shadowed sun' with which nature had equipped Miss Knox she wore . . . [a] bloomer suit." It elaborated further on her appearance writing that she had cheeks of a "warm olive" complexion.[23] *The Referee* was even more descriptive and alliterative, calling her a "beautiful and buxom black bloomerite."[24] Such descriptions made it appear that the two most important things readers should know about Kittie Knox was that she was not White, but also, she was attractive. This may have been her undoing. Had she been considered unfortunate looking, perhaps the White women of the league would have taken pity on her, or considered her something more akin to a mascot, much like the perceptions of some Black male cyclists.[25] Undoubtedly, the fact that she could be considered a "light mulatto" blurred the lines too much for some members of the LAW to stand.

A prognosticative question was posed in the pages of *The Bearings* in 1893 that seemed to foretell Knox's future with the league so accurately that the writer may have actually known of her, or someone very similar. In a section titled "Flashes of Cycling Life" the writer, going by the nom de plume "the Idler," asked, "can chivalry be dead?" Very much concerned with the impending vote by the League of American Wheelmen on whether to limit their membership to Whites only it asked: if there is a vote "to exclude Sambo from the order. . . . [H]ow about Sambo's sister?" Then, laying out a hypothetical that would become reality, the section continued, "Let us suppose that a handsome young quadroon female amateur, eighteen years of age, should apply for membership. Would the southern members vote for

Tintype of unidentified man and woman posing together with their bicycles. Photo courtesy of the Cycling Photographica Collection of Lorne Shields, Toronto.

her? Or does the chivalry of the south apply only to women whose skins and finger nails are perfectly white? These questions are respectfully referred to the distinguished gentlemen at the head of the anti-negro movement."[26] In the case of Kittie Knox, however, it was not a question of whether she could become a member since she had secured that designation before the league's vote to deny future applications from non-Whites. Instead, she would become embroiled in a debate about whether a non-White dues-paying member should be allowed to *stay* in the league, even if they joined before the color line was drawn.

By 1895, Knox had become the subject of a significant number of reports on cycling. It was July 4 of that year when her notoriety became most apparent—after she won a costume contest in Waltham, Massachusetts. Even so, at that point, the headlines gave more attention to her outfit rather than her perceived race or beauty. Exclaiming, "bloomers won the race" and

CHAPTER 5

"bloomers have it" articles appeared in papers across the country like the *Washington Times* and *Wichita Daily Eagle*. The articles probably originated from the same correspondent given their uniformity in coverage and style. They informed readers that there was a "bicycle carnival" for more than six thousand people in Waltham, Massachusetts on July 4. It was explained that "the events were especially noteworthy because . . . of a contest between several women for a prize to be given to the one having the most approved female bicycle costume, the latter event being the first of its kind ever held."[27] It is apparent that this sort of costume contest was a more acceptable competition for female cyclists than a race to test their speed and strength. While there was a large audience, it was up to three judges to make the decision about which costume was "most approved." The judges were Charles G. Percival, Henry Haynie, and a Miss Shaw. There were six contestants and each rode two laps around the track before they were judged by the small panel.[28] This contest was considered "intensely interesting, as the verdict of the judges has been expected to, in a way, decide the question of preference between bloomers and knickerbockers and skirts, long or short."[29] First prize went to Kittie Knox who, given her skills as a seamstress and dressmaker, had undoubtedly created her own costume, which consisted of bloomers, "sack coat, an ordinary bicycle cap, and gaitors."[30] It was apparent, however, that while the panel of three judges may have approved of Knox's ensemble, there were others in attendance who disagreed. The reports made note that some people in the grandstands "showed their disapproval of the bloomer and knickerbocker costumes by roundly hissing their wearers." Most sources agreed that it was "some women" in particular who disapproved but the *Seattle Post-Intelligence* claimed it was "the men in the grandstands." It seems more likely that it would have been the women, rather than men to hiss based on other encounters Knox would have with the world of cycling's self-appointed arbiters of taste. As the previously mentioned arrest of the woman wearing bloomers in Little Rock shows, this was an article of clothing that was still very controversial in 1895 so it comes as little surprise that there was some disagreement about whether they should be the style of the future. The fact that the winning costume of bloomers was worn by a woman who was not White only exacerbated Knox's rejection by the women in attendance. Other accounts of the day claimed it was indeed her race, not her clothing, that caused women to hiss in dis-

The New Woman 91

approval.[31] Either way, whether it was her costume or her complexion, she met the most disapproval from other women, not men. Male members of the league apparently treated her more cordially. In fact, at times it seemed the male members' reaction to her presence was a little too accepting, as far as the "ladies" of the club were concerned.

Indeed, the attention Knox received from White men appeared to make White women jealous. It was not simply that she was physically attractive, nor was it that her clothing was risqué. More so, it was that she used her knowledge as a seamstress and dressmaker to outdo the White women in their own fashion parades. Knox's experiences would seem to mirror the parable published in The Bearings over a year earlier in which a young White man and woman are sharing their respect and admiration of Black people with one another at a ball until a young Black woman enters the scene with a young Black male as her companion. The fact that it was set in Springfield, Massachusetts, less than 100 miles from Knox's hometown of Boston, raises the possibility that the story, written to seem like a parable, may have been based on actual events. That young White woman who believed in racial equality soon changed her mind upon seeing "a negro girl with a white satin dress cut low—very low—and trimmed with orange watered silk ribbon half-a-yard wide." It was gorgeous and the "colored man with a dress suit on" who accompanied her "danced every dance that evening."[32] This was enough to make both White subjects in the story disavow their support for racial equality as they soon learned that even their own sanctuary of White gentility could be "invaded." The young man grew even more upset after attending a similar ball in Cottage City that July and seeing "half-a-dozen-colored couples on the floor dancing with reckless abandon and enthusiasm."[33] The addition of a similar scene at Cottage City makes the parable seem even more likely to be based on actual events. In fact, there was indeed a ball for cyclists held in Cottage City in June of 1893 and Kittie Knox was there with at least two other female Black cyclists, Viola Wheaton and Benzina Reese.[34]

Viola Wheaton came from a well-respected Cleveland family as is evidenced by the Cleveland Gazette's frequent comments on Viola's appearances at various social functions. She was married to William Hamilton, eventual President of the Riverside Cycle Club. One of her brothers even joined the club.[35] Similarly, Benzina Reese had familial ties to the Riverside club as well. Her cousin, with whom she lived, George Lewis, was secretary for the club.[36] A report on the "summer girl" in the *Indianapolis Freeman* felt it was worth tracking all three of the women's activities. In June it reported that Knox and Wheaton, "two of Boston's fair ones," were "graceful" and "active members" of the Riverside Bicycle club. Two months later it reported that both Knox and Reese would be staying in Cottage City from August until September.[37]

The League of American Wheelmen often hosted balls or dances for their members. These could be organized for both national and local meets. Due to the popularity of the league at the time, their formal balls could attract very large crowds—such as the ball at the 1895 national meet of the LAW in Asbury Park with an expected attendance of around 5,000 guests. This was the same event where Kittie Knox set herself apart from all the other women in the league. She proved to be, "probably most talked of of any one person [t]here, danced every number on the order and added to her reputation as a clever wheelwoman by proving herself a model of gracefulness on the floor."[38] As "the only colored person in the building" her appearance clearly triggered an immediate backlash.[39] One report posited, "her presence was the cause . . . of much subsequent discussion on the race question in general and its connection with the league in particular."[40] Another report claimed, "The pretty and young cycling women down here all wear the walking-length skirts, and the costume that the bloomerites call irrational. That is all the pretty ones, except the mulatto girl from Boston, Miss Kitty Knox, who was first discriminated against on account of her color. She wears bloomers and is so very attractive that a lot of White men wearing League of American Wheelmen colors, and who had as well been in some other business, are constantly dancing attendance on her." Some of the men were apparently questioned about their actions and in defense they said they only did it to "show that the league makes no discrimination against colored persons and believes in equal rights." The report continued, "These young fellows made her quite the lion of the evening at the ball last night by dancing with her, and she enjoyed the sensation she created as the only colored person in the building."[41] *The Wheel* emphasized the point that after Knox appeared on the scene "A number of the ladies present left, but Miss Knox remained and participated in the dancing, with White men as her partners; in fact, she seldom lacked White escorts during the week."[42]

The fact that her presence upset many White women to the point that they would leave was widely reported.

As the White women stormed out of the auditorium the question on some minds was whether they were embarrassed, jealous, mad, or all three. It soon became clear they were indeed mad and simply leaving the dance in protest was not enough to quell their anger. The *New York Herald* reported, "Among the visiting bicyclers is a bright young mulatto girl, from Boston, and the many snubs which have been placed upon her by many of the women culminated last night in dozens of them leaving the ball at the Auditorium, because she was not only there, but first upon the floor in the waltz, which took place of the grand march."[43] It also commented on the potential long-term fallout from Knox's presence at the ball informing readers: "A dozen of the wheelwomen at the Ocean House Headquarters tonight declared their intention to leave the National League if Miss Knox stayed a member, the dozen being the most important and most influential wheelwomen at the meet."[44] While the dozen who left the dance were not exactly commended for their actions, they were in no way portrayed as inexcusable. Some reports went so far as to paint Kittie Knox as a provocateur. They blamed Knox directly for all the controversy surrounding her, arguing that it was a matter of "misguided chivalry" on the part of the men present but that Knox herself was also at fault for being "not at all averse to her notoriety."[45] *The Wheel* took a similar stance on Knox a few months later writing, "Kittie Knox, the young negro woman who earned some notoriety by appearing at the ball during the league meet at Asbury Park, has once more forced herself into print."[46] A little more subtly, The *Bearings* placed the blame on Knox by identifying her as the woman "who created such a furore at Asbury Park."[47] Given its precedents, it is unsurprising that the cycling media would make Kittie Knox out to be a young woman simply bent on getting attention rather than an individual who endured racist acts while attempting to exercise her freedom. She represented something bigger than herself and the idea that she was attempting to make a point about racial equality seemed lost on White writers. They chose to perceive her actions as purely egotistical and selfish.

The question of whether Kittie Knox was deliberately trying to call attention to the way Black cyclists were treated or just merely trying to ride her bike is not easily answered but it seems there was at least some inten-

94 CHAPTER 5

tionality in her actions. It is also true that she made that point whether it was her intended purpose or not. Lorenz Finnison argues that Knox was a deliberate activist and attributes it to her father, whom Finnison suggests was an activist himself, but also someone who died when Knox was just eight years old.[48] Though she joined the league in 1893, she did not receive much notice or mention until 1895, when the national meet was nearby. Why did she seem to emerge at that point? The 1894 national meet was in Denver so perhaps she did not attend in that year due to the distance and concerns about acceptance out west. Arriving in Asbury Park with a large contingent of her fellow Bostonian cyclists might have made her feel more comfortable, but at the same time, it is not like Boston was free from racism or restrictions, even against Black cyclists. The Massachusetts delegates to the LAW (many of them from the Boston area) did indeed vote against the Watts Amendment but it was becoming increasingly clear that Boston area cyclists, as a whole, were not exactly excited to diversify their ranks.

In November of 1895, less than two years after Massachusetts delegates voted against the Watts Amendment, the Boston Wheelmen, a White cycling club, drew their own color line. It was around September of 1895 that the club advertised a century run that appeared to be open to all riders. After receiving applications and entrance fees from several Black riders, the Boston Wheelmen returned them, including one to Kittie Knox, with the explanation that "at a suddenly called meeting of the organization it was voted that the club draw the color line and return the applications sent in by the colored people."[49] Knox was planning on riding a tandem bicycle with a "young physician" but when her application was denied he "got very indignant" and withdrew from the event. A Black councilman named Charles H. Hall went further. After claiming to have been personally invited by club leaders and then being denied, he filed civil suits against Charles L. Razoux, William B. Handy, and William Temple for $300. Hall said that he did not ask for an application or invitation but that he was "repeatedly urged to go on the run by some members of the club whom he holds responsible for his trouble."[50] Hall charged that Razoux, Handy, and Temple aided and abetted in color discrimination.[51] Members of the club explained that the color line was drawn after the applications of Black cyclists appeared accepted because "it was found that some of the lady participants on the run might object to their presence." Upon reporting the news, The Bearings concluded, "Therefore it looks bad for the future of the colored riders in

The New Woman

95

this city."[52] Women's objections to cycling with those who were not White were clearly strong and carried great weight. The fact that Black men had been active cyclists for several years and the arrival of Kittie Knox, Benzina Reese, and Viola Wheaton was relatively recent suggests the White women objected to Black women on bicycles more than they objected to Black men on bicycles. The very idea of it threatened their own thoughts of cycling as demonstrative of White gentility. Black men could be dismissed as a lower-class sort of rider seeking financial gain, such as professionals, but it was not as easy to categorize Black female cyclists the same way due to the lack of opportunity for women to race professionally. In some ways, White women may have been projecting their own feelings. After all, they were no strangers to being told they were lesser cyclists themselves.

Early in 1895, the Massachusetts Bicycle Club considered excluding all women from their club. The *Bearings* reported that the club had "tried the co-education idea in its membership, and it has failed, if a rumored change in the constitution can be taken for a sign. It is not improbable that at the next meeting of the club an amendment will be offered to the constitution to the effect that men only may be admitted to membership." Women represented a small percentage of the membership, less than twenty women total. Some of the male members believed if membership was limited to men only, "many of the old-time riders who were once members of the Massachusetts will once more associate themselves with the club."[53] This was extremely similar to the rationale used in arguments for the color line in the league. Increased exclusivity would generate increased membership. Apparently, the Massachusetts club did not actually go through with the vote, or at least they did not have to because once "the ladies were given to understand that they were not wanted . . . , they resigned in a body. . . ." The result was allegedly a restoration of peace among the club, which had only voted to admit women to membership around "a year or so" earlier.[54] In some instances, it is clear that while women may have been agitating to ensure their clubs were segregated by race, there were also men who wanted their clubs free from women in general, let alone a Black female cyclist like Kittie Knox. It is clear then that Knox endured discrimination on two fronts.

When Knox first arrived at the Asbury Park national meet, she quickly learned that she would not be welcomed with open arms. The *Savannah Morning News* reported, "When Miss Knox, whose appearance and dress had been objects of admiration all day, walked into the committee room at the local club house and presented her league card for a credential badge, the gentlemen in charge refused to recognize the card, and the young woman withdrew very quietly and went her way."[55] *The Referee* also reported on the initial denial of Knox's league privileges in Asbury Park and that she was refused accommodations at some hotels as well, but clarified that she got the league privileges eventually. Curiously, this news was included with a short article titled "Rescued from Thieves." It claimed that "two women cyclists" were "rescued . . . from two negro thieves" by three male cyclists. Without a break, the very next sentence mentioned Knox and her troubles as if the two stories were related.[56] The *Bearings* reported on Knox being denied credentials and that she was also refused admission "at several places of entertainment" but it added, "She, however, joined in several runs, and has been doing the best that she could to enjoy herself. Vice-President Geo. A. Perkins says that she must receive all the privileges accorded other League members, or there will be trouble."[57] Specifically, Perkins was talking about rumors that Knox had been refused service at a café in Asbury Park that was apparently affiliated with the league. Any hotel or restaurant affiliated with the league was under an obligation to provide services to all members. To that point, Perkins said that if reports could be confirmed that she was denied services at a café or hotel, he would "strongly recommend that the League take it up and prosecute."[58] Kittie Knox seemed to take it all in stride. At the initial refusal to recognize Knox's LAW membership card, she reportedly "withdrew very quietly" although another report said, "she straightway demanded protection."[59] In spite of the embarrassing scene she certainly "joined in several of the runs" and continued "doing the best that she could to enjoy herself."[60] There was even one source that claimed she denied "she had any trouble at the league headquarters."[61] The fact that it was only one source that reported this makes it seem a little dubious, but it is entirely possible that Knox shrugged off the kerfuffle that ensued when she presented her league card. It certainly did not stop her from participating.

Kittie Knox's apparent success and good showing at the Asbury Park meet elevated her status, particularly among Black cyclists. Two weeks after the national meet at Asbury Park, she traveled to Philadelphia where she was hosted by the Meteor Wheelmen. This club was mockingly referred to as "the 'uppah crust' among the local Ethiopian devotees of the wheel."[62] So excited they were by her endeavors, they "showed her a 'bang-up' time— escorted her to the Tioga races, tendered her reception, followed by a collation in the tastefully decorated clubhouse, and wound up with a fireworks display."[63] She was celebrated by the Black cycling club in Philadelphia and her reception shows that she was a woman of influence. This was true on multiple levels. As a woman, she challenged gendered ideals with the cycling costumes she designed. Today, we would call her a trendsetter since the contest she won was considered to be a test that would set the standard for cycling attire in the future. As a Black cyclist, she laid claim to her rights to the road and League of American Wheelmen events even though they had recently made a decision to bar Black cyclists. Their decision was not retroactive, however, and since she became a member before the decision went into action, it was much more difficult for the league to dismiss her.

Kittie Knox was remarkable, but it is also important to point out that she was not a solitary Black cyclist, she was not even a solitary Black female cyclist. There is evidence of many more unnamed Black female cyclists such as Viola Wheaton, Benzina Reese, Anna Morrison, and the cycling club for Black women in Brunswick, Georgia. Many of the other women may not have belonged to the same socioeconomic group as Knox and they most likely did not ride as often nor were they as visible when they did. Those factors, combined with the fact that they probably were not members of the LAW meant that there was very little chance that they would have made it into the pages of the press. Their seeming invisibility today should not lead us to assume they were all together absent. Indeed, the evidence, while scant, does suggest otherwise.

Kittie Knox, Benzina Reese, Viola Wheaton, Anna Morrison, and others show that Black cyclists' participation ranged wider than competitive aspects. While Knox was apparently a strong and skilled rider, she did not appear to participate in races even though there were women's races at the time. She did compete in at least one costume contest, but she mostly seemed to use her bicycle for social mobility in accessing middle-class pursuits like leisure and gentility. Still, there were times that she proved her strength and endurance on organized rides. She was also notable for showing the world a woman could be both strong and attractive. Her mere presence at cycling events made a statement that was powerful enough to clearly threaten the preconceived ideas of the White female adopters of the wheel. Black female cyclists like Knox challenged ideas of race, class, and gender in a way that was deeply unsettling for the White middle class, even those who may have considered themselves forward thinking when it came to the idea of race. As Knox's experiences show, however, the opportunities for cycling in integrated settings were becoming less and less frequent, even for those who were members of the league before the color line was drawn.

6

Six Days in a Row

Melvin T. Dove completed revolution upon revolution upon revolution. The turning of the cranks, which turned the wheels, and the slow turning of his handlebars left to complete circles on a wooden oval track. The air was stale, humid, smoke filled, and occasionally ringing with cheers from the stands. Most of this was hardly noticeable to Dove as he grew distant. His strength, his energy, and his will had all slowly seeped out of his body and into his machine. This was his sixth day in a row at it and many of those "masculine virtues" of the period were now gone. Reduced to something more like an irritable and unreasonable toddler over the last 130 hours, he took turns on the oval with his teammate, Woody Hedspeth. Together, they raced all hours of the day and night, one racing while the other rested and vice versa. In earlier editions of this annual International Six-Day Bicycle Race, some men made the effort solo, resting as little as two hours over the course of the first four days. They took their meals on the bike, drinking milk, broths, teas, and soups as well as choking down oatmeal when it was handed to them in a canister.[1] Regulations were introduced in 1899, however, that mandated it be a team competition.[2] Even though Dove and Hedspeth had worked themselves to exhaustion, they were well off the winning pace. Still, they would get paid. They rode a combined total of more than 1,900 miles over the six days.[3] This initial experience in six-day racing at Madison Square Garden would stick with Dove. It was not exactly a positive experience, but he would do it again. At least one more time.

Six-day bicycle races were an interesting phenomenon at the dawn of the twentieth century. They drew a significant number of spectators and remained one of the most popular forms of bicycle racing in the United States for more than twenty years. Their popularity was due, in part, to the controversy surrounding these tests of human endurance. Described as "one of the most disgusting, demoralizing, and pernicious contests parading in the guise of 'sport' known to humanity," the six-day spectacle had its fair share of detractors.[4] Six-day racers played the role of lab rats as the gallery of observers checked in on them now and again—when they found it convenient to take a break from their merry making in the grandstands. Over time, the riders slowly revealed the effects of prolonged aerobic intensity coupled with short periods of rest. It was such an extreme test of the human body that police officials were even called in to make sure the event was not overly dangerous.

The journal *Medical News* likened the racers to rabbits, rather than rats, arguing that the six-day race could be "utilized to corroborate Mendel's statements" that if animals "were placed on a flat surface, and the surface caused to rotate continuously a number of times per minute during a few days, the animals would develop all the physical manifestations of general paresis." In direct comparison, it argued, "In reality, going around the short circular track in the Madison Square Garden is practically the same as being whirled on a revolving table, save that there is added thereto the element of physical effort and consequent physical exhaustion." Rather than advocate for their immediate cessation, the article went on to propose that six-day racing be used for a real-life experiment on human subjects. It concluded, "we feel convinced that one trial of this will so eradicate six-day bicycle races from the program of sports that they cannot be resuscitated as long as the memory of the present generation continues."[5] Given the tenor of the article in *Medical News*, it was perhaps unsurprising that the New York Legislature stepped in the very next year to regulate the six-day events by passing a statute prohibiting bicycle racers from riding more than twelve hours out of twenty-four in a race, thus leading to the first team competition in the International Six-Day Bicycle Race of 1899.[6] The new statute, as well as articles decrying the inhumanity of the six-day grind, however, had little impact in turning the public away. Proving that there was no such thing as bad publicity, many spectators turned out just for the cruelty of the six-day race.

Six-day racing presented more than a simple opportunity to watch someone suffer, however. The races were also popular because of the bacchanalian atmosphere in the stands. They attracted both the depraved and the high-brow socialite. Somewhat akin to prize fights of the era, while six-day races attracted men of all classes, those of the upper class often attempted to keep their appearances low-key, as one would when "slumming." One report on the six-day races declared the crowd at the races to be far more interesting than the race itself. It elaborated on the point explaining, "the real fun begins about midnight, when the concert halls and theatres pour their crowds into the Garden. Class distinction is utterly forgotten after this hour and woe unto him who considers himself on a higher plane, socially, than his neighbor." To demonstrate the egalitarian nature of the stands, the description included a story of a "young scion of Fifth avenue" being pelted with rotten fruit when he expressed indignation at being unable to quickly make his way through the throng of "shop girls and their 'gentlemen friends.'" The man was eventually escorted away from the scene by police, but the spectators' need for excitement was not quelled by the altercation. Soon after the race's next sprint was finished, they found a young newspaper boy to razz. Discovering him sleeping with his head atop the day's papers, which he had failed to sell. The crowd woke him and then began pestering him with requests to entertain them with a song. The boy relented and stood on a stool while the crowd silently listened to his rendition of "She May Have Seen Better Days." When he finished, they erupted in drunken applause with a reporter taking the boy's "tattered cap" from his head, placing a dollar in it and passing it around. The people crowding the stands were there clearly looking for thrills, with little interest in who won or lost, except for the gamblers who had money on certain riders. If there was the slightest lull in the action on the track "dozens of expedients [were] resorted to, in order to stir the bunch up."[7] Six-day races could attract all walks of life, including Ernest Hemingway as well as Al Capone and his entourage.[8] Of course, the races also attracted the types of petty-thieves and grifters who elbowed their way among the crowd looking for easy opportunities. Even the racers were not immune. Such was the case for two of the competitors, Galvin and Root, who allowed a young boy they had only recently met to serve as their mascot and valet. At first, they declined but upon observing his condition and hearing the desperation in his voice, fearing he would starve or freeze to death, they relented. The boy ate like a king for the few days he worked for them and then when they asked him to take their clothes to have them pressed, he chose to abscond with them instead. Galvin and Root believed he took them to a pawnshop.[9]

The similarities between the six-day races and prize fights went beyond the socioeconomic diversity of the crowd. There were even intentional ties formed between the two biggest sporting events of the day. Former heavyweight champion Jim Corbett fired a blank round in the starter's pistol at Madison Square Garden to begin the 1903 edition of the International Six-Day Race. He himself had "used the bicycle extensively when training" for upcoming boxing bouts.[10] The connections between the six-day race and a prize fight did not go unnoticed by those in attendance either, but as one writer put it, "with all the spectacular brutality of the prize ring it is far less brutal than . . . a six-day bicycle race."[11] The men on the velodrome at Madison Square Garden could lose ten or more pounds in the course of six days. They were described as six days of "prolonged torture" that "taxes human endurance to the extreme of brutality, and after it is all ended it has proved no useful fact to the individual or to the public. . . . Its purpose is in the gate receipts only. . . . It is made as sensational as possible to awaken public interest. A band of men struggling to do something that men never did before, or to beat the records of all men who had gone before, appeals to the spirit of the masses. . . . It may be said to the credit of human nature, however, that but few of the visitors can perceive the cruelty of the competition."[12] Much like prizefights or the burgeoning sport of football, the masculinity of six-day racing was both abhorred by some and embraced by others. The exception for the six-day was that there were occasional six-day events for female cyclists. Visitors to the six-day races would have been privy to spectacles of racers being lifted by their trainers and put back on their bike after taking short breaks from the machine. Riding over 1,000 miles in six days was only part of the challenge, the bigger obstacle for many was the severe sleep deprivation they endured. It was reported that hallucinations, childlike psychosis, irritability, and mania were all observed among the athletes in a six-day race. Some riders felt that not only were they being persecuted but that their own trainers were trying to poison them. Others had to be restrained from jumping off their bike and going into the stands to attack the spectators. One report included details about a Black cyclist named Gray who "was kept going for days through fear of his trainer, who threatened him with personal injury if he quit, and at times stimulated him with the sight of a cane or a whack over the back. Men would go asleep on their wheels and tumble to the floor. One rider's arms and hands were so benumbed by injections of cocaine, used to deaden the aches, that he could not feel the handlebars."[13]

Perhaps the only reason the races lasted a mere six days and no longer was the belief that things should stop after the sixth day because blue-laws made it difficult to race on Sunday. Keeping it a "day of rest," the six-day races often began just after midnight on Sunday and did not stop until midnight on the following Saturday. Completing such a race in first place could earn a rider as much as $1,500 in 1897 with second and third earning $800 and $500 respectively. Payout ran on down to eleventh place with a prize of $75.[14] There were also prizes that could be won in the middle of the race. As a tactic to keep the racers on their toes or to create a temporary moment of excitement in what could become a boring and somewhat monotonous event, race officials would pick laps at random to be intermediate sprints, or primes. The winner of the prime would be awarded a prize, ten dollars for instance, or a set of racing wheels.

Like prizefighting and even horse racing, bicycle racing was an opportunity for social mobility that was particularly appealing to the working classes. These were opportunities for men, no matter their race or social status, to earn equal payouts. For a Black cyclist, this was undoubtedly enticing. This was one of the few opportunities where they could earn wages that were equal to those of White men.[15] This compounded the manly rewards of six-day racing because, as historian Louis Moore argues, economic independence was essential to Black constructions of manhood.[16] That economic independence and the attainment of manhood it conferred was fundamental to the appeal of bicycle racing. It was, therefore, the danger, the requisites of strength and endurance, as well as the money that could be earned, which all made the six days so symbolic of manhood during the period.

While the six-day races could be lucrative, some of the better-known cyclists made it a point to avoid them. Freddie Spencer explained his aversion to the format saying, "If I could make $600 in two minutes riding a match race, why the hell should I ride twenty-four hours for $600?"[17] "Major" Taylor, the best known and most successful Black cyclist, did at least one six-day race when he was eighteen. The fact that he shied away from them during his career suggests that he too preferred shorter races, generally of five miles or less. This was not necessarily because he lacked the stamina for longer races. Bicycle historian Peter Nye argues that it was due in part to the fact that there was a greater chance of "pocketing" in longer races.[18] This was a tactic that Taylor experienced a lot during his career. When pocketing, three to four riders would work together to box the favorite in and keep them from freely sprinting to the finish line. In the shorter races, it was a little more difficult to accomplish, especially if it was short enough for someone like Taylor to keep the tempo so high as to stay at the front. At other times, Taylor would hang back behind the bunch and then make his finishing kick from there, starting it a little earlier than he would otherwise. Fortunately for Taylor, he was not desperate enough to have to race the six days if he preferred shorter races.

For Black cyclists like Melvin T. Dove, Ulysses Grant Scott, and Woody Hedspeth, all who were less successful than Taylor, any time they could race for a prize, cash in particular, was a worthwhile opportunity. This was especially true when the event attracted up to 20,000 spectators at a time, like the six-day races at Madison Square Garden.[19] The six-day races were the best opportunities to demonstrate their speed, power, and skill before a large crowd. Beyond that, these races were also about masculinity in a more literal sense because they were a test of the limits of man. With the goal of using the bicycle to prove they were not inferior, but in fact superior to other men, there was no better venue than the six-day races at Madison Square Garden. These were the attributes that helped induce Dove and Hedspeth to race as a team in the 1903 edition of the International Six-Day Bicycle Race at Madison Square Garden. Well before Jim Corbett fired the starter's pistol, some began expressing concerns that "the bitter feeling" which had been prevalent between riders throughout the season might "crop out again" at the six-day race—the last major event on the calendar. In particular, the usual "marks" were the foreign riders, but the article also specifically mentioned that at the 1902 edition of the race, Woody Hedspeth "fell in a mix-up and had his shoulder dislocated. It was hinted that Hedspeth had been made a mark of by several of the riders whose prejudices regarding the race question are very strong." Conversely, however, it was pointed out that in 1903, Hedspeth would be riding with Dove, who "has always been popular with the riders, but whether there will be any feeling against him in the coming race remains to be seen."[20] Reports on the 1902 six-day claimed that the "mix-up" that led to Hedspeth's injured shoulder was actually caused by his White teammate, Alex Peterson, while he attempted to relieve Hedspeth on the track after only the twenty-seventh mile of racing.[21] As it would turn out, Dove and Hedspeth did not end up being much of a factor in the final results of the 1903 race. They were well off the winning distance with no hope of catching up but continued to race because they earned at least $50 a day to stay in the contest. They were pulled from the contest on Saturday afternoon, the final day of racing.[22] The payout for their six days of riding must have been worth the effort. Otherwise, Hedspeth and Dove would have withdrawn from the race as soon as it became clear that they had no chance of finishing in the money. For other cyclists like Spencer and Taylor, however, the relatively paltry reward was not worth the toll and the risk.

That risk, as one evening newspaper described it, could bring the complete destruction of a cyclist's mental health. *Medical News* also issued a damning article on the six-day races. It argued, "The six men whose brains have given away to this terrible strain are among the leaders in the van, and it is the efforts that they have put forth to hold their coveted positions which have cost them their sanity. These men are fit for little else than a ward in a lunatic asylum."[23] *Medical News* also used the event as an opportunity to discuss the morality of even casually spectating at such an event. Commenting on the inhumanity, it pointed out the contradictions in how "a people who decry cock fighting, dog fighting, and even 'ratting' for amusement, and who are horrified beyond expression and tolerance at the thought of [bullfighting] . . . should permit one of the most harrowing spectacles that can be imagined to continue without protest, or indeed refrain from taking matters into their own hands and stopping it *tour de force* is cause for wonderment."[24] The difference, of course, was that the cyclists in a six-day race seemed to participate under their own volition. As Spencer's comments and reports on the events would suggest, however, some of those participants could be considered desperate, or merely deranged. While Dove many not have exactly been desperate, he, like most professionals, was clearly motivated by the potential monetary gains and the psychic rewards of competing against, and possibly besting, White men before extremely large numbers of White spectators.

Dove's diminutive status in comparison to Taylor was continually reiterated through the cycling press and their tendency to refer to Dove as the "amateur Major Taylor" at times, even calling him Melvin "Taylor" Dove or Major Taylor Dove on occasion, since the first two initials of his name were M and T. According to his death certificate, Dove's middle name was actually Thomas. By 1904, Dove was clearly working to shed his amateur status, however, which suggests he had found considerable success on the bicycle. Seeking more wealth and fame, along with twenty-one other cyclists from the northeast, Melvin Dove turned professional for the 1904 season. Many of those men were actually "asked" to make the change while it was reported that Dove had already been racing as a pro in 1903.[25] Of course, Dove's move from amateur to professional would present some challenges, especially since White cyclists had worked out an agreement so that "Major" Taylor would be the only Black cyclist permitted to race as a professional. By early spring, the start of the 1904 season, it was clear that the line would hold firm.

In March, the "Racing Notes" section of *The Bicycling World and Motorcycle Review* reported, "M.T. Dove, the New York negro racing man, whose initials are said to stand for 'Major Taylor,' was a spectator at the races last Sunday at the Vailsburg track. Dove is in a somewhat embarrassing position, as he has been turned out of the amateur fold by the N.C.A. [National Cycling Association] Board of Control but is not allowed to compete as a professional. When 'Major' Taylor gained permission to ride through an agreement between the N.C.A. and the American Racing Cyclists' Union, it was stipulated by the professional riders that no more negroes were to be permitted to race as professionals." The only solution for Dove seemed to be racing abroad. The report continued, "Dove has had some correspondence with French promoters, and hopes to go to Europe to race this year."[26] There had been rumors, however, that Dove and Hedspeth were both going to Europe at the close of the season in 1903. The fact that Dove had little choice, if he wanted to race as a professional, was glossed over, however, and instead his decision was attributed solely to greed for money. An article in December 1903 lamented, "The success of a few riders in making money in Europe during the summer has excited the cupidity of so many American racing men that there is danger of there not being enough good men here next summer to make a respectable showing at the St. Louis Exposition." Some riders, such as Walthour and Bardgett, already had contracts to race in France but Hedspeth and Dove were described as "going over on speculation."[27] There was certainly still a great deal of resentment in the world of cycling for those who sought monetary gains from participation in the sport. For Black men like Dove and Hedspeth, however, men that were one or two generations removed from slavery, the bicycle offered not just physical mobility, but also social mobility. To them, earning money for their talents was not shameful, it was a rare chance at living a comfortable life as a free man in a time and place where there were very limited opportunities for such endeavors. Dove was somehow blamed for putting himself in the predicament that restricted his eligibility for racing in the United States. Leading with the color of his skin, *The Bicycling World* used the headline "Black Dove to go Abroad" for a short article that postulated he was "inspired, doubtless, by the comparative success of Woody Hedspeth, his black compatriot" to go to Paris. It also explained, "For several years Dove has been the soiled bird of the amateur flock, having committed all sorts of offenses in the effort to have himself professionalized. The crack professionals on this side of the water, however, refused to compete with him, and, perforce, the N.C.A. compelled him to mingle with the 'amateur white trash.' . . ."[28] For Black cyclists in the United States, it seemed the choices were to either race as an amateur or to leave.

The treatment Dove received from the press only added to his difficulties. For instance, he was made the poster child for something of an exposé on the "prostitution of amateurism." The state of amateurism in cycling was considered by some to have "sunk to such degrading depths" in 1904 and was "reeking with the slime and filth of maladministration . . . by the National Cycling Association."[29] The problems were evident in 1903 as "the sport ran riot and was permitted to practically run itself." There were unsanctioned meets without penalties, amateurs openly accepting cash, and the amateur champion allegedly worked out a deal so that he could have the cash value of all the prizes he won rather than the actual prizes. Those issues were allowed to slide by the cycling press, however, since the NCA admitted to its own dereliction and assured everyone it would do better in 1904. This is the main reason why the NCA officials "made an outward show of housecleaning by professionalizing a number of tainted amateurs, and later—and without outward show—quietly reinstated them."[30] One rider who represented a particularly upsetting example of this was Melvin Dove. With a contemptuous tone the same report said, "The stench was already sufficiently nauseating when last week it leaked out that Melvin T. Dove, the New York negro rider of some notoriety, had

108   CHAPTER 6

been whitewashed and restored to the amateur ranks. Action in Dove's case is so absolutely disgusting that words fit to characterize it are hard to find. It lays bare the entire rottenness and impotency of the N.C.A."[31] Dove's sin was that he not only made money from racing, but he openly talked about it. Making no secret of it, Dove allegedly "boasted that he has always sold his prizes and has accepted cash whenever and wherever he could get it." The most blatant example of the NCA turning a "blind eye" to his flouting of the rules of amateurism was when they allowed him to ride as a professional "'teaming it' with another negro, 'Woody' Hedspeth," and even though they did not win a prize at the end of the six-day races, they "were paid money for training expenses and 'appearance'."[32] It is curious that Dove was the target for the brunt of the complaints against the NCA while the White "amateur champion"(Marcus L. Hurley) was not even named. Hedspeth too did not receive the same level of attention, most likely because he had already taken up the practice of racing abroad for the most part and he was not winning prizes as an amateur in the United States.

When asked how the NCA could allow Dove to race in amateur events after it had declared him a professional, the explanation was the "time worn agreement with that paper organization, the American Racing Men's Union." That agreement was "fairly well known" due to its terms that "no negro, Major Taylor excepted, shall be permitted to ride as a professional." A spokesman for the NCA explained, "if Dove is permitted to so ride, the white men who race on bicycles for a livelihood will 'strike' and forgo their livelihood, and the Vailsburg track become a barren waste." For the author of the exposé, possibly the editor, Ritchie Betts, this was not an explanation so much as it was a "disgraceful confession of the N.C.A's impotency and inability to fairly and decently control and regulate the sport it set out to control and regulate." It reportedly showed the NCA was "at the mercy of a so-called 'union'." If that was the agreement then, as the article pointed out, the men of that union essentially nullified those terms when they agreed to race against Dove "and his black mate in the six-day races."[33] This then was how Dove's case purportedly "laid bare" the fact that "American amateurism as it [then] exist[ed] [was] a howling and disgraceful farce." The article closed by taking a stand that championed the ideals of the leisure class stating, "it is because of faith in the sport and in amateur sport, and in behalf of the men, it matters not how few, whose efforts spring from love of sport and not love of lucre, that his protest is uttered. The spirit of amateurism is too precious to be throttled by a few men whose interest in it is shallow. . . ." The sport was in need of "rescue" and this author hoped holding the NCA accountable for the state of amateurism was key.[34]

For Dove and all Black cyclists except "Major" Taylor it seemed a catch 22, unless they were independently wealthy. Even at the amateur level, the competition was stiff enough that it required consistent training to the extent that having a job, especially one requiring physical exertion, was disadvantageous. Racing as a professional meant you could earn enough in payouts and prizes to offset the inability to work during the cycling season. In the United States, only Taylor could do so. The calls for the ideals of amateurism were an attempt to keep the playing field unlevel in a way that benefited the upper classes. Of course, this also had direct racial implications.

The Amateur Athletic Union (AAU) was brought into the debate in the following week's issue of *The Bicycling World*. The AAU was founded in 1888 with the goal of ensuring uniform standards for amateur status across all sports. It was best known for the work it did in helping prepare American Olympic athletes. The modern Olympics, which were resurrected in 1896, largely through the efforts of the Frenchmen Pierre de Coubertin, were firmly grounded in those same ideals of amateurism, a primarily classist and masculine ideal that men should compete for the love of sport. The Secretary of the AAU, James Sullivan, in reference to cyclists who took part in the six-day races for money, said "that under no circumstances would such riders be recognized as amateurs by the A.A.U., nor could they compete in amateur sports, because they had clearly violated the very foundation of the amateur law." Of Melvin T. Dove, who *The Bicycling World* lumped in as one of the many "money-grabbers," it was stated explicitly that the AAU "does not and will not recognize [him] as an amateur."[35] The fact that the magazine appeared most upset about Dove being allowed to continue racing as an amateur was not lost on President A. G. Batchelder of the NCA, who suspected that it came down to the issue of race. Upon receiving questions about why Dove was reinstated, which were submitted by *The Bicycling World*, Batchelder laughed and said he "supposed that the editor of *The Bicycling World* came from the South."[36] The explanation, however, remained consistent that Dove was reinstated to amateur status because the White professional racers refused to race against him.

110   CHAPTER 6

It seems likely that Batchelder knew for sure that the editor of *The Bicycling World*, Ritchie G. Betts, was indeed from the South. Though he lived in New York at the time, Betts was something of a recent transplant. He was born in New Orleans in 1869 to a mother from Alabama and father from New York. By 1887, while working for the Southern Division of the Illinois Central Railroad, Betts had proven himself a devotee of the bicycle, helping establish a cycling club in New Orleans at age 18 and entering his role as a leader in all things cycling in New Orleans. He put his eighth-grade education to use and began working as the southern correspondent to *The Wheel* based out of New York. By 1891, he had moved to New York to become assistant editor of the magazine.[37] There he would move on from editing *The Wheel* to serving as editor of *The Bicycling World and Motorcycle Review*. Given his hardline stance on amateurism, it is little surprise that he would ultimately go on to serve as a governor of the AAU.[38]

While it is clear that Betts's opinions on race influenced his editorial decisions, it should be pointed out that his thoughts went further than mere words. As a formerly competitive rider, he had a considerable amount of experience with racing and service on cycling club committees. In fact, he served in a position of leadership on the Racing Board of the Metropolitan Association of Cycling Clubs. This very same board made headlines in 1894 when it voted to ban Black cyclists from competing in the annual Irvington-Millburn Road Race. In years prior, they had been free to enter but in 1894, perhaps emboldened by the League of American Wheelman's decision to draw the color line just three months prior, the racing committee followed suit. One explanation for the move held that it was due largely to one Black cyclist in particular, David Simmons. It was not that he had done anything wrong, per se. He had in fact raced in the Irvington-Millburn in 1893. Some believed, however, that it was due to the fact that he performed so admirably at that race that the committee decided to ban him and all other Black cyclists. One paper posited that the move was orchestrated primarily by Fred Hawley. Hawley was secretary of the race committee in 1894. Simmons had apparently finished second to Hawley in the "citizens" category of the race in 1893 and the theory was that Hawley was afraid Simmons would beat him in 1894. It went even further in its comments against Hawley saying that Simmons was 70 percent White and Hawley himself was merely "two shades better off." The cycling magazine *The Bearings* claimed that the daily newspapers were mistaken, however, and that Hawley actually voted to allow Simmons to ride.[39] It did not name a ringleader of the action against Black cyclists. Regardless of whether one person orchestrated the move, or it was several members of the committee is hard to say, but the committee's decision did not seem to deter Simmons.

Even though his entry was refused, Simmons vowed to take the start and threatened legal action against the Metropolitan Association of Cycling Clubs (MACC) if anyone stopped him from racing. The MACC was the sponsor of the event and it was their racing committee that had made the decision to bar Black cyclists. Simmons's threat was apparently effective because the MACC soon overruled the decision of the racing committee. *The Bearings* reported on the dispute saying that the decision to over-rule was "favorably commented upon generally." While the magazine did not seem hesitant to air the dirty laundry of Betts, Hawley, and the MACC racing committee, its reporting on the race did not seem any more open-minded than much of what could be read in *The Bicycling World* once Betts became the editor a few years later. *The Bearings* continued that even though it was a decision that was viewed favorably, "only one colored rider started. His name is J.C. Diggs of Newark and fully twenty of his clubmates were on hand to see him through. David Simmons, Alex Schwalbach's colored representative, did not start. Diggs resembled a Zulu more than anything else at the finish of the race so much dust had he collected on his face during the contest."[40] It is curious that Simmons did not take the start since he seemed so adamant about participating in the event. No further comment was made about his failure to start. The racing committee (Betts included) was so upset, by the club's vote to over-rule their decision that the entire committee resigned. Some were mad enough that they wanted to resign before the race was even over, but others thought it best to perform their duties in organizing the Irvington-Millburn first and then resign immediately after the race was over.[41] Because Betts agreed with the racing committee in their decision to bar Black cyclists and then to resign after that decision was overruled it seems that, in 1894 at least, he was far from an ally.

After commenting on Betts' southern roots, Batchelder explained that they reason why White professionals raced against Dove in the six-day race but then refused to race against him later was because they thought it best not to "raise any eleventh hours disturbance." They consented to race against him but, "the circuit sprinters stated that he would be barred from outdoor short racing."[42] It was a curious case. On one hand, it seems to validate "Major" Taylor's preference for shorter races due, in part, to the fact that it was much easier for riders to work in a combination to shut him out from winning in longer races. The White riders may have been confident that they could form a combination against the Black cyclists at the six-day races if it proved necessary. Of course, Dove and his teammate finished well off the winning pace. It begs the question, were the professionals at ease with Dove's entry because they did not see him as a threat in the six-day discipline or, was there an agreement worked out so that he and Hedspeth could race for six days, making their $50 a day, as long as they did not try to win? The fact that the promoter allowed their entry was undoubtedly driven by the potential added revenue. It is likely that the promoter, Patrick T. Powers, who is well known for his efforts on behalf of minor league baseball, would have been happy to include Black cyclists in the program due to a belief that it would generate more gate receipts. "Major" Taylor would certainly encounter promoters who embraced this rationale as they implored him to participate in their events.[43]

For a program that also included "foreign" racers, the diversity of the field in the international six-day races actually played well for many of the attendees, especially those who were susceptible to getting caught up in the story lines with strong nationalistic undertones. Publicity for the races and programs distributed to the spectators upon admission would have apprised the reader of who was on each team, where they were from, and any other details that might make that particular racer a fan favorite, or even a heel. To that same end, a new rule was introduced for the 1903 edition of the International Six-Day Race at Madison Square Garden in which each respective team would be expected to wear their team colors throughout the race. Coincidentally, that same year, the cyclists coming from Europe had shaved off their mustaches, which had apparently set them apart from the American riders in prior years. It began as a bit of a lark when one rider dared another (Gougoltz) to shave half his mustache while they were passing time aboard the steamer on their way to New York. The dare was accepted under the condition that all the other cyclists present do the same. It is unclear how long they donned the asymmetrical upper lip adornment, but they all had the steamer's barber remove what was left before disembarking the ship.[44] Fortunately for the large crowds at the 1905 six-day race, there were the team colors, which the cyclists were somewhat compliant in wearing, to keep who was who straight. It was enough for one

Six Days in a Row 113

unruly spectator to throw a drinking glass from the second balcony onto the track striking Gougoltz's front wheel at 6:30 in the morning. The glass shattered and resulted in punctures for four other riders.[45] That the Black cyclists in the 1905 edition, Dove and Ulysses Scott, were made marks, along with the foreign riders like Gougoltz can only be assumed based on comments made about the prospect of the Hedspeth-Dove team in 1903 and the fact that they were cast as foreign riders. Whether the spectators loved or hated the sight of a Black cyclist in the velodrome at Madison Square Garden, it added up to more profit.

Ulysses Grant Scott, another Black cyclist from the era, was apparently not at the stage in his career where he could turn down the opportunity for a cash payout. He was around four years older than Taylor, being 31 in 1905 (the year he would race a six-day with Dove at the Garden) but wins carried more seniority than age in the world of cycling and in that category, Taylor was far ahead. Dove, on the other hand, was around the same age as Taylor, 26 in 1905, yet he too did not find the same success as Taylor. It undoubtedly perturbed *The Bicycling World* to no end that once again, in December 1905, Dove would race the six days at Madison Square Garden against professionals. This time it was with Ulysses Scott. Apparently, the White professional cyclists had agreed once again to race against Black cyclists who were not "Major" Taylor, and the organizers of the Madison Square Garden event also allowed it. True to the exploitation of nationalistic sentiments of the era, Dove and Scott would be profiled as both the "African team from Manhattan" in the pages of *The Bicycling World* and the "Afro-American Team" by the *New York Times*.[46] They raced against other teams, mostly categorized by place but some by religion such as the "Mormon Team." Other teams were given names like the Little Old New York Team, Yankee-Western Team, Irish Team, Mexican Team, and German American Team among many other variations. *The Bicycling World* pointed out that Dove and Ulysses Grant Scott "who bears the euphonious name" were there, "to give color to the contest" but the White riders were reported to believe "the clouds will soon pass" in reference to the two Black riders.[47] The White riders proved to be quite the prognosticators on that point. Dove and Scott were eliminated from the race by the second day. Dove suffered the misfortune of being caught up in a crash, along with several other cyclists, during the first fifteen minutes of the race. Soon after relieving him, Ulysses Scott, five years Dove's senior and nineteen pounds heavier, managed to lose a

114 CHAPTER 6

lap on the other riders. Dove was visibly upset at the prospect of being a lap down so early and it was not long before Scott lost another lap. By the time they resigned on Monday night, they were so far behind that the scorers had stopped keeping track of their laps.[48] Since they withdrew so early, it is unlikely that Dove and Scott earned the same amount that Dove and Hedspeth earned in 1903. The fact that they gained little from the appearance led *The Bicycling World* to remain relatively subdued about Dove and Scott's participation.

The Bicycling World did, of course, still make fun of Scott. Specifically, it derided his name in their coverage of the six-day race, quipping, "Ulysses Grant Scott—his name gives an inkling as to color."[49] Given his treatment by the magazine, it was something of a surprise that it did not take the early withdraw of Dove and Scott as an opportunity to say something insulting about their supposed character or lack of stamina. There was, in fact, a common racist stereotype during the era that while Black athletes were sometimes very fast, they were unable to succeed in contests that were of long duration. Black boxers, for instance, were often thought to have that weakness and White boxers were therefore led to believe that they would win if they simply forced Black boxers to "go the distance."[50] White sport writers also seemed to have few qualms offering prejudiced opinions about the character of Black athletes in general. Writers covering cycling certainly jumped at the opportunity to drag Dove through the mud one year earlier, after he was involved in a physical altercation at the Vailsburg track. During a ten-mile amateur race, Dove took off in a sprint for the intermediate prize but as he came around the pack, a rider named Rupprecht swerved, knocking his rear wheel into Dove's front wheel. Dove was thrown to the track and barely missed having his head caved in by the wheels of the twenty other racers on the track. He was so upset that he waited at the edge of the track to attempt to grab Rupprecht on the next lap but Dove was intercepted by Robert Hunter, who grabbed Dove by the throat. They fell off the track into the grass. At that point, Hunter allegedly kicked Dove a few times, which is how Dove explained the bleeding cuts on his head after the altercation. It ended up taking two policemen to subdue Dove but even after they got him back to the changing area, he refused to forget the matter. Picking up a 2-foot-long iron bar with heavy nuts on the end, he stormed out, intent on "getting even." The officers were able to wrestle the bar away from him, but he broke free from them and ran back out on the track to find Hunter.

As he and Hunter were squaring up for another round the police grabbed Dove once again, much rougher this time, escorted him back to the changing area, and then arrested him, taking him to the "Vailsburg lockup."[51]

The Bicycling World added its own flourishes to the story this time with a joke on Dove's name and multiple allusions to the color of his skin. In bold it said, "Black Dove Runs Amuck" explaining in the first paragraph that the meet could have been called 'The Fluttering of a Soiled Dove' in reference to the controversy over his amateur status. "Fortunately," it continued, "or unfortunately, however, the particular Dove concerned is of a crow color, and, although 'whitewashed' by the N.C.A. after having grossly soiled the amateur rules the kalsomine was not thick enough to offend the real thing in doves or to conceal the inkiness of his hide. He is Dove only in name, and of markedly African persuasion. . . . He acted like an untamed Hottentot, and did not subside until he reached the police station."[52] In the early 1900s, the term hottentot was mostly used for the Khoikhoi or people of Khoisan descent, but it was also used disparagingly for all people who were perceived to have African ancestry. The most well-known example of the word's usage was with "Hottentot Venus"—a Black woman of Khoisan descent who was put on display for European audiences in the early nineteenth century as a sort of exotic spectacle due to the size and shape of her buttocks.[53] The fact that J.C. Diggs (mentioned earlier) was compared to the Zulu and Dove was called a "hottentot" almost seems more than coincidental since both the Zulu and Khoikhoi were from southern Africa and they were both clearly associated with the continent of Africa in general. The article calling Dove a hottentot described him as someone who was innately different from the average "American" by alluding to a supposed connection to Africa and focusing on the color of his skin when it specified that he was a "black" Dove. It also summed the incident up as a moment in which people witnessed "Dove's reversion to savagery."[54] Both Rupprecht and Dove were suspended by the NCA for the incident, Rupprecht for thirty days, Dove indefinitely. Dove was also fined and lectured by Recorder Jaeger of Vailsburg. The fact that Dove pleaded guilty was attributed to the "lenient" fine of five dollars according to *The Bicycling World*, but he was warned that if he came up on similar charges in the future he would be sent to jail. In a remark that was full of supremacist undertones, Jaeger said to Dove, "The sport in itself is clean, but a disorderly person can and does make it unclean, so that the public becomes disgusted, and will justify me in being severe in such cases.

116   CHAPTER 6

Kindly remember that, and tell your friends."[55] It is unclear what he meant by "friends" whether that be other cyclists in general or a specific group of cyclists with whom Dove was assumed to associate.

Melvin Dove was, of course, not the first nor the last to find it necessary to defend himself while racing a bicycle. Other cyclists found themselves embroiled in physical altercations because of crashes and other antics around, and on, the track as well. The coverage of such instances of fisticuffs by *The Bicycling World* seemed, however, much more neutral in tone when the principal actors were White men. A few months earlier, in a very similar example to Dove, a racer named William S. Blizzard was involved in a crash at the Vailsburg track along with two other White cyclists, J. Frank Galvin and W. S. Fenn. Readers were informed, "While Galvin was sitting on the edge of the track waiting for someone to loosen the straps which held his feet to his pedals, Blizzard ran to him and struck him in the face twice. When Galvin stood on his feet Blizzard was waiting for him and attacked him again. The spectators formed a ring around the pair, and Galvin was giving Blizzard a good trouncing when the police interfered. Blizzard was arrested but allowed to go the next day by the Vailsburg authorities. The pair were suspended for the rest of the day by referee Batchelder."[56] There was no comment about the character of either man, nor were there any suppositions or allusions as to what compelled these two men to settle their disagreement with their fists. Neither were described as "reverting to savagery." Neither were derided. There was no mocking of their names, even though Blizzard would have seemed an easy target. The cut-and-dried coverage of this particular "row" was contrasted by coverage in the *New York Times*. With the headline, "Police Arrest Cyclists," it was described as an event marred by "disgraceful scenes." These "belligerent incidents" between Blizzard and Galvin, the paper said, were just a few of the "fistic encounters" of the day. Another racer, Floyd McFarland was "struck . . . severely" by Hadfield and a spectator then jumped in on McFarland's behalf. The spectator was arrested and fined $10.05.[57] *The Bicycling World* reported on the McFarland incident but used the same matter-of-fact tone to relay that story as well. For *The Bicycling World*, these were simply instances of heated rivalries between red-blooded men, which were to be expected from time to time.[58] There was a separate column about McFarland and Hadfield's decision to settle the matter once and for all at Manhattan Beach. There they stripped down and had a bare-knuckle fight that was "fair and square."

It was characterized much like a boxing match where two men tested their strength and power, not an animalistic or savage affair. McFarland was described as having "danced nimbly around Hadfield. He feinted several times for the head, and finally landed a terrific smash on Hadfield's left eye."[59] Those events at Vailsburg in July involved no less than five men yet none were lambasted like Melvin Dove would be for the fight he had a few months later at the same track. Melvin Dove was actually there at Vailsburg racing on the day in July with Blizzard, McFarland, and others, but he avoided the various physical altercations and, since he did not have a good finish, there were no comments about his color or race. One explanation for the difference in tone between *The Bicycling World* and the *New York Times* could be that *The Bicycling World* simply did not want to scare off potential spectators, trying to maintain an air of dignity, at least that was the case when it was a story about White cyclists. On the other hand, the *New York Times* writer may have been of the opinion that cyclists were a nuisance, as was common during the era.[60] Given the *New York Times'* decision not to report on Dove's altercation in October yet *The Bicycling World* used it as an opportunity to excoriate Dove—giving particular focus to his color and race—suggests that NCA President Batchelder may have been correct in his insinuation about the editorial decisions of *The Bicycling World*. There was a pronounced bias against Black cyclists like Dove.

The fact that Melvin Dove fought the rider who caused him to crash might at first seem like a temperamental reaction to what could have merely been an accident, but it was much more than that. Along with "pocketing" Black cyclists, like Taylor often complained of, another tactic would be to intentionally crash cyclists who were made marks, Black cyclists in particular. Regardless of this tactic, Black cyclists like Dove were so adamant in fighting against racism, claiming their rights, and proving their equality that they would risk life and limb in pursuit of their goals. The mere act of competing against White men was one way of confronting racist myths but when Black cyclists like Dove resorted to physical altercations, they were not only making a statement by being so bold as to defend themselves, but they were also literally fighting back against racism. Dove's verbal or written response to the racism he faced does not survive; the same seems to be true for all the Black cyclists from that era, aside from Taylor, but in these instances, their actions speak volumes. They show just how frustrating and tiresome it could be. They show how the constant overt and subtle racist acts endured day-in and day-out weighed on them. There were some, like David Simmons, who fought racism through the courts. When Simmons threatened to sue for being denied entry into the Irvington-Milburn race, he simultaneously signaled his willingness to fight back against racism and his cultural savvy by pursuing upper-class tactics as a way to seek justice. This was more than ten years before the formation of the NAACP, which was created in 1909 specifically to fight racism through the use of the American judicial system. Black cyclists like Dove, Simmons, Hedspeth, Scott, and others made it clear that they had not bought into the idea that they were inferior to White men and they were intentionally using the bicycle in a myriad of ways to prove this. They did not ride bikes simply because they were good at it, or because they found it entertaining. They rode bicycles to proclaim their own ideal of manhood.

The six-day grind, like bare-knuckle fighting, or the battle royal, would have seemed at least one version of cycling that would always have room for anyone brave enough, or desperate enough, even Black cyclists. It is important to consider ideals of masculinity inherent in such an event too. As *Medical News* reported at the time, this was an opportunity for spectators to see men taxed so strenuously that they were transformed into irascible children. From that perspective, the six-day race could be seen as an experiment in subduing men through labor. The men who prevailed then, were those who could not be broken or reduced to children. Even though this would have been an opportune moment to try to prove the racist stereotype of Black men being childlike, Black cyclists' access to six-day races was measured. What was more appealing for promoters was not the spectacle of subduing a man so much as the diversity of the participants that could be used to draw spectators. Much like the Olympics, the International Six-Day Bicycle Race was a competition that was ripe for spectators with any sort of nationalistic, racist, or jingoist sentiments. While these things, and the possibility of being made a mark or serious injury may have scared some men away, the opportunity for exposure and financial reward was too much for others to ignore. These were also some of the best attended bicycle competitions in the United States. If you wanted to make a name for yourself in the world of cycling, the six-day grind was certainly one avenue to explore. Even though there had been increasingly overt attempts to segregate cycling by 1903, Black cyclists made use of the few opportunities that remained.

Six Days in a Row

When the League of American Wheelmen voted to draw the color line in 1894, some Black cyclists may have remained unfazed. For them, it might not have been all that surprising. At the same time, it would not have exactly been the end of the world. After all, they would still be able to compete in races and Black cyclists could create their own clubs if they wanted—as they did. The thought that it merely meant Black cyclists could not be a part of the LAW, however, perhaps missed how that vote would seemingly encourage other organizations and associations to draw the color line as well. The NCA certainly followed suit, as did several velodromes and governing bodies that organized road races, such as the MACC's momentary ban. Black cyclists like Dove, Hedspeth, and Scott found themselves with few options, especially when it came to entering the most prestigious races since all, except Taylor, were disallowed from racing as professionals. This was true even when it came to the six-day races—arguably the most dehumanizing and damaging form of bicycle racing that existed at the time. Although, the transition to a team event by 1899 gave the six-day a little more air or respectability, making it seem less like a simple death march. The rules in place at the time stipulated that Black cyclists were allowed to race, even against White cyclists, as long as they did so as amateurs. The double-edged effect of those rules kept most Black cyclists from being able to devote themselves to racing full-time since they could not earn as much money and would have to continue to work to support themselves. The other effect was that it kept all but "Major" Taylor from challenging the fastest White cyclists in the United States. Unwilling to accept the unfair restrictions placed against them in their own country, many Black cyclists found their way around the barriers. In a show of defiance and bravery, they left the United States and raced for even larger prize purses in Europe and Australia.

7

Going Abroad

On August 13, 1903, Marshall "Major" Taylor and Woody Hedspeth made their way from the rider's quarters behind the finish line, through the tunnel, and onto the infield of the Buffalo Velodrome in Paris, France. Of the many races that would take place that day, on that circular wooden track with steeply banked turns, the Americans, Taylor and Hedspeth, were to headline in a team race against two French riders, Jue and Bourotte. Their respective nationalities, however, seemed to pale in comparison to the color of their skin. French newspapers wrote about the event as a competition of "blacks against whites," since Taylor and Hedspeth were Black while Jue and Bourotte were White. The setting seemed straight out of a novel. There was no more fitting venue for the Americans to headline abroad than the Buffalo Velodrome of Paris. It took its name from a captivating demonstration by the American Buffalo Bill Cody, during the Indo-American Exhibition of 1889. First constructed in 1892, a major renovation in 1902 refashioned the velodrome in an American style, with wooden planks instead of cement blocks, running lengthwise around the 300-meter track.[1] The renovation not only made the track faster, but it also made room for more spectators.

Among the crowd of around 8,000 spectators surrounding the entirety of the oval, both Taylor and Hedspeth were well known. French cycling fans certainly knew of Taylor. He won the world championship for the one mile-sprint in 1899. He had also raced extensively in Europe and set

Going Abroad

an important precedent for other Black cyclists. This was reiterated by the fact that the French commonly referred to Hedspeth, who came shortly after Taylor, as "the second black" or "black number two." The race between Taylor, Hedspeth, Jue, and Bourotte consisted of four heats: a 1,000-meter race in which Taylor finished first and Hedspeth fourth; a tandem team race, which Taylor and Hedspeth won; a pursuit race "won by the whites," and a final heat pitting Taylor against Jue in a 300-meter sprint.[2] Taylor won the final sprint and the Black team took the overall victory. There were several of these races throughout France. For promoters, it was a chance to generate more ticket sales through an athletic contest that masqueraded as a battle for racial dominance. For Hedspeth and Taylor, it was an opportunity to demonstrate their abilities and show their racial pride, especially when they won. Of course, it was also a chance to earn a significant amount of money. This race should have proved they were just as good as White cyclists. A few Whites may have thought so, but most would have been more likely to qualify the event as merely proving *some* Black cyclists were as good as *some* White cyclists at racing bicycles in one particular instance and nothing more. Taylor's autobiography makes it clear that he saw himself as equal.[3] He even hoped the story of his achievements would help encourage the young Black Americans. Hedspeth's actions seem to suggest the same, but his motivations are not as explicit as Taylor's since he was rarely, if ever, asked and he left behind no personal effects. Consequently, much about Hedspeth is unclear.

Aside from the locations and results of many of his races, Woody Hedspeth's background is difficult to ascertain. Written as Woodie Headspeth, Hedspath, Hedgepath, and Hepspeth across numerous sources, he was likely born in central Kentucky, near Marion County. "Levenon" Kentucky is listed as his birthplace on a 1921 passport application, which was a likely misspelling of Lebanon, Kentucky. His parents are listed as Frank Hedspeth and Mattie Johnson. The 1870 census shows a Black farmer named Frank Hedspeth of the appropriate age living near Lebanon, Kentucky, in neighboring Taylor County. In the 1880 census there is a Frank and Martha Hedgepeth in Green County, which borders Taylor County. They were married and living with an infant daughter named Lilly at the time. Eighteen years later there would be a marriage certificate for one Lilly Headspeth in Marion, Indiana, which is where Woody claimed to reside. Her parents were listed as Frank Headspeth and Martha Yonsey. Mattie is often a nickname for Martha. Similarly, the last name of Yonsey could have easily been a misunderstanding of Johnson. These are just a few of the difficulties of tracking the life of working-class Americans at the turn of the century. Even Woody Hedspeth's birthday is questionable. The dates of June 15, 1881, June 15, 1884, and July 14, 1884 all appear in different sources. In spite of whether he was actually born in Kentucky or not, Hedspeth considered himself to be from Indianapolis, which was in another county named Marion—just like the Kentucky county where his life may have begun. It is likely that he moved to Indianapolis at a relatively young age. His status as resident of Indianapolis was often how he was identified in the media once he became a renowned cyclist. In fact, he was the first cyclist the *Indianapolis Recorder* mentioned as an example of how "Indiana ha[d] produced some of the fastest riders in the country."[4] It was a bit surprising that his name came first since "Major" Taylor was also from Indianapolis.

Hedspeth saw success early in his career at "colored fairs" in Kentucky and even at some well-known tracks in larger races such as those at Ravenswood in Chicago and the Newby Oval in Indianapolis. He began to experience considerable notoriety as early as 1899—the same year Taylor would be crowned world champion. The Newby Oval, being something like his home track, would have undoubtedly served him well in the training to one day, as unfathomable as it may have been at the time, race at the Buffalo Velodrome in Paris, France. Similar to the Buffalo Velodrome, the Newby was a quarter mile oval constructed of white pine boards with banked turns. The boards were actually laid with the rougher grain facing up but then a wire brush was used to remove the splinters and the board would be dipped in a sealant before they were secured to the track with nails. The seating capacity was also the same as the Buffalo Velodrome, holding around 8,000 people.[5] These were advanced facilities. The Newby Oval boasted of its ability to host races at night that were "as light as day" due to the sixty arc lights installed around the track and grounds.[6]

Hedspeth's star rose quickly. He apparently made quite an impression with spectators in 1899 when he demonstrated his ability to finish a mile in 1:49 3/5 at a time when "Major" Taylor's record stood at 1:22 1/5. He was soon bestowed the title of the "fastest colored rider in the country, barring the Major" and officials at the Ravenswood track offered to pay his expenses and track rights for the 1900 season.[7] Of course, Hedspeth's prowess was mostly described in segregated terms. He could be considered the fastest colored rider, but not the fastest rider. The Marion County championship race, held at the Newby Oval, was open only to White cyclists in 1899. As the *Indianapolis Journal* put it, "the colored riders of the city had an opportunity to show what their muscles were made of" but that was in events "open to colored riders exclusively."[8] They were free to beat each other but not White cyclists. While the Black cyclists tore around the track, on the Fourth of July in 1899, a day that undoubtedly held special meaning, the majority White crowd cheered them on yelling, "go on ink!" and "ride like the police were after you."[9] Hedspeth took first in the final heat of the day and as the evening came to a close, the bright lights of the track and the cheers of the crowd were replaced by the thunderous explosions of gunpowder obliterating blackness. For the White fans, it was an occasion to celebrate independence. For the Black cyclists, it was a time to reflect on what had yet to be achieved.

Hedspeth, when part of a team, was most often paired with other Black cyclists such as Melvin Dove and another man simply referred to as Germain, but that was not always the case.[10] At the Six-Day International Championship of 1902 in Madison Square Garden, Hedspeth, who was reportedly well known as the "Black Demon" teamed up with Alexander Peterson, who was known as the "Terrible Swede." At first, Hedspeth's eligibility was in question, because he was Black, but after examining his palmarès, management at the track and other riders accepted his entry. Hedspeth's record proved that he was more than qualified, but as a Black athlete, being qualified was relative. At the time, he held the one-hour unpaced record, taking it from the former world champion, Charlie Miller.[11] Hedspeth accomplished the feat in July 1902 when he covered twenty-six miles and nineteen yards in the hour at a track in Dayton, Ohio.[12] His record was "allowed" by the National Cycling Association (NCA) but like other Black cyclists, his past accomplishments did not guarantee that he would be allowed entry into a race, or even be granted a license. Burdened by recurring debates about their eligibility, much like Hedspeth would face in 1902, and drawn by the opportunities to race for significant prize purses abroad, it was little surprise that other Black cyclists would decide to follow "Major" Taylor's example by crossing the pond to race in Europe.

The draw of racing opportunities in Europe was enough to attract White cyclists from the United States as well. One report in *The Bicycling World and Motorcycle Review* at the end of 1903 seemed nervous about what it

124   CHAPTER 7

described as a likely exodus of American cyclists. It explained, "The success of a few riders in making money in Europe during the summer has excited the cupidity of so many American racing men that there is danger of there not being enough good men here next summer to make a respectable showing at the St. Louis Exposition." Names like Walthour, Bardgett, Root, McFarland, Lawson, Taylor, Hedspeth, and Dove all were included. The only rider of note not going, the White champion cyclist Frank Kramer, was described as the only one without the "European bee in his bonnet" and one who "continue[d] to refuse good offers to go to France."[13] Some of these men had already raced in Europe in 1903 and planned to return in 1904. Of course, the chance to make more money would be attractive to professional riders, but the article ignores the fact that three of the riders mentioned, Dove, Hedspeth, and Taylor, were Black cyclists who were not only pulled toward Europe but also pushed to race outside the United States because of challenges they faced entering races at home. While Taylor was permitted to race as a professional in the United States, even he was uncomfortable in many of the venues outside of the Boston area.

All three of these riders would go on to win considerable accolades abroad. While Taylor won higher honors in his racing career outside the United States, Woody Hedspeth's international career was actually more prolific, spanning more than twenty years. Hedspeth began racing in France by 1903; shortly after recovering from the injury he suffered during a crash at a six-day race in Madison Square Garden.[14] The French magazine, *La Vie Au Grand Air* dedicated a section to "les Americains sur nos velodromes" in which Taylor and Hedspeth featured prominently. The cover showed Taylor mounted on his bicycle just at the edge of the infield, while Hedspeth stood next to him, holding him steady in preparation for the start of the race. The magazine was quick to point out that Hedspeth had come to Europe to compete because, unlike the United States, France made no distinctions based on race. It was noted that Hedspeth could not obtain a racing license from the American governing body, the NCA.[15] Hedspeth would eventually not only race in France, but also in Belgium, Switzerland, Germany, and Russia.

Soon after Hedspeth arrived in Europe, while not winning races outright, he began achieving some promising results. By June of 1903 he had some close finishes, including second place in a trial heat on a Parisian track.[16] He returned to the United States to race in the late fall of 1903, but was back to Europe by May of the 1904 season. Among representatives from ten other

"Les Americains sur nos Velodromes," Woody Hedspeth supporting Marshall "Major" Taylor on the track in a French velodrome. *La Vie Au Grand Air*, June 5, 1903, 363.

countries, Hedspeth would finish second in a heat of the one lap scratch race held in London in 1904.[17] By this time, he was determined to stay in Europe for an extended period. Applying for a passport on September 14, 1905, at the United States Embassy in Paris, Hedspeth stated that he had been temporarily living in Paris since last leaving the United States in May of 1904. At that time, he stated that he would return to the United States within two years and that his purpose in applying for the passport was to be able to race in Russia. This application was made around two months after the International Cyclists' Union decided at its annual meeting in Antwerp, of which Hedspeth was in attendance, to address the question of the color line existing in the United States. M. Rousseau of France introduced a resolution "to place white and negro riders on an equality in the United States." The American journalist conveying the story was confused by the wording of the resolution adding, "whatever that means." In the subsequent debate, it was decided that the ICU would address a letter to the National Cycling Association of the United States on the matter. Apparently thinking Hedspeth was the main reason why such a discussion even arose, the same journalist made sure to point out, "'Woody' Hedspeth, the American 'chocolate drop,' was among those present at Antwerp.[18] Black cyclists were making the racial disparities in the United States an issue of international proportions. Similarly, Black boxers would also "pursue French sympathy" and "become a popular medium through which French sportswriters critiqued U.S. racism and Anglo-Saxon imperialism more broadly."[19] Well before the arrival of the Black boxer Jack Johnson, Hedspeth and other Black cyclists had made a convincing case before French crowds that they were equal to White cyclists, and they deserved equal opportunities. White America, however, refused to acknowledge the same.

Hedspeth's decision to race abroad did lead to more attention from the American cycling press, but it in no way made him their darling. As with many riders who went abroad, the expectation was that they win. Otherwise, why bother? It was not until May 1906 that *The Bicycling World* would report, in less than exuberant fashion, that Hedspeth had indeed won. The short article, under the headline "Hedspeth wins a race at last" made a quick note that, "'Woody' Hedpseth, the negro with not too white a reputation, has at last won a race on the other side, where he has taken up his abode." This happened at the Steiglitz track in Berlin a month prior to the article's publication and there was no explanation for the comment about his reputation. The writer seemed to cast doubts on his status adding that he was serving as a "masseur" for a German rider named Bader and downplayed his win by describing it as "by an 'eyelash',"[20] This was in stark contrast to coverage of the results of the White American rider, Bobby Walthour, who was also racing abroad. In describing his lack of success in the 1906 season in Europe, *The Bicycling World* at least attributed previous victories to him, introducing him as "Robert J. Walthour, of Atlanta, Ga., the world's champion pace follower" and it explained that he was more successful in Europe the previous year.[21] Hedspeth, on the other hand, who held at least one record of his own, could find himself subjected to scorn even when he won.

Hedspeth's origins were also written about in terms that were much less concrete than White riders. This made it seem as if he were a nomadic racer with no real home or citizenship and therefore no loyalty to a specific place.

Going Abroad 127

Occasionally, Hedspeth was "of Indianapolis" or "American" but affixed to those identifications was nearly always "negro" or "colored" rider. In contrast, when announcing Walthour's plans for the season, Walthour was "the only American to contest the world's championships" in Switzerland while "Hedspeth, the negro" was there as well, riding in the sprint races, but he allegedly only served as "figurehead."[22] Hedspeth would be described as an "American negro" but even then, attaching his race or even a description could serve to segregate his accomplishments from "true" Americans. Reporting on his success in Brandenburg, Germany on May 7, 1906, one article began, "Woody Hedpseth's ebony hued skin glistened with perspiration and delight. . . ." Even though he was described as an "American negro" he was also described later in the article as "the Europeanized descendant of Ham."[23] The explanation that Black people were descendants of Ham allowed Whites to justify their racism and the mistreatment of Black people based on biblical grounds since it was Ham and his descendants that were cursed because Ham awoke his father, Noah, while he was sleeping and saw him naked. "Descendant of Ham" was a term used less often than "colored," or "negro," et cetera, and while it was certainly intended mainly to make the reader aware of the subject's race, it also gave a sort of fatalistic answer to the question of race. Peter Jackson, the Black boxer, and many others were written about in similar terms. Jackson was actually referred to as "a despised descendant of Ham."[24] Thus Jackson, and Hedspeth alike, were stripped of their agency and reduced to innate sinners with no self-control and a degeneracy on a level that set them apart from White men.

The fact that Hedspeth had not only gone to Europe to race, but that he was staying there on a semi-permanent basis earned him the ire of American cycling fans who treated him as something of a traitor, even though it was clear he could never "truly" be American because his citizenship always came with parameters or certain racial qualifiers. Hedspeth was also easily susceptible to a loss of his vestiges of Americanness, sometimes being described as the "Germanized" or the "Frenchified negro." Nearly five months after winning in Berlin, a story describing him as "the Germanized American negro" proclaimed that Hedspeth "actually won a race recently" in Munich. Even then, the same author felt it important to point out that he was Bader's trainer, which called attention to the fact that he was in the service of a White German.[25] Conversely, the White cyclist Oscar Schwab who, similar to Hedspeth, lived and raced abroad was described as "the

128   CHAPTER 7

former American." Hedspeth was the "Frenchified negro."[26] It was easier for Hedspeth to seemingly change nationalities because he never actually held firm American citizenship in the White mind. Schwab's American past endured while Hedspeth's was written over, corrupted, or erased. With the constant inclusion of qualifications, he was depicted as more of a hybrid. At first, he was not American because he was Black. Later, he was not American because he moved abroad. Indeed, Hedspeth was even included among a list of "foreign candidates" for six-day races to be organized in the United States by P. T. Powers. Among the French and German sounding names such as Trousselier, Dussot, Gorgoltz, Doerflinger, Parresiuex, Ingold, and Catteau, there was "Hedspeth, the negro."[27] Hedspeth also lost his citizenship in a more literal sense when, in 1913, he was forced to apply for an emergency passport at the American Embassy in Berlin. As Elizabeth Pryor argues, "for colored travelers . . . the passport was an object of desire because it denoted U.S. citizenship. Colored travelers battled passport rejections with much the same vigor as they fought segregation on public conveyances."[28] Those fights began in the nineteenth century but even by the 1910s, the passport was still desirable, and often necessary, because of its power of affirmation. Hedspeth had apparently left his passport at home and it was the sole piece of evidence to confirm that he was in fact an American citizen.

Hedspeth was not the only Black cyclist to travel to Europe, of course, Taylor did the same and there were at least five other Black cyclists to leave America for the chance to race in Paris. White cyclists like Bobby Walthour, Oscar Schwab, Floyd McFarland, Owen Kimble and many others also made the voyage. They were all looking for opportunities, but White cyclists were mostly drawn outside the United States, whereas Black cyclists were pushed and pulled abroad. The trend of Black cyclists going to Europe was not lost on *The Bicycling World*, an American periodical, which proclaimed, "Paris seems to be the 'nigger heaven' for black-skinned riders, there being five in the Parisian city at the present time."[29] This was by no means a sympathetic treatment of Black cyclists who essentially had few options to race professionally in the United States. Instead, they went abroad for those professional opportunities rather than remain amateurs and forfeit the chance to race for cash prizes. The article was not meant to invoke nationalistic pride about the exploits of the readers' countrymen against European cyclists either—something which many of the articles about White Americans racing abroad seemed intent on doing. Instead, it took on a critical tone.

In mentioning that another Black cyclist, William Ivy, was among the riders abroad it was intentionally disrespectful and pointed out that his most notable accomplishment was winning a 30-mile race around Thanksgiving and then boasting about the "easy feat" all winter while working and saving money at a Palm Beach hotel so that he might return to Europe to race. The list of Black cyclists in Paris included Hedspeth, "Major" Taylor, Germain, Vendredi, and A. C. Spain with an additional quip that "should Ike Lindsay decide to go across, Paris will have them all."[30] In failing to acknowledge all of their potential motives, that this was the best, perhaps only, option for these men if they needed to earn a living in the sport, the writer worked to reinforce racial stereotypes that undergirded decisions to restrict Black cyclists' ability to race in United States in the first place.

Without taking the time to explain why Black cyclists went to Paris, the article left room for readers to make their own assumptions why the men were there. Also, by focusing on Paris, ignoring the fact that some of these men were racing in numerous cities throughout France, Germany, and Belgium (even beyond), the author insinuated that it was the city itself that the men were attracted to, not to opportunity to race their bikes. Paris was not exactly the "city on a hill" or a beacon of the tenets of White Christian morality. Because of this, the reader was free to infer that these men were there to fulfill their supposed base, immoral desires in a city of vice such as Paris.[31] Popular French artwork of the era, such as Edouard Manet's *Olympia*, Henri de Toulouse-Lautrec's *La Toilette* and Henri Gervex's *Rolla* were just a few of the many popular works of art coming out of France that displayed prostitutes as provocative central characters in Parisian life. There were enough works of this variety that the Musee d'Orsay in Paris opened an exhibit in September 2015 dedicated to the subject—*Splendour and Misery: Pictures of Prostitution, 1850–1910.*[32] That is not to say that Americans were widely aware of these particular works of art, but their popularity coupled with the reputation of the Moulin Rouge would have undoubtedly filtered into American's ideas about Parisian culture. As Miranda Gill shows in her study of nineteenth century Paris, popular conceptions of the city imagined it as a place of "fantasy in which eccentric fashions, enigmatic appearances, and illicit eroticism were closely entwined."[33] It was not only the prostitutes that the city was known for, but also what one journalist and former policeman referred to as "semi-prostitution," which included courtesans, kept women, fallen women, demi-mondaines, actresses, and even married women who experienced financial gain through their illicit affairs.[34] Gill highlights the elements of class conflict as courtesans and demi-mondaines participated in the parade of conspicuous consumption that could be seen at sporting events attracting the public masses. These women would have been scorned by the wealthy elites because of their nouveaux riche status, much the same as professional athletes, such as the Black cyclists in Paris. No matter how much money they earned or what they bought with that money, they would never be accepted as equal among the upper classes.

There are further similarities between the prostitutes and "semi-prostitutes" of Paris (and beyond) as well as the Black men. Just as exotic women, or those of questionable repute, were often referred to as poule or biche (hen and doe), similarities between Black men and animals in the United States have also often been drawn with references to them as bucks.[35] Similarly, in his study of Black boxers, Louis Moore argues that sportswriters often compared Black fighters to horses, thereby allowing "whites to fetishize over the black body while denying black men humanity or equality."[36] There was a clear fascination, or obsession, with the bodies of the two respective groups, Black athletes and prostitutes. The corsets, crinolines, and necklines of the clothing adopted by prostitutes and semi-prostitutes would draw attention to their bodies just as the shorts, photographs of flexed muscles, and bare torsos also showcased the body of the Black athlete. These depictions did less to humanize the subjects than to turn them into commodities that could be consumed by the public. Just as the use of a prostitute's or courtesan's body could be temporarily purchased, the spectacle of the Black athlete's body could be temporarily accessed through buying a ticket at the gate, or buying a newspaper that printed images of those athletes, and money could be exchanged, made or lost, through gambling on expectations of the physical capabilities of that body.

Black cyclists who wanted to race as professionals may have had few options but there is some evidence that they actually preferred European racing. This could be explained by the simple fact that Black cyclists were permitted to race as professionals abroad, whereas Taylor was the only one to be granted a professional license from the United States governing body NCA. Both Hedspeth and Taylor made separate decisions to extend their stay in Europe. Hedspeth benefited from the fact that by the time he went abroad, Taylor was already there with contacts and a knowledge of the lay of the land. He could help Hedspeth settle in. Taylor first made the decision in 1901, when he was reportedly "so pleased with his successes in Europe that he Intend[ed] to remain there indefinitely."[37] He actually canceled engagements in America to do so. He was not simply staying because he had nothing to do, he stayed out of preference. He even passed up the opportunity to race in the American championship of 1901. Taylor chose to do so because he did not encounter the same level of racism in France that he did in America. The *Cleveland Gazette*, a Black owned newspaper, made note of this arguing, "In France there is not the same prejudice against Afro-Americans that Taylor found here (in America). In a private letter it is said that he was seen in a box at the opera with a party of which he was the only one with a dark skin."[38] It is little wonder then that Taylor would want to prolong his stay in Paris. Not only was he permitted to enter races against the best competition, but he was treated as an equal off the bicycle as well. Still, simply inviting Taylor out for a night among friends at the opera, his manager Victor Breyer, who offered the invitation, could have merely been flaunting the fact that he was responsible for bringing this exotic man to the city. He could have been commodified there too. Breyer was responsible for helping plan Taylor's European excursion. As the editor of *Le Velo*, he was also a prominent member of the French cycling scene.[39] Regardless of how sincere the feelings of equality may have been among the White Frenchmen who watched and raced against Taylor, it was surely a welcome change in his eyes, to be treated with more respect and comradery.

The idea of Europe as a place of relative racial harmony was well established among free Black Americans by the middle of the nineteenth century. Historian Elizabeth Pryor shows that many traveled to Great Britain and Europe at that time, where they experienced the "perceived egalitarianism" of Europe firsthand. There, she writes, "they wanted to . . . see if the promises were true that abroad African Americans could experience true freedom of mobility, a right that eluded them at home." They did. Pryor argues, "they found that freedom could be heard, seen, inhaled, and touched when they found themselves abroad."[40] This was certainly also true of the Black boxer George Godfrey, who traveled abroad to fight in 1887, as well as other prominent Black fighters of his era who did the same and it was true of Black cyclists a decade later.[41] As Pryor argues, "free people of color in the early nineteenth century established two important ideals of black protest . . . that access to transportation, the processes of travel, and indeed mobility itself were core features of American citizenship." Secondly, "they

132   CHAPTER 7

insisted that black people had a right to independent movement."[42] The decision of Black cyclists to travel then was indeed an act of Black protest.

In the United States, news circulated as early as March of 1901 that Taylor was a celebrated figure in Paris, owing to his cycling success and "gentlemanly deportment."[43] By April, the Black newspaper the *Topeka Plaindealer* was reporting on Taylor's treatment in Europe. It deliberately held a mirror up to the United States. In a direct comparison, it stated, "What will our friends(?) think now, a 'nigger' who could not ride on a thirty-cent track in his own free America nor eat in a 2x4 eating house, is now riding on the Park des Princes, Paris, France that costs something like $100,000, and eating at the beautiful Hotel Scribe—the beauty of it all, he is not passing for white, although black, he is not passing for black; but passes only as an American-some of our friends(?) would follow the example of this great American lad who will do much to uphold the greatness of his country."[44] Black American boxers had a similar experience and the historian Theresa Rundstedtler points out that traveling abroad led these athletes to "develop a critical eye for white American racism along with the creativity to protest it. Their well-publicized experiences outside the United States gave their black American fans a picture of life in the world beyond the confines of Jim Crow America."[45]

The French cycling magazine *Le Velo* reported on April 12 that Taylor had secured his first victory in Berlin on the previous day. *Le Velo* claimed Taylor was so fast that he was "another Zimmerman and probably a better one."[46] In contrast to how Woody Hedspeth and other Black cyclists were often compared to "Major" Taylor, French journalists and Black newspapers compared Taylor to the White American cyclist Arthur Zimmerman. He was from New Jersey and became a world champion cyclist by 1893. Like Taylor, Zimmerman also traveled to Europe for the purpose of racing, except Zimmerman did it in 1894. That was around six years before Taylor would go abroad. Three months after his first victories in Europe, the French were still "wondering whether Taylor w[ould] be another Zimmerman or fail like John S. Johnson." Similarly, they called Taylor the "black Zimmerman."[47] John Johnson, a White cyclist and the first to ever ride a mile in less than two minutes, seemed to have a promising career but found it hard to escape Zimmerman's shadow. "Major" Taylor, on the other hand, proved to be a great sensation in France as he was "followed everywhere by curious throngs that seem[ed] never to tire of their latest novelty" and as many as 50,000 people were expected in attendance when he took on his French rival for the world championship in their first match scheduled for May 15, 1901.[48] The fact that he was a Black cyclist from America would have undoubtedly turned heads and drew a crowd, at least at first. If he had not demonstrated he was a true contender, however, his popularity would have quickly diminished. His success against European cyclists solidified his status as more than just a passing novelty.

The coverage of Taylor's endeavors abroad for the Black readers of the *Cleveland Gazette* and *Topeka Plaindealer* is of notable contrast to the predominantly White audience of *The Bicycling World*. Black newspapers' tendency to write about Taylor as a source of racial uplift makes it unsurprising that their attention was also focused on Taylor's reception and reputation in Europe, not just his results. In a section reporting on Taylor's travels, the *Topeka Plaindealer* stated explicitly that it would "do all in its power to" celebrate the achievements of men and women who were making good for themselves and the race.[49] Conversely, cycling news outlets such as *The Bicycling World* seemed more partial to White riders like Robert J. Walthour by not just reporting his results but adding minor details such as, he "demonstrated to the enthusiastic satisfaction of his home folks at Atlanta, Ga., that all the nice things said about him by the New York daily newspapers . . . were well merited."[50] In proclaiming "no one can ride like 'our Bobby'," *The Bicycling World* argued it was no surprise that "a large and uproarious crowd greeted the idol in spite of the frigid weather." There was a noted contrast to reports on the very same page that "Major" Taylor was to go back to Europe to race. Regarding that development, *The Bicycling World* simply said, "'Major' Taylor, the former negro crack [will] get into the game again" as it was reported that "the negro is willing to leave his comfortable fireside at Worcester and go abroad to fill out the contract with Breyer and Coquelle that he broke two years ago and for which the National Cycling Association suspended him for one year. When Taylor jumped his contract because, it was popularly supposed, of fear of meeting Frank Kramer, he went into retirement in Worcester and has been almost forgotten."[51] From *The Bicycling World's* perspective, rather than an exciting development, this was a story about delinquency, one where Taylor would finally pay the debt he owed his White managers. That he was to race again was "a big surprise" but according to *The Bicycling World* not good news or something people might get excited about. Furthermore, the inclusion of unsubstantiated

134   CHAPTER 7

rumors served to condemn Taylor to retirement for refusing to meet a White cyclist (Kramer) who could presumably beat him on the track. Thus, Taylor retired merely because he was afraid of being beaten.

The real reason for Taylor's temporary retirement was a combination of factors. By 1903, he began to feel a loss of physiological stature. He was also experiencing more racism abroad from officials and riders, primarily his American compatriots who had also traveled to Europe and Australia. Taylor was hurt by the realization that to many of the promoters and other racers, he was simply a means for them to make more money. They did not genuinely care about him or whether he had the chance to race. This was coupled with the fact that he observed dwindling crowds both abroad and in the United States. At home, he believed cycling was on the decline. He was correct. Abroad, he felt he had lost his appeal. All of this weighed on him, and of course, the three to four races per week were taking their toll, not only physically but psychologically as well. He claimed he had "collapsed and narrowly averted a nervous breakdown" in July 1904. In spite of all that, the biggest factor in his decision to stay home was his newborn baby girl Sydney; named in honor of the Australian city where he had felt most welcome.[52] Taylor stayed home for the 1905 and 1906 seasons to be a family man, but he quickly grew restless.

On March 7, 1907, *L'Auto* announced that Taylor had made the decision to return to cycling with the headline, "Resurrection of the Negro."[53] By April, Taylor, along with his wife, daughter, and around 1,900 other passengers, boarded the French liner, the *Provence*. Coincidentally, just nine years later, on February 26, 1916, the *Provence* would be the subject of one of the "worst French disasters" of World War I as it was torpedoed by the German U-35. The fleet ship, by then an auxiliary cruiser in the service of the French navy, reportedly listed so quickly that many lifeboats could not be used and nearly 1,000 troops went down with the ship.[54] In 1907, however, the *Provence* regularly made its transatlantic trip from New York to Le Havre, a major port in Normandy, in around six days. That would be the Taylor family's experience in April 1907. "Major" Taylor likely chose a French liner for his family and himself because it would not have been as strictly segregated as most American liners. This was, after all, the height of Jim Crow segregation in the United States and integrated travel on public conveyances would not be federally enforced until fifty years later. One of the more disturbing examples of this being the treatment of gold star mothers in 1917. In spite of the fact that the federal government provided mothers and wives round trip accommodations aboard an ocean liner so they could visit the final resting place of their sons and husbands who perished in World War I, it was still done according to Jim Crow's rulebook. At the news the voyage was to be segregated, and with encouragement from the NAACP, many of the Black mothers decided against making the trip. The 279 Black women who did choose to make the voyage were allegedly placed on cargo vessels with headlines in newspapers proclaiming they were put aboard a cattle ship, while White mothers were provided much more elegant accommodations aboard luxury liners. In spite of the questionable accuracy of that particular detail, the cattle ship rumor became accepted as truth in part because it was so plausible.[55]

"Major" Taylor averted a similar fate when he sailed to Normandy. He had accepted the offers of European managers and agreed to race for at least two months in Europe, but he also entertained the idea of returning to race in the United States by late summer or early fall.[56] As Taylor made evident in previous years, the fact that he was married and now had a little girl weighed heavily on his thoughts of whether to race at home or travel abroad. Since getting married, he was accompanied by his wife on his travels and now his daughter would be doing the same. This was the primary cause for Taylor's disappearance from the cycling circuit around 1904. In an interview with his hometown paper, the *Worcester Telegram* he said, "I can't ask my wife to go around the country and abroad with me like I could before the little girl came, and I won't go away alone. If I could find something congenial to do, I think I'd stay home for awhile."[57] The apparent boredom of living off his savings while driving his car around town and the abandonment of his extremely disciplined training regimen—as evidenced by the weight he gained from 1904 to 1907—was too much for Taylor. This was the primary factor in his decision to return from what ostensibly appeared as full-blown retirement. The depression from languishing in Worcester and the general boredom it brought on was apparently enough to erase from memory all the negative aspects in the cycling world that burdened his career in 1904.

As their careers show, the simple fact that Black cyclists seemed to prefer to race in Europe, when they could, does not mean that their experiences abroad were entirely free of racial prejudice. Hedspeth's experience being labeled black number two was one thing, but there were also instances of prejudice that were meaner in spirit. Such was the case when Taylor, upon

136   CHAPTER 7

arriving in France in 1907 with his wife and daughter, was soon asked to
vacate his room by hotel management. Shortly after the incident, Taylor
reacted by saying that "in America it would not surprise me at all" but he
was a little more taken aback that just as he was asked to abandon his room
at Savannah, Georgia, hotel in 1898, he was now being asked to abandon
his room at a French hotel in 1907. His eviction in France, however, came
at the request of White American guests of the hotel.[58] Of course, Taylor
also faced racism from his White compatriots who had also gone abroad
to race. Upon returning to France in 1907, Taylor encountered his old rival
Floyd McFarland who had been involved in pacts with other White riders
against him. When asked if Taylor would be able to reclaim the speed he
was supposed to have lost through the retirement, McFarland answered,
"Oh sure, the damned nigger can get back to where he was before. . . . As
an American, he really disgusts me, but as a bicycle racer, I couldn't be
happier. Make no mistake about it, he's the best advertisement for bicycle
races. Everybody will profit from him being here."[59] This was not a shocking
statement, considering it came from McFarland, but it alluded to feelings
Taylor had years earlier; when he began to see himself as someone who was
being used as a meal ticket by so many others in the bicycle racing industry.
While Black cyclists did face racism abroad, the most blatant examples
often resulted from the actions of White Americans who had also made
the journey. Still, Black cyclists' overall experiences abroad seemed much
more positive than their experiences at home.

In spite of those positive experiences, Black cyclists, excluding Hedspeth,
ultimately came back to the United States. Taylor was popular enough that
he clearly could have continued to earn a living if he had stayed in Europe,
but even he chose to come home after a while. *The Bicycling World*'s claim
that Black cyclists preferred racing in Europe is then not entirely accurate.
The journal even contradicted itself on the point. In April 1908, it reported
that where Taylor would race that spring and summer was still in limbo.
Regarding Taylor's conundrum, it said, "At present the Worcester negro is
figuratively 'betwixt the devil and the deep blue sea.' He has a good offer
from Europe, but would *prefer* [emphasis mine] to ride in the East if there
are sufficient week-day meets to make it interesting."[60] By "East" the article
meant the East Coast of the United States, which would have been close
to Taylor's home in Worcester, Massachusetts. It used "East" as contrast
to the opportunity to race in the West at Salt Lake City. While Taylor may

have preferred to ride on the East Coast, he made the decision that it was in his best interests to return to Europe to race in 1908.

For the Black cyclists who traveled abroad, the goal was not merely to escape racism in America, especially if it also meant abandoning their home. Rather, they exerted their independence and likewise their masculinity by employing their physical mobility in the pursuit of social mobility. It was a protest against segregation. They did not all proclaim their actions were done on behalf of their race. They may not have seen themselves as "race men," but that does not mean they worked in vain or that their actions were apolitical. When White individuals and White led organizations attempted to deny these Black men the opportunity to race against White competitors and earn money doing so, men like Taylor, Hedspeth, Ivy, and Spain, found alternative routes to earning a living in the occupation of their own choosing (cycling). For some, to call it earning a living may be a stretch, since they obviously worked odd jobs in the off season to support themselves. While the pay may not have been enough to support the cost of living during the off season, there were psychological rewards to earning pay that was equal to White men.

Their success on cycling tracks at home and abroad did not end segregation, it did not seem to change the opinions of most White Americans. It did, however, build the confidence and courage of others to move forward. Black newspapers used Black cyclists as proof of equality. European newspapers used the episodes to highlight the inequality and racism in the United States, which Europeans perceived as disparate from race relations in their own corner of the world. Regardless of their intentions, these men made a statement by crossing the ocean in pursuit of financial independence. They were confronting spectres of the Atlantic and disrupting the wake of the Middle Passage. It was a declaration of manhood. Their mobility was an exercise of freedom to an extent their immediate ancestors struggled to even fathom. It was not only an attestation of that freedom but also a statement and, perhaps unconsciously, an effort to demand more of their supposed citizenship. The bicycle made the dream possible, but it was these courageous and determined Black cyclists who made it a reality.

8

Home Trainers and Vaudeville

Guaranteeing that their musical numbers would include "all the latest hits" the Florida Blossoms Company opened their show with five men and women on stage; dressed in evening gowns and full dress-suits. Considered "one of the best colored shows in the business," the Florida Blossoms were quintessential Vaudeville. The variety of acts they offered included plenty of music and performances by "premier buck and wing dancers who [were] in a class by themselves." King Williams delighted audiences with "the greatest act ever put together by a colored man," which included an assortment of performing dogs, cats, monkeys, goats, and geese. His animals could "do everything but talk." Mr. Chas (Mush Mouth) Miller then stupefied the audience with "ten minutes of nonsense." After intermission, the curtain was opened by "The Great Adams trick cyclist, who [was] second to none." He often "closed the olio" as well. This was the part of the show concentrating on comedy sketches, often including the headlining act.[1] Given the placement of his act at pivotal points in the show, it was apparently well received by the crowds who came to see the Blossoms' "good clean and moral show." There was an emphasis on the "clean and moral" character of Vaudeville shows in comparison to the reputation many minstrel shows and other traveling acts had developed over the years. Vaudeville was proclaimed to be family entertainment. The acts then, had to be more wholesome than those of Vaudeville's rivals. The wholesome atmosphere helped the Blossoms draw crowds that could be impressive in size. They "play[ed] to capacity houses every night in and about Washington, D.C." Sometimes, however, the crowds were "far below average" all depending on the time and location.[2]

Traveling Vaudeville shows like the Florida Blossoms were "put up" with the help of cast members, like a traveling circus, and then torn down at night to begin travel to the next town. In the South, they tended to travel in a seasonal pattern following the agricultural rhythms of the region. They would go to Georgia when the peaches were in season then on to North Carolina during the cotton harvest and on to West Virginia and the Mississippi delta in a similar pattern. The hopes were that people would be more willing to spend their money during these periods, as a lot of laborers and farmers had just been paid.[3] The managers of the Florida Blossoms, Pete and Frank Worthey, made regular adjustments to the order of the performance. Of course, the cast sometimes changed as well, with one of the most well-known performers of short tenure with the Florida Blossoms being Bessie Smith. She went on to become a prominent blues artist during the Jazz Age. By that time, she was recognized as the "Empress of the Blues" but while performing with the Florida Blossoms in 1909 she was billed simply as a "coon shouter" or the "Tennessee coon shouter."[4] Early in her career she made about ten dollars a week, but audiences were also known to throw money on the stage for her. Stagehands would then scoop it up, often collecting an additional three to four dollars for Smith.[5] The cost for entry was anywhere from ten cents up to one dollar and fifty cents for the most expensive box seats in bigger cities during Vaudeville's prime.[6] From the 1890s until the late 1910s, Vaudeville was the most popular form of entertainment in America, with audiences spending around $900,000 a week.[7]

Numerous Black athletes and entertainers were able to earn decent wages by climbing atop the Vaudeville stage, but it did not provide shelter from racism. In her biography of Bessie Smith, Michelle Scott recounts how Black Vaudeville performers "encountered virulently racist white communities and could not find establishments that would house and feed them. W. C. Handy recalled that during his travels in the late nineteenth and early twentieth centuries, a white mob in Missouri lynched a member of his traveling review for a supposed incident of 'impudence,' white supremacists also fired bullets at the train carrying the black performers as it passed through some towns in Texas, and the entire group of enter-

140 CHAPTER 8

tainers stocked up on arms for self-protection."[8] No doubt this would have made the performers think twice about entering certain communities and some may have second guessed whether they wanted to risk their lives to perform in Vaudeville at all. The fact that the group traveling through Texas armed themselves for self-defense, however, shows that while some may have been scared by such racist antics, they did not quit. Of course, they could also face less overt and less violent attempts at derailing their success. In Tennessee, a local newspaper referred to the Florida Blossoms as yet "another colored minstrel aggregation" and reported that "most of the audience" among the small number in attendance, were "of a like color with the performers." The column went on to tell its White readers, "We want to congratulate our people over staying away from such a show, especially in these troublous times. The money spent for seeing these kind of shows can easily be spent to a much better advantage."[9] This was only two weeks after the "East St. Louis Race Riot," a labor dispute that lasted for three days. The East St. Louis race riot was also a tragic event that exemplified the racial unrest of the period. Among the many violent acts perpetrated, the race riot culminated with angry White mobs firing their guns into the Mississippi River in attempts to murder the Black people struggling to swim away to safety.[10] This was just one of many examples of the virulent racism that was plaguing the United States during the early twentieth century. It was up to the managers of the Black troupes, like the Florida Blossoms, not only to negotiate these sorts of incidents, but they had to do it while hiring performers, planning shows, and sequencing the acts to make the show as entertaining as possible.

While the performers and the order of performances experienced many changes, for the Florida Blossoms, the Great Adams's comedic trick cycling was a consistent part of the show. This and other novelties such as magicians, strongmen, sharpshooters, animal acts, acrobats, contortionists, and trapeze artists were all a regular part of Vaudeville.[11] The Great Adams was one of many trick cyclists performing in Vaudeville around the United States, but according to the *Indianapolis Freeman*, he took up "where others leave off."[12] Indeed, there were other Vaudeville cyclists like Mace Lawrence of John W. Vogel's Mastadon Minstrels. Lawrence was called "America's greatest trick cyclist." There was also James Pickett, a former track cyclist doing a juggling act with the Sunny Dixie Minstrels. Pickett could allegedly "ride any kind of wheel any kind of way." There was Lester McDaniels, who

Home Trainers and Vaudeville

was said to "deserve the title of king of cyclists, a trick cyclist, magician, and comedian."[13] By the 1910s, many cyclists had made their way from the track to the Vaudeville stage. Undoubtedly, they were drawn by the opportunity to earn money for their labor. For some, Vaudeville was a natural extension of their talents and a convenient outlet, but it was also more than that.

In some ways, these Vaudeville shows were a response to, or correction of the traveling minstrel shows that had come before. The minstrel show, with its stock characters of White actors in blackface performing racist antics was, after all, where the term Jim Crow got its start. As the historian Elizabeth Pryor points out, the racist commentary present in the minstrel shows was often a statement about mobility. She argues, "Most dangerously, the Jim Crow caricature was a colored traveler, epitomizing the problems of unregulated black mobility."[14] The Black Vaudeville performer was then acting both out of protest and reclamation. The performances of Black characters could now be done by Black actors, not Whites in blackface. It is also true that the very fact that Vaudeville troops traveled throughout the United States made a point not unlike that of the Black athletes who traveled abroad to compete. Performing in Vaudeville could be liberating and a statement against racism because it was another opportunity for Black performers to exert their freedom of movement as well as the economic independence that came through the wages they earned while on the circuit. In these respects, performing in Vaudeville had a similar appeal to the Black cyclists as did traveling abroad to race in foreign countries. Of course, it appealed to other Black athletes too, like the boxer Jack Johnson and the jockey Isaac Murphy.

Some of the Black cyclists who landed in Vaudeville made their way there incrementally. This was the case for Hardy K. Jackson, who raced on the track before moving on to home-trainer races, and then on to Vaudeville. Each discipline represented a novel spectacle of sorts. Track racing, particularly the six-day variety, drew crowds who were interested in how the delirium of riding for six days in a row affected riders. Home-trainer races, while popular for a shorter time, also impressed spectators by the athletes' ability to keep their balance on a narrow set of drums, or rollers, generally two feet in width. For added excitement, both roller races and track racing were well-suited for gambling.

Home trainers were also referred to as rollers. As the name suggests, they were specifically intended for cyclists to use in their own homes, al-

Hardy Jackson in a home-trainer race. Photo courtesy of Joanne Schumpert.

lowing them to continue training when the weather was not cooperative or when it was just simply more convenient to stay in one place and still work out. The rollers, or drums, on the home trainers were around two feet in diameter and mounted to two bars by an axle that ran the width of the large drum. There was a small platform in the middle because the circumference of those drums positioned riders so far off the ground. There, they balanced their bicycles on a total of three rollers, two for the rear wheel and one in the front. A cord connected the rear drums to the front so that both the front and rear wheels of the bicycle would spin while the rider pedaled. In the more advanced setup, there would be a circular sort of model track, or velodrome, between the riders with figurines representing the riders. As they pedaled, the figurines moved around the model track, with a start finish area marked on the model. The most sophisticated designs even included a natural backdrop with trees, leaves, and a path, much like a green-screen would serve today. The riders' names were sometimes tacked up to the front of the rollers but in Jackson's case, sometimes his identity was reduced simply to "black." All of these embellishments were designed to improve the spectators' viewing experience.

Of course, the balancing act required to stay on the rollers could be thrilling enough. Accidentally riding off the edge came with potentially serious repercussions since the wheels were so high off the ground when

Home Trainers and Vaudeville

they were balanced atop the rollers. There may have been different scales, but it was not uncommon for eight laps of the figurine around the model velodrome to equal one mile—similar to some of the shorter indoor tracks of the era. The races were usually head-to-head and the progress and speed were marked by a few different types of analog display. They were also often shorter distances, five miles for instance, however, there were many that were much longer. The prospect of Hardy Jackson taking on a rider named Herman Hintze in an extremely long home-trainer race was reported to sound "like a joke, but it isn't; the two men are in earnest and that a 100 miles race on the rollers contains the gem of novelty goes without saying."[15] This probably would have taken the two somewhere in the neighborhood of four hours to complete. It also would have necessitated consuming fluids and possibly taking on some calories. Riding on rollers was one thing, but racing on them for several hours was something new and it sounded like it was Jackson's idea.

Maintaining balance on the rollers was hard even with both hands on the handlebars, eating or drinking while racing someone else on rollers added a considerable amount of difficulty to the endeavor. Still, many riders became well adept at riding the rollers and some even ventured beyond simply riding them to performing on them. They performed tricks while balancing atop the rollers such as riding with no hands or removing their warm-up pants, or perhaps even hopping their bicycles onto the rollers to begin riding without the use of the platform. This was a natural extension of the sort of trick riding that was done in Vaudeville acts and it is little wonder that short roller routines ended up on stage. Much later, in the 1980s, the sort of trick riding done on Vaudeville stages would be resurrected by what came to be referred to as flat land BMX riding.

Some cyclists made the transition from track racer to roller racer to Vaudeville performer, which is unsurprising. Bicycle racing in the 1910s, and the bicycle in general, struggled to hold a candle to the glory and popularity it experienced in the 1890s. Roller races could take place in much smaller venues, with less expense, and in Vaudeville the bicycle was only featured for five to ten minutes out of ninety-minute program. Of course, roller racing was also featured in Vaudeville shows. At the Howard theater in 1911, the *New York Age* told readers regarding a "'monster bill' in polite vaudeville," that "the work of the second and third numbers on the bill was something different from what has been seen in this city in a long time.

Unidentified competitive cyclist and his trainer in Camden, NJ, circa 1900. Photo courtesy of the Cycling Photographica Collection of Lorne Shields, Toronto.

A new and thrilling feature of the bill were the roller cyclists, consisting of Hardy Jackson, the 100-mile roller champion of the world, and George Harris, the roller champion of Pennsylvania."[16] On the Vaudeville stage, as opposed to venues that only featured roller races, it was easier to hold audiences' attention since the acts were generally around six minutes or less. A race could also be run while other Vaudeville acts were performed simultaneously, especially the comedic routines.

It is unclear how many cyclists transitioned from track racing to the home-trainer races but along with Hardy Jackson and James Pickett there was also William F. Ivy, who was born May 22, 1879, in Massachusetts. Later, he moved to Atlantic City. His parents, two former slaves, had moved to Massachusetts from Virginia, much like the family of other Black cyclists, such as David Drummond. His father was from South Carolina and died young when he fell from a tree. Similarly, his mother, from Richmond, Virginia, died at the age of thirty-three during childbirth. William Ivy persevered, making significant achievements in life. He graduated from grammar

Home Trainers and Vaudeville

145

school when he was 18, attended his local Baptist church regularly, and he was in overall good standing within his community.[17]

By the press, William Ivy was described as having a "cream tint," which may have been important in distinguishing him from other Black cyclists at the time. At other times he was referred to simply as a mulatto. One of the roller-race series in which Ivy competed was held at Madison Square Garden and described with the headline, "Racing Fast but Standing Still." The accompanying story reported that home-trainer racing continued all week and the machine "gave good service until that time, but on Thursday night . . . the inevitable happened . . . one of the rollers unfortunately got out of order and it was not until several events were run off that the discrepancy between the two machines was noted."[18] *The Bicycling World and Motorcycle Review* laid the issue out by beginning with a description of Ivy as "a strapping big negro . . . who pushes a bicycle geared to 131 inches. Ivy once won a road race and after that thought of going to Europe, but changed his mind and began riding on the home trainers. He has become quite proficient, too, as evidenced by his good riding in the series, although he apparently 'lay down' in his heat of the inter-club team race on Thursday night, which fortunately was one of those declared no race, else Ivy might have received a dose of punishment."[19] Sanctions for throwing the race is what the writer meant. The following week's publication reported, "charges have been lodged with the N.C.A." against two of the riders "W.F. Ivy, the big, husky mulatto, who played a large part in the sport; and against Otto Brandes, one of Ivy's several white rivals."[20] The NCA was the governing body for bicycle racing in the United States, after the League of American Wheelmen relieved themselves of that responsibility. Specifically, the article stated that the accusation against Ivy was of "'throwing a race' in one of the heats of the three-mile team championship" due to the fact that he rode really fast for about a mile but then really slow, losing his lead and only speeding back up after it was too late. An ally of Ivy explained that due to the fact that there were no prizes for that event, Ivy was saving himself for subsequent races. The article also pointed out that it was a little "unusual" to bring charges since one of the rollers had malfunctioned and all of the events from the night in question had been declared "no races."[21] There was a secondary story in the article that "on Wednesday of last week, when Ivy went to his quarters to get his bicycle he discovered that four nails had been driven into the tires, and that the sprocket had been hammered badly out

146   CHAPTER 8

of true. Later one of the Garden attendants claimed that he recognized Brandes as a man who had done the damage."[22] The chairman of the NCA was tasked with sorting the matter out but it is unclear how it was resolved, or why exactly Brandes would sabotage Ivy's bike if they were indeed in league together to intentionally throw the race. The attack on Ivy's bike, if carried out by Brandes, would suggest there was, in fact, no agreement between the two. Regardless, the home-trainer races seemed a short-lived fascination as news of such events fizzled over the course of a few years. Perhaps it was the difficulty of keeping the machines accurately calibrated or maybe it was the lack of high speeds and lower consequences involved with crashing on trainers that failed to thrill fans for very long. The rollers apparently did, however, maintain some ability to thrill crowds when they were used as part of a trick riding routine, rather than simply using them for races.

Trick riding became an alternative way of earning money with bicycles. It was not long before there were more than a few cyclists of color making a living with the bicycle outside of racing and beyond the repair stand. In a setting where exoticism was celebrated and the ability to hold an audience's attention for three minutes was desirable, a cyclist who could perform amazing tricks while also offering the occasional laugh was a fairly common ingredient on the Vaudeville stage. For Black cyclists and entertainers, trick riding did not seem to generate the same fear and paranoia in White audiences as racing. That is not so surprising, however, since the image of the Black man as a non-threatening clown who performed for Whites, rather than against them, was one role in which Black men were more easily accepted. The historian Joseph Boskin has researched why this was so, arguing that these men, and others like them, were stereotyped as Sambos. He discusses how the figure of the Sambo was represented in various forms, such as images, artifacts, as circus and stage performer, worker, and athlete. Boskin argues, "The entertaining grin was just one aspect of a large notion, the presumption that Sambo was an overgrown child at heart. And as children are given to impetuous play, humorous antics, docile energies, and uninhibited expressiveness, so too one could locate in Sambo identical traits."[23] The big smile and comedic aspects therefore, would have been crucial for White audiences, especially when it was a male performer. Boskin explains, "to make the black male into an object of laughter, and conversely, to force him to devise laughter, was to strip him of masculinity, dignity, and

Home Trainers and Vaudeville

self-possession.... The ultimate objective for whites was to effect mastery; to render the black male powerless as potential warrior, as sexual competitor, as an economic adversary."[24] It is also true, however, that some Black men performed this role with the intent of assuaging White fears. Acting as though they were harmless was a tactic for earning favor and therefore more money and less suspicion, which meant greater freedom.

Since a trick is akin to deception, performing tricks on a bicycle did not threaten the concept of White superiority in the same manner as winning on the track, especially when the trick riding routine included comedic antics and a smiling face, like that of the Great Adams. Undoubtedly, while people may have been wowed by the stunts, there were also those who believed that it was a meaningless skill that did not prove physical superiority. This was, after all, one of the ways in which Marshall "Major" Taylor gained notoriety and "earned his stripes" early in life—because of the trick riding he would perform outside of the bicycle shop where he worked in the 1890s. The fact that he did so while wearing a soldier's regalia, which the owner had loaned him to wear for the occasion, is how he got the nickname Major.

It is little surprise that after the prohibitions against Black cyclists became more concrete, with regard to segregated clubs and events in particular, some turned to trick riding as a supplemental stream of revenue. It was a far cry, however, from the world of cycling when it was a promising endeavor—when it still seemed possible to attain the level of fame and fortune "Major" Taylor had achieved. It had become much more difficult for all cyclists to make a comfortable living from their mounts by the 1910s, especially in comparison to the 1890s. The six-day races were one of the few cycling events that could still draw a crowd. The whole industry had gone from feast to famine, precipitated by the meteoric rise of bicycle sales beginning around 1896 and soon burning out like a shooting star within the course of just a few years. Bicycle production in the United States would remain high until 1900 but by that point, manufacturers had well outpaced the demand, which was as fleeting as daffodils in spring.[25] For several reasons, the thrill of riding bicycles seemed to soon fizzle with many Americans as the bicycle lost its newness.[26] Even though it had not surpassed the bicycle in affordability or practicality, by the 1910s, the personal automobile, and even the prospect of flight, offered more exciting possibilities than the now old technology of the two-wheeled steed. While cycling's star was falling, Vaudeville's was on the rise.

148   CHAPTER 8

Due to the circumstances, the presence of Black cyclists on Vaudeville stages demonstrates the agency of these athletes. Each obstacle to using the bicycle for a lucrative career was met with a creative new solution. Hardy K. Jackson was a quintessential example of that agency. According to the 1910 census, he was born around 1872 in North Carolina. By 1910 he was employed as a Vaudeville actor. Jackson's agency is most apparent when considering his entrepreneurial endeavors. *The Bicycling World and Motorcycle Review* called attention to his energy and passion, identifying him as a "press agent, wireless telegraph reporter par excellence, proprietor of International Cycle Works, President of the International Cycle Association, janitor at No. 305 W. 41st St, and husband of noted colored suffragette—Mrs. Hardy Anastasius [*sic*] Jackson."[27] The next year he would be referred to as the "colored champ." He was also part owner of the Dinnel & Jackson Velodrome, which was located at the West 41st Street address in Manhattan. It does not seem that it was the traditional sort of velodrome with a long circular track, but rather a venue for home-trainer races. There were not many stories that mentioned the velodrome, making it an unlikely venue for a lot of races, or races that were considered prestigious for the era. Of course, this could have been an intentional snub. Other tracks, like those at Revere, Vailsburg, and Madison Square Garden received much more coverage. However, some race reports from the time did mention results of events, such as when J.B. Hawkins "lapped the colored challenger [Jackson]" in a home-trainer race at the Dinnel & Jackson Velodrome.[28] Home-trainer races occurred in other locations as well, like the Lafayette Theater in Jersey City. While some reports about Jackson's results looked bad, like the one mentioned previously, due to his prowess atop the rollers on the home trainers, cycling magazines adopted the moniker the "colored champ" for Hardy Jackson. He was more than just a home-trainer racer, however, as he had a notable career on the roads and tracks before he came to home trainers. On Thanksgiving Day in 1904, his speed earned him a pair of opera glasses as a prize at the Brower Wheelmen's road race. *The Bicycling World* took the opportunity to make an elitist joke that "the colored rider [Jackson] didn't know what to do with" them.[29]

Hardy Jackson participated in a considerable number of races and group outings. He was, for a while, a member of the Navarre Wheelmen Club for Black cyclists. *The Bicycling World* noted that Jackson was also a bicycle

A black-owned bicycle shop? Photo courtesy of the Cycling Photographica Collection of Lorne Shields, Toronto.

salesman, pointing out that he had a bicycle store at 325 West 39th Street in New York City. This was only a few blocks from the Jackson and Dinnel Velodrome and it was the same address that was listed as his home address in census reports from the time. Even if the attention he received from the White press dripped with disdain, all of his go-getting was apparently having an effect. By 1912, the Black newspaper, the *Indianapolis Freeman* referred to Jackson as "the famous cyclist" and announced that he would be at the Ford Dabney theater.[30] The status that he was gaining among cycling circles likely led to an elevated social status, which would have undoubtedly impacted his employment prospects. Census records suggest as much. The 1910 census lists his occupation as Vaudeville actor, which was a step up from his occupation as "carpenter" in 1905 and "stone operator" in 1900. His family had moved from Gainsborough or Gaysburgh, NC, to Elizabeth, NJ, when he was around the age of six (approximately 1877). He left school at twelve years of age, in the fourth grade. In spite of the early end to his education, so that he could help his parents at home, his status

150 CHAPTER 8

as a telegraph operator suggests that he was literate and certainly intelligent. Census records confirm this, listing him as able to read and write. Jackson's cycling career, in spite of that fact that his prominence in the sport came relatively late in life (around age 30), spanned a relatively long period of time. It was certainly a longer career in cycling than many other Black cyclists. In interviews, he claimed he was still racing as an amateur, possibly just to fill space, at the Revere track in 1928 for around $4 per day.[31] That would have been when he was around fifty-six or fifty-seven years old, a very advanced age for competitive cycling before there were divisions specifically for such men.

Although Jackson claimed that he began riding by the age of nineteen, there is not much evidence that he was a serious or competitive cyclist until around eleven years later. By that point, he had elbowed his way into race reports in the major news outlets for cycling. They show that as early as 1902 he was racing at the Vailsburg track. In July of that year, he would take second place in the quarter-mile race for novices.[32] He would not have been allowed to race with the professionals even if he wanted to due to restrictions against all Black cyclists except "Major" Taylor. It seems that by that point Jackson was at least racing in integrated competitions but to say Black cyclists were accepted as equals would be a gross exaggeration. Jackson experienced unfair treatment—on and off the track. In 1906 he was arrested for "reckless riding" when he and two White men allegedly ran into three White women, one with a baby in her arms, as they were disembarking a streetcar. The women were knocked down and an off-duty police officer from the Tenderloin District of Manhattan was able to quickly apprehend the cyclists. The magistrate held Jackson for $300 while his two White compatriots were fined $3 each.[33] This would not be Jackson's last brush with the law and it gives a glimpse of the racism he faced outside the world of cycling.

As far as sanctioned cycling was concerned, Hardy Jackson was still racing in 1909, but his physicality seemed more acceptable when it was demonstrated against competitors who were deemed his equals, other Black cyclists. On August 22, 1909 the Newark velodrome hosted an event that included the exploits of the champion, Frank Kramer. *The Bicycling World*, however, reported, "One of the features that gave the 'fans' more delight than any other event on the card was the unlimited match pursuit between those two New York colored champions—Hardy A. Jackson and William A.

Home Trainers and Vaudeville

Penn. Jackson and Penn fought bitterly, but the race ended when Jackson passed his dusky rival at 4 miles 1 lap. Jackson was mightily pleased when the 'bleacherites' referred to him as 'Major' Taylor."[34] Undoubtedly, that would have been quite the complement, since Taylor was one of the fastest men in the world, but it is also another example of fans' inability to think about Black cyclists as anything other than Black. Regardless of who the current champion was, or who had the most titles, any Black cyclist that showed promise could expect to be compared to "Major" Taylor, regardless of his build, style, or particular talents. All Black cyclists from the 1890s to 1920s could expect that. In a race held at the Garden in 1908, which included Jackson, Penn, and Earl Adams among others, *The Bicycling World* wrote, "The future 'Major' Taylors got a cheer when they lined up 11 strong for the one mile colored championship."[35] Jackson and Penn perhaps had more in common with one another than with Taylor. Both were born in Virginia, as were their parents, and both moved to New York City at an early age. Both were literate, as was Taylor, but Taylor was from Indianapolis. Regardless, it is clear Black cyclists were often seen as one in the same.

Even though there were integrated races, these thoughts, or comparisons of, and lumping of Black cyclists together shows a desire to keep them segregated from White cyclists. Jackson was often limited to segregated races. At Madison Square Garden, before 4,000 fans, he found that even then, his principal event was the half-mile handicap amateur, "for colored riders only." It was won by John Brewer of Keysport, NJ. Earl Adams of Montclair got scratch, or second, and Jackson, who was affiliated with the International Cycling Association by that time, took third.[36] It is somewhat curious that there was a segregated event at all. Were there enough fans who desired to see a race between Black cyclists only or was it a concession by the race organizer and an attempt to make a little extra money? "Major" Taylor's experiences suggest that there was a desire to see Black cyclists race against White cyclists in a sort of mock race war, but the novelty of such events may have worn off quickly, especially if Taylor was successful against his White competitors. Integrated races had grown too controversial.

Readers would have surely picked up on the cynical and contemptuous treatment Hardy Jackson received in the pages of *The Bicycling World*. For instance, it reported that one race in particular was "conducted by the 'International Cycle Association of New York,' an organization that exists largely in the expansive mind of one Hardy Jackson, a colored bicycle dealer.

152 CHAPTER 8

. . . Jackson not only lies awake nights thinking up impressive names, but also striking prizes."[37] The article went on to imply that maybe Jackson did not actually pay the $35 promised to the two headlining athletes, both men by the name of Alphonso. It also appears that one of them was Black and the other White since the title of the article was "Whites and Blacks on the Rollers." It was reportedly "one of the most 'exciting' bicycle races ever held in New York City, Alphonso Johns of New York, and Alphonso Davis, of Washington battled on the home trainers in Mutual Hall."[38] The quotation marks around the word exciting suggests that it was a quote from Jackson and one that the writer for *The Bicycling World* found dubious. In that race, Alphonso Johns fell three times, which might have made the race more exciting than other races on the home trainers where nothing seemed to really happen other than the spinning of wheels and perhaps the slow movement of a small figurine around a model velodrome. There is not much else provided in the coverage of the race to make it sound particularly exciting, but the magazine may have intentionally overlooked more details regarding the race if they came from Jackson, since the article insinuates that he was prone to embellish a story. This is a reputation that would follow Jackson, as other accounts would portray him as what would colloquially be referred to as a "big talker," yet most of these accounts were written by White men and there was certainly a stereotype that confident Black men were merely lying about their credentials, possessions, wealth, or status.[39] The distrust of Jackson, therefore, could possibly be attributed to the racist preconceptions of the people reporting on his actions. He certainly seemed to be what some would call a mover and shaker. The fact that he owned and helped operate a velodrome, no matter its size, created the International Cycling Association, was a competitive cyclist himself, and sold bicycles shows that he had his hand in multiple facets of the sport. As a telegraph operator, he would have even helped promote the sport. The incredulous and condescending tone that White writers adopted then, might seem somewhat curious. The fact that they never pointed out an outright lie of Jackson's suggests that the treatment he received was based solely on the color of his skin.

On other occasions, *The Bicycling World* also took a patronizing tone when reporting on the exploits of Hardy Jackson, and many other Black cyclists as well. In an article titled "Hardy Jackson Winner at Last" the magazine explained, "after waiting 15 long years, during which time he has been most assiduously plugging along, victory came to Hardy A. Jackson, the most assiduous colored cyclist in Greater New York . . . and victory tasted as delicious as an ice-cream-chicken-watermelon feast to Jackson, take his word for it."[40] He was further described as a "great home trainer, meet promoter, rider, dealer, prize donor and leading spirit of the 'International Cycling Association of New York City'" which included "Jackson, an Italian, German, Frenchman, American and just a mongrel. . . ."[41] The article went on to explain that there was "no question about Jackson's victory. He won, and in a most picturesque finish, his lean ebony frame leading a bunch of twenty riders across the tape in a soul-stirring finish. Jackson is thirty-four years old and has been riding a bicycle for over fifteen years. He had never won an open race, and that is why the handicapper was kind to him last Sunday, giving him 4 minutes, next to the limit." Here, the article was making the point that Jackson did not win the race so much as it was given to him out of pity. It continued, "About a half mile from the finish some one jumped out and the rival 'Major' Taylor got on his rear wheel when the leader tired after making his sprint, Jackson saw his opportunity and, ducking his kinky 'haid' he raced for the tape an eighth of a mile beyond. His toothpick like legs hammered away at the pedals like they meant to get there, and they did, about a length in front of Mourice Van Dendries [sic], who had started from the three minute mark."[42] Using "haid" as a colloquial version of head was no doubt another elitist mockery of what the reader was to assume was Jackson's own parlance. Of course, there was also the ever-present comparison to "Major" Taylor.

The list of examples in which Hardy Jackson was treated with prejudice goes on. Even though he was born in the United States, of parents who were also born in the United States, when he was not being compared to "Major" Taylor, Jackson was often considered a representative of Africa, rather than the United States. In one race, it was reported that because of the five riders who participated, William van den Dries, A. J. Seldney, Ernest Bleuzat, Hardy Jackson, and Frank McMillan, "five countries were 'represented'"—Holland, America, France, Africa, and Scotland.[43] The fact that the writer categorized the entire continent of Africa as a single country is not all that surprising and further demonstrates the inability of White audiences to see people of color as individuals, rather than a monolith.[44] The writer did at least place the word 'represented' in quotations, maybe an attempt to point out the flawed conflation of race and nation in this example. All this taken together suggests that while writers who covered the cycling industry would occasionally write about Jackson and list all of his endeavors, they did not exactly take him seriously. To say that there was "no doubt" about his victory insinuates that maybe there was doubt about some of his other victories, which conjures up that old stereotype once again that Jackson was dishonest and a master of hyperbole.

All of these athletes, William Penn, the Great Adams, William Ivy, and Hardy Jackson in particular, represent the ability of the Black cyclist to negotiate the changing nature of bicycles and bicycle racing. As the novelty of the bicycle played out, the manner in which it was used ventured into new realms. The races that were most popular among spectators shifted toward the six-day variety due to the physical demands it put on cyclists. For a time, the races on home trainers also captured the public's imagination, but that seemed rather short-lived as athletes like Hardy Jackson and James Pickett made their way to Vaudeville over the course of a few years—in their search for lucrative careers.[45] For most Black cyclists in the United States, other than "Major" Taylor, it was seemingly impossible to reach the status of professional racer. Most raced as amateurs and this designation meant that they were technically disqualified from winning cash prizes. Still, it was possible to sell prizes won, such as the opera glasses Hardy Jackson earned, but that was more of a hassle than winning a cash prize. In spite of this, amateur Black cyclists kept competing and were somehow able to cobble together enough income from their cycling endeavors to survive. Of course, many also worked other jobs, sometimes repairing bicycles, but oftentimes they worked in other trades unrelated to bicycles, like carpentry, or as porters. It is unclear how they self-identified since the census data for many of these men often list some other occupation, such as machinist, or mechanic. It is rarer to see bicycle repairer or bicycle racer listed as their occupation, which makes it seem that for many, cycling was thought of as a hobby or side-job, rather than their full-time occupation. The designation of amateur and restrictions against them racing professionally made this their reality since they were unable to easily earn enough money from bicycle racing to support themselves or a family.

As cycling's popularity among American audiences declined, the number of races, prizes, and reports on race results all dwindled in size. Naturally, those who were not independently wealthy simply could not afford to spend the little free time they had pursuing athletic achievements, especially when it came with expenses like those of race entry fees, club memberships, and the cost of buying and maintaining top of the line equipment. Hardy Jackson did, however. While working other jobs, he would continue to race at the Revere cycle track (velodrome) into 1928. He made $4 a day doing this, but the work was not consistent as he could only race a few days per week and it was mostly during the summer months.[46] Otherwise, he worked as a steamfitter, carpenter, janitor, and other similar jobs. Many of the early entrepreneurs who came to bicycles during the golden age of cycling left bicycles for motorcycles and cars as soon as the bicycle craze began to lose steam. Jackson, Penn, Adams, and Ivy all continued to use the bicycle but in slightly different ways—from race tracks, to trainers, to the stage. By the time Vaudeville and the six-day race craze were on their way out, these cyclists were at advanced ages. Some Vaudeville performers even made their way into film, beginning with silent pictures and the bicycle was still seen, on occasion—featured in the performances of stars such as Buster Keaton or Charlie Chaplin. By that point, the bicycle was mostly a prop, however, and it is unclear if any Black cyclists did so. Most of the early recordings of silent films featuring Black actors have been lost or destroyed over the years.[47]

This then is not just a story of the agency of Black cyclists in their ability to continue to employ the bicycle in their pursuit of social mobility. Sadly, none of these Black cyclists, other than "Major" Taylor, really became wealthy from their cycling endeavors but many did experience some temporary financial gains and certainly a good deal of notoriety. The bicycle itself is an important factor in how this played out, due to how it slipped in status from once enjoying immense popularity as an object of sport and leisure to an object of little interest for most adults. As the bicycle's novelty wore off, so did American's interest. This, coupled with the barriers Black cyclists faced, which were often erected by White cyclists, is what led to creative solutions to overcome, or get around, those barriers.

These men's lives also show that from cycling's beginning through its downfall, Black cyclists were present. Their presence adds significance to what we already know about "Major" Taylor. Even his story is not as well known by the general public as it should be, but it is important to note that he was not the only Black cyclist during this period. Calling attention to this allows us to see that it was not just one unfortunate Black cyclist who faced discrimination in the sport, it was much bigger than that. There were many Black cyclists and while most did not find the same success as Taylor, some of them faced even stiffer barriers than he did since he was a sort of "token" for American cycling due to the fact that he was the only Black cyclist consistently allowed to race as a professional. There is little to suggest that any of these cyclists came from wealthy families. Hardy Jackson's father was a carpenter and his mother "kept house." Their socioeconomic status, then, was not what served to exclude Black Americans from attaining greater heights in cycling, it was something else and it was bigger than the League of American Wheelmen's decision to add the word "white" to the membership requirements in their constitution. These athletes defied the odds and fought hard. They were strong, confident, and enterprising, yet examining the entire arc of their lives shows that none of them were truly successful on a personal level—if we measure success as living happily ever after. Pursuing the question of how this could be so, sheds light on the power and pervasiveness of systemic racism in our country. A discussion of these cyclists' full lives, including what happened after they stopped racing and riding, is also helpful in understanding how and why their achievements were forgotten over time.

9

Once Was Lost

When he finally retired from competitive cycling, for good this time, "Major" Taylor had amassed a considerable amount of money. It was enough for him to construct a large home in Worcester, Massachusetts, and to afford the first automobile in that city. In fact, he owned three large houses in Worcester and a few plots of land beyond that. He rented the investment properties for extra income and in his financial prime, he had between $35,000 to $75,000 in cash. As the historian Andrew Ritchie points out, of Black men in the United States, Taylor was one of the wealthiest in 1910.[1] In spite of this, Taylor would die alone and destitute. It was not the case that he merely lived an extravagant lifestyle and spent all the money. Rather, it seems that failed business ventures and a limited support network were the primary causes of his financial ruin.

After hanging up his bicycle in 1910, Taylor's interest in motorcycles and cars grew. Possibly encouraged by the success he saw his old friend Birdie Munger experience in the automotive industry, Taylor applied to Worcester Polytechnic Institute. He wanted to apply his engineering talents, which had been demonstrated in modifications he made to his own bicycle, to cars and motorcycles. Taylor recognized he needed more training in the area and he was sorely disappointed upon receiving a letter of rejection from the technical school. The official reason was the fact that Taylor did not have a high school diploma, but Taylor and his daughter Sydney believed

158   CHAPTER 9

a more likely reason they did not simply waive that requirement was due to his race. Sydney added that despite his upstanding reputation, "there were certain things that blacks just could not do."[2] Seeing it as merely a temporary setback, Taylor plowed ahead and targeted automobile tires as the area in which he would make his mark. Andrew Ritchie recounts that his first, and most substantial, investment in time and money was toward the development of a "sprung tire" that would help cushion the ride and eliminate some of the failures that arose due to the rubber tires that were being used at the time.

Two years after retiring from cycling, Taylor was already looking for a company to test his new idea to improve automotive tires. He settled on the Iver Johnson Company, a company with which he had worked during his cycling career. By 1914, the Major Taylor Manufacturing Company, makers of the "Metal Taylor Tire," was created. The president of Iver Johnson and Taylor invested equal shares of $15,000 each with other co-investors and shareholders contributing toward the initial investment as well. The company was rather short lived, however, apparently failing in its endeavors before production of the tire even began. Fred Johnson was able to bounce back from the failed business venture, but Taylor's financial wounds were much more serious. Additionally, Taylor's financial losses brought conjugal strife. His wife did not agree with the venture and the failure added significant stress to his marriage. Nevertheless, he tried to rebound through a series of other enterprises. First was an automotive oil company, called the Excello Manufacturing Company, from 1913 to 1915. Four years later, the Worcester city directory listed Taylor as a partner of a company called Taylor and Quick. That was short lived as well. In 1922, he was listed as the owner of "Major's Tire Shop," and by 1926, his occupation seemed downgraded even further to simply "auto repairer."[3] In spite of his dwindling economic prospects and sapped cash reserves, Taylor continued to tithe regularly to the John Street Baptist Church in Worcester and he gave generously to any special projects undertaken by the church. His daughter claims he even angered his wife with his generosity—allowing tenants to live at his properties rent free when they struggled to make ends meet.[4] Ultimately, he was forced to begin liquidating his estate, selling properties, taking a loan out on his own house, and selling gifts of precious jewelry given to his wife and gold coins given to his daughter as birthday presents.[5] He simply could not afford to maintain all the possessions he had acquired in his prime—as a professional cyclist.

Slowly, the relationship with his wife Daisy continued to unravel. He had written much about his devotion to her and it seemed she and his daughter, Sydney, were a major part of his decision to leave the world of bicycle racing behind. As his finances and marriage continued to deteriorate, so did his health. Of course, his poor health led to even more significant financial burdens. Just after becoming ill, in 1925, Taylor was forced to sell his final possession of significant value, his home of twenty-five years on Hobson Avenue in Worcester. Taylor had gone from being the landlord of multiple properties to a mere tenant—moving his wife and daughter into a small apartment.[6] The psychological toll on Taylor, in tandem with a weakened immune system, culminated in a recurring and debilitating case of shingles, for which he was hospitalized on numerous occasions.[7] His situation became so desperate that friends tried to step in on his behalf. Spearheaded by a very wealthy White man named Henry Worcester Smith, there were calls in the local newspapers for the public to intervene financially on Taylor's behalf. In those articles, Smith made appeals for monetary assistance, recounting Taylor's financial problems and poor health. The checks were to be sent to Smith. Within a week, over $1,200 poured in from New England, Canada, and as far away as Australia.[8] Taylor was grateful, but it was a blow to his pride to be forced to come to terms with just how far he had fallen.

Perhaps in an effort to regain some dignity and to ensure an enduring legacy, "Major" Taylor's last great undertaking was to write and distribute his autobiography, *The Fastest Bicycle Rider in the World: The Story of a Colored Boy's Indomitable Courage and Success Against Great Odds*. Taylor recognized how important it was that his story not only be told, but also remembered. He likely assumed that writing the book would be the hard part and sales would be much less work, but he overestimated demand. At over 400 pages, all the details he had poured into the book seemed to weigh it down, hindering its commercial success. Taylor was used to hard work, however, and believed if he just worked a little more, he could fix the problem of meager sales and so, he walked door-to-door selling copies of his book at $3.50 per copy. Published in 1929, it was not long before he had exhausted the potential consumers in Worcester and he began to travel more extensively in his car, now packed with books. First, he went to New

York, then he toured New England after that. He poured himself into selling the book with the same vigor he had put into writing it. To a man used to training hours upon hours, six days a week, on a bicycle, this would have been something of a cake walk—except Taylor's body was worn out. Andrew Ritchie argues that the time on the road came with other stressors, putting the final nail in the coffin for his marriage.

In 1930, one year after dedicating himself to selling the book, his wife Daisy left him. She moved to New York and his daughter Sydney, now married, moved to New Orleans. Taylor, apparently deciding there was not much left for him in Worcester, drove his car toward Chicago for an extended stay. Since he was originally from Indianapolis and had a brother and sister living in Chicago, it is unsurprising that he chose to visit the Windy City.[9] It is unclear whether he planned on a brief stay or something more long term, but he soon checked-in at the YMCA on South Wabash Avenue, a branch that catered to the Black community on Chicago's South Side. This was not the first time Taylor had sought refuge at a YMCA and from its doors he would exit every day to hit the pavement to solicit sales for his book.[10] Sales would never really take off, however. Somehow, Taylor was able to survive on the proceeds, but just barely and not for long. By 1932, Taylor was still in Chicago, still staying at the YMCA, but his health was fading fast. Suffering from prolonged hypertension and myocarditis, in March, biographer Andrew Ritchie believes Taylor suffered from a stroke or heart attack. He was admitted to Provident Hospital, which specialized in cardiology and like the Wabash YMCA, it also catered to the Black community of Chicago's South Side. There, Taylor underwent heart surgery. Still, his condition did not improve. A month later he was moved to Cook County Hospital, where he would live out his last days.[11] In his autobiography, Taylor tried to express the great weight both physical and mental, of being a Black man in the United States. In addressing all the questions he had encountered of why he quit racing when he did, he explained that the people did not "realize the great physical strain . . . and the utter exhaustion I felt on the many occasions after I had battled under the monster prejudice, both on and off the track."[12] In death, he could finally shed that burden for the first time.

It is quite possible that he was alone when the time came. No contact was made with his wife or daughter and so the only potential visitors would have been his brother and sister, the friends he made since beginning his sojourn at the YMCA, and James Bernard Bowler. Bowler was a Chicago city commissioner and former professional cyclist who would go on to become a United States Congressman. Taylor surely knew him from his racing days, since their careers overlapped, and rekindled their relationship while targeting former cyclists when selling his book. Bowler was an influential friend who had helped Taylor gain admission to Provident Hospital, which was a private institution.[13] Reading the speeches made at Jim Bowler's memorial, his similarities to Taylor stand out. Bowler, described as a "champion of champions" whose name was a "household word throughout the Nation" was also "a man of his word . . . [who] never deviated from the simple virtues." He was considered "deeply religious" and "never too busy to help those in the humbler stations of life" as well as a devoted husband.[14] He was celebrated for all of those attributes, and they were described as what made him a "great American" and a successful politician. Marshall "Major" Taylor, infamous for his tee-totaling and obstinate refusal to race on Sunday, even when faced with fines, was all of those things as well. Yet the paths of Bowler and Taylor diverged so drastically after their racing careers came to an end. Taylor was much better known as a champion cyclist than Bowler, but unlike Bowler, he was unable to ride the wave of his notoriety after hanging up his bicycle. Bowler had at least one glaring advantage over Taylor, he was White.

Though they both suffered heart-attacks, Jim Bowler died at the age of eighty-two, while serving as a United States Representative. "Major" Taylor died at the age of fifty-three, homeless, destitute, and alone. Even then, fifty-three was relatively old for a Black man, for whom the average life expectancy was around forty-seven. When Bowler passed, twenty-five US Representatives and two Senators rose to eulogize the man. One week after Taylor's death no one had even come to claim the body and so he was "buried at public expense in a 'pauper's grave' in a plain wooden box, in the welfare section of the Mount Glenwood Cemetery, a Jim Crow burial site about thirty miles south of downtown Chicago."[15] Jim Bowler deserved no less than what he received. Taylor, on the other hand, deserved much more.

On November 26, 1924, Woody Hedspeth boarded the S.S. Baradine to make his way from the Port of London to Melbourne, Australia. As the twin-propellers of the class B steamship began to spin faster, Hedspeth and two other cyclists settled in for the voyage. All three, Hedspeth (the lone American) and two Frenchmen, Lucien Faucheux and Ernest Védrines, were under the care of Thomas Cook & Son of Ludgate. Thomas Cook, formerly a preacher, had become what could be considered the first travel agent in the world during the second half of the nineteenth century.[16] By 1924, his family had expanded the business to become a limited liability company, offering packages for international travel. At this point, Hedspeth was forty years old, which is relatively old for a cyclist, or any elite endurance athlete. Comparatively, his French companions were twenty-four and thirty-three. Most of his competition would have been somewhere between 20 and 35. Hedspeth had been racing for more than twenty years, which was remarkable and would have seemed unachievable had he remained in the United States. His talents on the bicycle allowed him to travel extensively in his lifetime. Moving from Kentucky to Indianapolis as a child and then making regular excursions around the Midwest and Northeast as a cyclist. Hedspeth went even farther, traveling to Paris by 1903, and on to Australia, Switzerland, Belgium, Italy, Spain, the British Isles, and Russia. Of all the places he had been, he chose a six-story building at 36 Rue Nollet in Paris, just a short walk from Montmartre and a quick bike ride to the Velodrome d'Hiver constructed by Henri Desgrange (father of the Tour de France) as home.

Woody Hedspeth's ability to race as a professional in Europe and live an otherwise less restricted life than what the United States offered was a great lure. In contrast to "Major" Taylor, who would return to the United States, the allure of Europe seemed to overcome any bouts of homesickness Hedspeth may have experienced. He was able to leave his mom, dad, sister, and two brothers behind showing an obvious preference for life in Paris to that of the United States.[17] It is hard to say whether it was the day-to-day life as a Parisian or the fact that he could continue to make a living as a professional cyclist that was most attractive. He certainly did not turn his back on the bicycle, at least never for long. There were a few gaps in his palmarès but never more than a few years.[18] Hedspeth even began to build his own family in Paris. In 1907, in a quick blurb about the most recent cyclists to obtain professional licenses from the National Cycling Association, his recent marriage was announced in a less than exuberant tone. It identified Hedspeth as, "the negro who has married a white woman and settled down in Paris between races. . . ."[19] The fact that she was White was added for obvious effect. The woman was a Rosalie Le Maître, a French cabaret dancer.[20] Whether they were actually married, however, is doubtful. They did have a daughter together, who was named Geneviève Le Maître but in an official document, Rosalie was listed as the mother of his daughter, not his wife.[21] The fact that neither woman took the name Hedspeth also indicates they were not married. More than likely, they lived together as a family for an extended period, but the specifics are unclear.

Hedspeth's racing career continued until at least 1929 but there is scant evidence that he raced in the United States after the International Six-Day Race of 1903 in New York City. As an older, more experienced, cyclist he undoubtedly mentored many European racers. While sailing from the Port of London to Australia, he had ample time to share tips and tricks with the 23-year-old French racer, Lucien Faucheux. Even when not racing, Hedspeth could find work in the world of cycling by serving as a trainer. It was apparently enough to keep him going. Whatever his income and living conditions may have been, he did not appear eager to leave Europe. It was not until Paris was captured by Nazi forces that Hedspeth finally accepted it was time to return home to the United States.

By 1941 Hedspeth was still living in Paris but now it was part of Vichy France. If he had chosen Paris over the United States because of greater freedoms he had there, he surely found that not to be the case living in under Nazi occupation. As this was the case, it is little surprise that Hedspeth began the process of repatriation to the United States in 1941; he may have had no safe alternative. As a part of the Red Cross repatriation group 14, he was evacuated to Lisbon, Portugal, so that he could board a ship to carry him back to the United States. Sadly, he never made it aboard and it was there in Lisbon that he would take his final breath, dying at 1 p.m. on April 16, 1941. The primary cause of death was "intestinal tuberculosis," but he was also suffering from typhus. Typhus, generally a flea-borne bacterium, could have led to complications like delirium, skin rashes, bleeding, and shock while the intestinal tuberculosis would have led to weight-loss, abdominal pain, fever, and anemia. Hedspeth was buried five days later at the Benfica Cemetery. Local authorities ordered that his body not be disinterred for at least five years and the attending physician ordered that his remaining personal effects be burned. What effects he did have were described as "old, mostly in poor condition, and almost valueless." Hedspeth was considered "destitute." The only names listed as relatives were Rosalie and Geneviève Le Maître, but Rosalie was not even contacted about his death. Instead, the

164 CHAPTER 9

first person given notice was a man named Jim Gibson who was notified three days after his death via telegraph. Geneviève would not receive word until three days after that—nearly a full week after his death.[22]

Hedspeth may have found more suitable living conditions in Paris, but even there he did not escape the grip of racism entirely. There were the references to him as "black number two" and "ink." There were doubtless other incidents as well. On the way back to France after racing in Australia for instance, Hedspeth, Faucheux and Védrines disembarked their ship in Cape Town, South Africa but found that no restaurant would serve them due to the presence of Hedspeth and the color of his skin.[23] Still, he preferred living abroad over returning to the United States. Even after becoming estranged from his daughter and her mother, Hedspeth stayed in Paris. The fact that he died alone and destitute, like "Major" Taylor, is heartbreaking and, unfortunately, it was not an uncommon end for the Black cyclist.

There were still other Black cyclists who could be considered even more unfortunate than Woody Hedspeth and "Major" Taylor. That certainly seemed to be the case for the few well-known riders who died while they were still young. Viola Wheaton of Boston, the young associate of Kittie Knox, was struck down by appendicitis in 1895; shortly after marrying an equally prominent cyclist, William Hamilton. She had barely entered her twenties. Five years later, death would come for one of Boston's most important cyclists. This time it was Kittie Knox. Knox was in her mid-twenties and single when she fell ill. The cause of death was listed as "chronic nephritis," an affliction of the kidneys that can be caused by an infection and is often associated with lupus.[24] Just a few years earlier she had established herself as a female cyclist who was both beautiful and strong. She had even experienced the rare privilege of sailing to Europe to ride her bicycle through the streets of Paris and went on to perform in Vaudeville.[25] What else might she have achieved with more time?

Like Kittie Knox, Melvin Dove was also successful enough on the bicycle to make his way to Europe, but he went there to race against some of the fastest men in the world. Dove, six years younger than Knox, would die six years after her at the age of twenty-six. Living in New York City at the time, Dove was one of the many victims of tuberculosis.[26] It was apparently the pulmonary variety, not the intestinal variety that would lead to Hedspeth's death. For Dove, it was a fairly sudden death. He was racing in December 1905, but his death certificate states that he died just three months later,

March 17, 1906 at a private home on West 134th street. Adding insult, his death appeared to go unnoticed by the major publications reporting on cycling in the United States. A few years after the fact, one did mention him, off-handedly, simply as being deceased.[27] All these cyclists were struck down in their prime so it is difficult to say what may have become of them. Dove certainly showed a lot of promise and Knox was remarkable in her own right. Still, the fact that none were White would seem to have placed a cap on what they could achieve due to the restrictive Jim Crow world in which they were living.

There was yet another group of Black cyclists who came to tragic ends not necessarily because they died in destitution nor were they struck down too soon. Perhaps even more tragically, these Black cyclists were forced to live out their final years in institutions for convicted criminals and those with mental health issues. David Drummond, William Ivy, and Hardy Jackson would all become inmates and/or patients, serving sentences that lasted late into their lives.

David Drummond was a well-known Boston area cyclist in the 1880s and 1890s. He came before Marshall "Major" Taylor and successfully transitioned from the high-wheeler to the safety bicycle. Drummond, who was a popular rider to call upon for assistance in pacing long-distance record attempts, seemed to have comparatively greater options open to him outside the world of cycling. City directories for Cambridge, Massachusetts listed him at first as a spar-maker, then a clerk, and a bicycle repairer after that. Outside of work, however, Drummond ran in some influential circles. As a member of the fraternal organization the Knights of Pythias, and in attending civic engagements that included the likes of James Monroe Trotter, Drummond was considered one of Boston's "distinguished colored men" in 1887. He was just twenty-seven years old at the time.[28] The U.S. census reports show him as living at home with his mother and father until around 1910. It was in that year that his address switched from the familiar Blanche Street domicile in Cambridge to the Worcester State Hospital.

It is unclear what led to Drummond's status as an "inmate" of the Worcester State Hospital by 1910 but it appears he was never released. In 1920 he was still there but listed as a "patient" instead of inmate and in 1930 there was no change of status. If he simply needed the care and facilities of a mental institution, it is perhaps not so bad, but the fact that he had been an able bodied, apparently bright, and distinguished young man in Boston, it

166 CHAPTER 9

is perplexing to consider what might have changed. It should also be noted that state hospitals did not have the most humane track records regarding treatment of patients in the early part of the twentieth century. Worcester State Hospital (WSH) was certainly no exception. The Gothic architecture of WSH's campus gave the stereotypical sense of foreboding we have come to associate with institutions of the era, when people were hidden away, never to return to society.

While Drummond was in residence at Worcester State, multiple reports of abuse and inhumane conditions in the hospital made their way into Boston area newspapers. In an article about the dangers of flies running rampant, the *Trenton Evening Times* reported on the effects of flies in many locations, including Worcester State. In 1910, it reported, Dr. Orton of the "Worcester State Hospital for the Insane found that flies, breeding in huge numbers in piles of hops used as fertilizer near the hospital, were infesting the hospital, carrying the dysentery germs from patient to patient."[29] That seemed only the tip of the iceberg with far more horrific descriptions of the hospital surfacing soon thereafter. In 1913, nurses working at the hospital who acted as whistleblowers reported instances of torture as some patients were "dragged by [their] hair . . . naked through hallways, [with] splinters from the floor entering their bodies." Other charges reported in the *Boston Journal* were, "the older nurses subdue patients with back-handed blows that cut the face and lips. One nurse has the reputation of being able to 'handle any patient.' Violently insane patients are allowed to beat themselves against walls of iron strong rooms. Homicidal patients endanger lives of patients and nurses. Inmates are forced to sleep in winter in cold rooms with one thin blanket for covering. No treatment is given for the cure of insanity." These specific details, as well as other "unspeakable cruelty and neglect characterize[d] the treatment of patients at the Worcester State Hospital for the Insane. . . ."[30] Shortly after the report came out, thirteen other nurses stepped forward to corroborate the story and add their names to the charges against the hospital—charges that were already signed by thirty-six attendants and given to Governor Foss.[31] These charges focused primarily on the women's wing of the hospital, but the allegations were strong enough that Governor Foss requested reports on "all deaths at that and similar State institutions."[32] The allegations were denied subsequently and some of the women retracted their stories, saying they signed under

Once Was Lost   167

"misapprehension and deception." Still, thirty-three women maintained their stories. All forty-three male attendants denied any abuse.[33]

The torture probe encountered more difficulties as "one or more" of the members of the State Board of Insanity were "opposed to the introduction of any further testimony . . . regarding alleged abuses at Worcester State Hospital for the Insane." One nurse in particular, who asked that she be allowed to present photos she had taken and read from her diary while working there, saw her request denied by the board.[34] The testimony that was offered seemed to prove the allegations and further reports found that "ninety-five percent of the male attendants at the Worcester State Hospital for the Insane drink or are habitual drunkards. . . ."[35] One of the male patients suffered eight broken ribs and many of the patients were "sheeted" (swaddled tightly in a sheet) so that they could not move. There were still more who were "doped" with "hypnotic and sedative medicines . . . to put them to sleep."[36]

Even though the aforementioned details were clearly disturbing, the climax of the probe appeared to be Dr. H. V. Hendricks's reluctant admittance that "'some' perfectly sane persons are confined against their will in the State Hospital for the insane. . . ." He explained that since there were 386 patients under his care, he only had 28–30 seconds to examine each one.[37] Still, the whole investigatory probe may have had little result. The next year a male patient died from internal injuries resulting from eleven broken ribs, but the hospital was not found to be at fault. Instead, the ruling was that the man simply had bones that were too brittle.[38] A year after that it was discovered that a male patient at Worcester State had not died from heart failure, as originally reported, but rather it was "blood poisoning resulting from burns sustained when he was put into a bath much too hot for him, according to the . . . autopsy. . . ."[39] None of the reports specifically mention the renowned cyclist David Drummond, so it is difficult to ascertain the extent of abuses he may have suffered, or whether he experienced poor treatment at all. In fact, Massachusetts does not release medical records without a specialized court order so there are many unanswered questions about Drummond's predicament. How he came to be in Worcester State and why he remained institutionalized for more than twenty years. It is likely that he was kept heavily sedated and as the reports show, once admitted, it would have been nearly impossible to obtain release from such a hospital.

168   CHAPTER 9

Given that the 1930 census describes his occupation as "swabs floors" while he was at the hospital, it does sound like he was at least mobile late into life. Still, it is hard to know if he suffered any injuries or what his general mental state was while there. David Drummond would ultimately die at WSH on January 7, 1931. The cause of death given was chronic interstitial nephritis (an inflammation of the kidneys that can lead to renal failure) and senile dementia. It is unclear when he was first diagnosed with dementia, or what the circumstances were for the diagnosis and hospitalization. Regardless, though he was a successful cyclist and one of Boston's more prominent young Black men, life after fifty was potentially fraught with inhumane treatment and "unspeakable abuses" for David Drummond. It was the indignity of his ending that makes his story so tragic.

As sad as David Drummond's story may be, he was not the only prominent Black cyclist to endure such hardships in the early 1900s. William Fleming Ivy would have a very similar experience. Ivy raced at Vailsburg for several years as an amateur but then raced in Paris during the Fall of 1908 and into 1909, at which point he won several long-distance races as a professional.[40] Ivy was one of the many Black cyclists who had gone abroad to race professionally. By late February 1909, however, he was back in the United States, living in Connecticut and competing in various races, including the home trainer variety.[41] His name appeared in reports on cycling events up until 1909, at which point William Ivy seems to vanish from the world of cycling. Sometime around 1913, just prior to World War I, Ivy joined Company A of the 25th Infantry in the Army. He would wind up being discharged before the United States entered the war, however. A World War I draft card states that he was a "previous service man discharged on account of disability Feb. 26, 1917."[42] That disability was not disclosed, but he was quickly arrested after his discharge and taken to Stockton State Hospital in California in March 1917.

William Ivy, like David Drummond, was diagnosed with dementia. Ivy's diagnosis was dementia praecox, a term that is no longer used but simply meant it was a chronic and deteriorating condition. He was thirty-seven years old. A doctor's remarks in his case file states, "I do not think he has been right for some time. He was drunk [on sherry and Sunny Brook whisky] 2 days immediately after he was discharged from the army and that was the immediate cause of his arrest. I am inclined to think it is a case of Dementia Praecox."[43] The affidavit of insanity included in his file said that he was "suffering from delusions, that he is employed by a business firm and is handling their business affairs, sent telegrams to the President of the United States and to unknown women." He also claimed to see a comet in the sky and believed he could bring world peace with a banner or flag.[44] These ideas were ongoing, not born out of inebriation. His file does not offer much elaboration on how exactly he believed the flag could bring world peace but there is some indication that it may have been connected to his ideas about cycling and exercise.

Deeper into his records from Stockton State Hospital there are indications that the determined cause of his "dementia" was syphilis. During questioning by a Dr. Conzelmann, he was asked, "Did you ever hear if you were diseased or not?" Ivy responded, "I was tested when they came in 1915—and in 1916 after I had the operation [to relieve chronic constipation] they said it was syphilis and I asked him where he got the blood test and he said, 'Haven't you ever had one?' and I said, 'No.' I said, 'I don't belong in this Syphilis ward.' Three or four days after that, they had another blood test and those whose blood was impure were ordered to take treatment at Scofield Barracks Hospital. I asked my Captain when I got back to my Company, why they wanted to put my case as syphilis, from the blood test, when I had no blood test and if I had it, why they allowed me to go without treatment, and he said 'I don't know why, I cannot judge here.' and I said, 'Well, it is very funny. Why did you take my money?'" This was in reference to the $133 he was given after being discharged from the hospital. During the interview at Stockton State, the doctor asked, "Then you were discharged not in line of duty?" and Ivy said that he was, once he "got to America" arriving back from Hawaii.[45]

There were several questions about the flag that he had designed as well as when he came up with the idea and began to believe that it could bring world peace. This, the doctor seemed to believe, would help clear up exactly when Ivy began to exhibit the symptoms of untreated syphilis. His flag, which he described as an "Ethiopian flag" with the colors yellow, white, and blue, could help "lead this race to see the Light and Word of God, so they will understand His coming." He had it designed in 1914 by "the Elrey people" while in the army but said that it was a "bicycle flag" that was to "go over the roof piece of the Fleming Home Trainers up in Connecticut." When asked about Fleming Home Trainers, Ivy responded that it was an exercise.[46] Apparently, Ivy had created his own home trainer business, giving

170 CHAPTER 9

it his middle name. He was asked about his cycling career too, as further evidence of weakened mental faculties. An attending examiner, Dr. Young asked, "you claim to be the champion Negro Bicycle Rider in the world. What was the time you made at the Paris meet—in the 24 hour?" Ivy responded, "728 kilometers," and then Dr. Young followed up by asking how many miles that would be. Ivy responded vaguely that "a kilometer is less than a mile but over half a mile."[47] He performed well when questioned on current events, and passed tests in the areas of math, reading, writing, and retention, yet still he was judged to be impaired. His file also states that he "had [a] sore on [his] penis in 1905, no secondary symptoms."[48] The doctors discussed his condition with Dr. Young, admitting that he did not know why Ivy was discharged from the army, but due to the fact that his memory seemed good and that he had a history of a chancre, which was believed to have been syphilitic, they agreed the diagnosis of dementia praecox was appropriate.[49]

A section labeled "Continuous notes" in his file at Stockton State showed that on both June 9 and July 2 of 1917, he seemed to be improving. The July 2nd entry reads, "Patient has shown marked improvement, developed superficial insight into his condition, got away from his expansive ideas and worked well on the Ward. He was today sent to Cleveland by the State Deportation Agent."[50] Ivy would end up in Rock Island, Illinois where he seemed to return to a somewhat normal life. A draft card from 1918 and the 1920 census both list him as a crane operator for the Rock Island Arsenal. He lived in his own home with his second wife, Alice Ivy, who was twenty-one years his senior. In 1921, however, the Watertown State Hospital of Rock Island requested his records from Stockton State, suggesting that his mental problems had worsened. His mental state must have been deteriorating slowly. It is likely that he was in and out of the state hospital for the next few years. In 1924, it seemed he was still somewhat independent. The *Chicago Broad Axe* reported that he was among many Masons and other citizens to welcome Grand Master Samuels to Rock Island.[51] After his second wife's death in 1928, however, he soon seemed to no longer have the capacity to live on his own. It is not clear when he entered, but by 1930, he was clearly living at East Moline State Hospital (formerly known as Watertown State) on a permanent basis and there he would stay. A letter from 1938 and a draft card from 1942 both show he was still a resident at East Moline State. The draft card specifies that he was a voluntary patient at the hospital, while other records list him simply as a patient.[52] Dying in 1956, Ivy lived out the last thirty years of his life in Rock Island, Illinois. As his mental state worsened, his memory and his athletic achievements were slowly erased from existence. Aside from his sister, Rose Ivy Tyler, who was listed as his next of kin, there did not seem to be anyone left to tell his story. Undoubtedly, even the people that Ivy shared his story with later in life listened to his tales with a certain amount of incredulity.

While David Drummond and William Ivy both ended up living out their final years in mental institutions, Hardy Jackson would spend a significant portion of his twilight in a slightly different institution, prison. Jackson, who *The Bicycling World and Motorcycle Review* believed was the "most assiduous colored cyclist in Greater New York" had at least one previous arrest in 1906, when he was thirty-four. He and two other White cyclists were "charged with riding bicycles recklessly" after they accidently ran into three White women who were disembarking a transit car. This was perhaps an early instance in which Jackson witnessed the uneven scales of justice as his two White compatriots were released after paying $3 fines but the magistrate "held Jackson in $300 for examination."[53] Apparently, he was released soon thereafter and continued as a competitive cyclist; transitioning into a home trainer specialist around 1909 and then into Vaudeville as a performer around 1912. By his account, he was married five years later, around 1917, to Ida May Chandler and they had four children, Hardy, Paul, Dorothy, and Irma. Having left serious cycling behind, to a degree, his primary means of supporting his family was through work as a machinist, but he did continue to earn some money from cycling—four dollars per appearance at the Revere Cycling track in the summer months.

Hardy Jackson would be arrested a few more times after that first incident in 1906. In 1920 it was for "A&B," which is safe to assume was an assault and battery charge but there were no further details. Otherwise, there were a few separate arrests connected to the charge of lewd and lascivious cohabitation. This charge was more severe than those he faced previously because it carried with it the penalty of a few years of incarceration.

By today's standards, the thought that you could be arrested for living with someone out of wedlock seems almost absurd but such laws against adultery have a long history in the United States; some of which even survived into the recent era. Convictions for breaking these laws, however, all but disappeared by the 1970s. Dr. Joanne Sweeny, Professor of Law,

172 CHAPTER 9

argues, "Early cases were routinely composed entirely of circumstantial evidence that was used to prove the act of fornication or adultery. Courts emphasized that because of the secrecy involved in illicit sex, it is 'ordinarily impossible to prove it, except by circumstantial evidence.'" She shows that "observations of how parties behaved together in public, illegitimate children, a 'disposition' towards adultery, and even reputation could all constitute acceptable evidence of illicit sex."[54] Some of the evidence, as Sweeney points out, could even be outright racist, "the defendant's skin color, former slave status, and hairstyle have been used as evidence of illicit sexual intercourse."[55] If those forms of "evidence" were factored into Hardy Jackson's case, he stood little chance of being found innocent. Sadly, it is unsurprising then that he was convicted of two counts of lewd and lascivious cohabitation and sentenced to one year, six months in prison, and a $100 fine.

He served a little over eight months of the sentence at Suffolk County House of Correction at Deer Island before being released in March of 1926. Though Hardy Jackson claimed that he and Ida May Chandler were married at home in 1917 (he even named the preacher who officiated and his church affiliation), other parts of his prison record claim that they "never had any ceremony performed either church or civil marriage." Ida was referred to as his common law wife in many parts of the paperwork and all four of their children were considered illegitimate. They lived together until 1924, at which point she left him. According to her account, he was previously married, but she did not find out until after a year into their relationship. He allegedly "applied for a divorce but never received it." Indeed, both the census of 1900 and 1910 report that he was married to a woman named Bertha Jackson and had been married to her since about 1892. They were apparently still living together in 1910. There were no children and Bertha died around 1925. In spite of discovering that he was married a year into their relationship, Ida stayed with Hardy and they had at least four children together. Jackson claimed that Ida was pregnant when he met her but there was no child living with them who was old enough to prove that story, however, it is entirely possible that she had a miscarriage and/or lost the child.

It seems unlikely that Ida was the one to report Hardy Jackson for lewd and lascivious cohabitation, since she would have been incriminating herself as well. She probably would not have been arrested, since men were charged more often than women, but she did fear that the legal infraction could lead to her losing her children. Therefore, the circumstances leading up to his arrest are curious. The materials in his record (from a subsequent arrest) suggest that his arrest for lewd and lascivious cohabitation came about through the surveillance and complaints of his "neighbors." Dr. Sweeny's study of the history of adultery and fornication crimes points out that a large percentage of arrests for adultery came through the willingness of community members to spy on one another, but she adds that "police officers were also quite proactive in trying to catch people in the act of illicit sex."[56] As this was the case, it is highly probable that the complaints came either from people who simply did not like Hardy Jackson for various reasons, or they arose in connection to earlier charge of A&B, which may have led police to observe his activities more closely. Reports in his file make it clear that he was not trusted, especially not by the legal officials responsible for compiling the reports. Jackson was, for instance, described as a man that was "too smooth to be true" on April 29, 1930. The "early history and general reputation" section of his prison file states, "It is a well-known fact that he lived for years with a woman to whom he was not married [Ida Chandler]. He also has had a reputation for 'having a good line of talk.'" The investigator added, "Jackson is regarded as a menace to society in Lynn [Massachusetts]. His mode of living has been the cause of comment for many years. It is common opinion that he should be segregated from society. An additional reason for animosity towards him is his readiness to defend himself. It is said that he can always 'hand out a good line.' He attempted his wiles even on Judge Dillon, but did not succeed." To say that there was hostility toward Jackson because he defended himself and that he was always able to "hand out a good line," or be excessively charming to the point of deception, gets at some of the less overt racism Jackson and other Black cyclists would have faced in the first part of the twentieth century, even in cities thought to be bastions of Black independence like Boston. The racism he encountered in the world of cycling was one thing, but outside those boundaries, the racism was even more pervasive yet often harder to define. His experiences show that the challenges Black cyclists faced did not let up once they dismounted their machines, especially if they had the audacity to defend themselves.

The arrest and conviction for lewd and lascivious cohabitation was more of a temporary setback for Jackson. His next arrest, however, would lead to

174 CHAPTER 9

ruin. It was in December 1929, at fifty-eight years of age, that his life would take a drastic turn after being hauled in by police in Lynn, Massachusetts. He spent two months in jail before going to trial and when he finally stepped before the court, he had no council other than himself. It was there, in the Superior Criminal Court of Essex County, that he was convicted of statutory rape. This was a much more serious charge than the previous charge of lewd and lascivious cohabitation. Jackson was sentenced to 9–12 years in prison, which he was to serve at Charlestown State Prison in Massachusetts—the same prison where Sacco and Vanzetti would serve time before their executions and the same prison where Malcolm Little would begin his transformation into Malcolm X.

True to his "assiduous" nature, Hardy Jackson had continued to occupy his time outside the velodrome at various tasks, operating a radio store at one point and working subsequently for Kay Jewelry Store in Lynn. It was in that context that he came to know the subject of the charges against him, Mary Martello. She was thirteen years old and met Jackson while working at his radio store. While there were no statutory provisions for marriageable ages in Massachusetts in 1930, the common law dictated that Mary was old enough to be married (twelve years of age for girls was acceptable).[57] The age limit for statutory rape, however, was sixteen.

Statutory rape laws had actually changed within Jackson's lifetime. Up to the 1890s, the age of consent was ten to twelve years old. Arguments for enforcing the law often emphasized the protection of "white females and their premarital chastity—as property" rather than the idea of consent. Dr. Carolyn Cocca argues, "Statutory rape was a property crime."[58] It was in that era of progressivism that "a collation of feminists [the Women's Christian Temperance Union in particular], religious conservatives, and white working-class men's organizations lobbied together to raise the age of consent. Working men joined in because statutory rape was largely considered a crime against working-class females perpetrated by middle class men.[59] Dr. Cocca adds that "Black women's groups did support the idea . . . but they worried that more stringent age of consent laws within a racist society would be used to target black males, who were stereotyped as uncontrollable rapists of white women. . . ."[60] Ultimately, Black women's groups did not join the campaign but still, it was successful and "all states raised the age to 16 or 18."[61] It was not overwhelmingly popular, however. Many legislators "did not take the protectionist ideals very seriously" and even mocked them at times, with sarcastic proposals to go ahead and raise the age of consent to eighty-one. Many states even considered rolling-back the age to previous levels.[62] Once codified, the laws were used in some surprising ways, such as families "us[ing] the laws to try to control their 'incorrigible' and 'delinquent' daughters." Even if they protested, the daughters were unable to stop the prosecutions.[63]

At the time of the complaint, Mary Martello was working with Hardy Jackson at the Kay Jewelry Store, where he was a janitor. It was her father who pressed the charges, after he grew upset with her for "staying out late at night." When she came home late, it was often in the company of Hardy Jackson. The "Narrative of Offence" in his prison record explains: "The girl was questioned by Inspector Remsen of the Lynn Police and an agent of the Mass. S.P.C.C. [Society for the Prevention of Cruelty to Children]. She admitted to them that she had been assaulted by Jackson some few times. Jackson's two young sons reported that the girl often called at their house on her way to school and she and their father went into a bedroom and shut the door. When they came out, they said that Mary always had some money. Jackson told of giving the girl money in $4.00 amounts. At first, he said that it was her pay for services at the jewelry store, but when the manager of the store denied that she received any such pay, he said that he gave her amounts additional to the pay to make up for amounts that he owed her for services when she worked at his store." More specifically, Mary claimed that on "two or three occasions" he assaulted her by "taking down her bloomers and having intercourse." She was examined by a doctor and while the results have been redacted, the examination apparently did not exonerate Jackson. Under "causative factors" in his file, the investigator stated, "Jackson has been known as a man of low morals. That no doubt is the result of early home environment." This, he believed, was the reason why Jackson "did not scruple to take advantage" of "a girl that was neglected" and allowed to "be out on the streets."[64]

Since he was fifty-eight years old when convicted, serving the minimum sentence of nine years would make him sixty-seven before he was eligible for release. His records show that in spite of mostly good behavior, the first request for parole was denied and he, like William Ivy, also began to suffer from mental delusions. Jackson reportedly began to claim he believed, "a South American snake charmer stole his wife away and in so doing installed a snake in . . . [his] body so that he would die a slow and torturing death."[65]

176   CHAPTER 9

That delusion was possibly based in some bit of reality since there was a man from Central America, Michael Harrison, who was single and living in Hardy Jackson's wife Ida Chandler's house as a lodger. One investigator remarked on a potential relationship between Chandler and Harrison, after witnessing Harrison entering the house surreptitiously though the back door and adding that he was a "very buxom looking gentleman . . . who certainly looked far from a colored man." Earlier in the interview Chandler had claimed both of her boarders were "colored."

Shortly before Jackson's chimera manifested, he had been transferred from the state prison to the state farm, which was a lower security form of incarceration where the prisoners spent more of their time outdoors working. The onset of these delusions, however, prompted the Superintendent of the state farm to ask that Jackson be returned to the state prison. While claiming a snake was in his gastro-intestinal tract and that it would calm down when he ate spicy food but become agitated when he consumed cold foods, he also expressed "many ideas about how he was convicted for a crime which he did not commit, because certain people wanted him out of the way." Unlike Ivy, Jackson's spell sounded more like a temporary hallucination. The idea reportedly, "suddenly left him; so that he now realized that it was only imaginary" and he showed no other signs of delusions after that point. The doctor's report in his file added that he "seems to have all the native superstition of his race." This report weighed heavily into the denial of parole in 1937, but his file from Charlestown State does not extend beyond 1937, suggesting he was released from prison sometime after that.

His family believes that after release from prison he moved in with his second oldest son, Paul Jackson, who was on record for visiting him often in prison and whose name was mentioned on an insurance policy Hardy Jackson had through Metropolitan Life.[66] There is little record of how he occupied his time after release, but Jackson would die in 1943 at the age of seventy. Both of Hardy Jackson's most serious offenses, netting him around ten years in prison, came down to the fact that he participated in sexual acts with White females to whom he was not legally married. The last thirteen years of his life would all but ensure that any accolades he deserved and any achievements he made in the sport of cycling would be erased from the annals of history.

For "Major" Taylor, Woody Hedspeth, William Ivy, Hardy Jackson, Kittie Knox, David Drummond, and so many others, the bicycle was instrumental

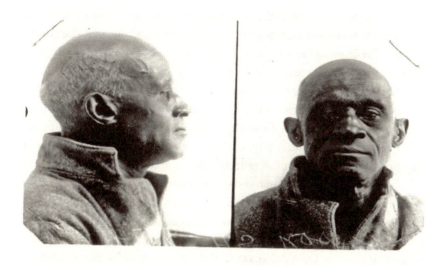

```
Hardy A. Jackson        #3974
     September 16, 1936
```

Hardy A. Jackson, inmate #17994, Charlestown State Prison, September 16, 1936. Photo courtesy of the Massachusetts Archives.

in the search for social mobility and greater liberties. It could literally take them around the world, but at the same time, it could only take them so far. It was used to secure travel throughout the United States and through Europe—even to Russia and Australia. Bicycles aided Black cyclists in their insistence on greater freedoms, but all of that was fleeting. Even on the bike, the path to freedom was not easy, but once the bicycle was put away any sort of status Black cyclists may have achieved soon vanished. One thing they all had in common was just how quickly they were forgotten once their cycling careers were over. This was true even for "Major" Taylor. Although he is the most well-known of all the Black cyclists, he too was largely forgotten, especially after the death of his contemporaries. Still today, biographers talk about him as the "forgotten" cyclist. If that is true of Taylor, then it is certainly much truer of Hedspeth, Knox, Ivy, and all the other Black cyclists of the 1880s through the 1910s. The sport changed considerably during that period and by the 1910s it was on its way out of favor with the American public. It had lost much of its appeal for the masses. Aside from the six-

178   CHAPTER 9

day races with their late-night crowd of gambling and drinking revelers. In America, cycling moved beyond adult interest and entered the child's realm.[67] Cycling magazines ceased production and newspaper coverage of cycling events was far less frequent.

Even in sports that remained popular, like prize fighting and horse racing, Black athletes faced similar circumstances. Isaac Murphy, the famous Black jockey who won the Kentucky Derby three times along with many other races, amassing huge payouts, died at the age of thirty-five. While the funeral and even his casket reflected the respect the community had for him, he was buried in an unmarked grave in a small Black cemetery in Lexington, Kentucky. By the 1960s, hardly anyone even knew where his body had been laid to rest.[68] Another well-known and successful Black jockey, Lonnie Clayton saw his fortunes dwindle after retirement and he was forced to move his family from Arkansas to California, where he would work as a doorman and eventually die of pneumonia. There were still other Black jockeys with tragic endings like Willie Simms, James Perkins, and Albert Isom.[69] In prize fighting there are even more examples with Jack Johnson being the best-known case as he was forced into poverty and a life on the run from legal authorities over trumped up charges of violating the Mann Act. The historian Louis Moore gives details of many other Black boxers going broke after retirement. "Sugar Ray" Robinson, Joe Louis, Henry Armstrong, Peter Jackson, and so many others saw their fortunes depleted by taxes and greedy managers.[70] Of course, the finer details of what happened to Black athletes after their careers were over differed but the final result of being reduced to a life of poverty was a trend that was certainly not unique to the sport of cycling. Horse racing and bicycle racing had much in common, due to the extent that Black athletes were pushed out and largely forgotten.

The Black cyclists of the 1880s through the 1900s had made important headway in using the bicycle for significant gains. Earning a living and sometimes a considerable amount of wealth from cycling, as well as winning status and esteem among the middle classes, was important to the struggle for equality. As their stories show, however, those gains were short lived. It would be hard to argue that "Major" Taylor and other Black cyclists broke the color-line in cycling because it reverted to a sport that was, and still is, mostly associated with the White middle class. The sometimes premature, and often ignoble ending of so many of the Black cyclists from this era led all these figures to become spirits that were lost. Their progress and deeds were increasingly difficult to observe as the sandstorm of time covered over the in-roads they had made. The fact that they became lost would only exacerbate future struggles for diversity and inclusivity in the sport of cycling from the 1930s into the present era. Remembering their stories, their struggles and their successes, is the best way to ensure that all they worked for was not done in vain. Many Black cyclists lived dedicated, yet relatively quiet, lives of protest. While they tell us much about the origins and diversity of the revolting Black athlete, they also present a broader picture of what life was like for Black Americans seeking freedom from the radically racist period of Jim Crow segregation in the Progressive Era.

Epilogue

Born Again

Through the 1920s, '30s, and '40s, there is scant evidence of Black cyclists competing professionally, or otherwise, in the United States. In fact, there was little press coverage of cycling in general. Six-day racing certainly continued in the 1920s and there were flashes of what looked like cycling's return in the mid-1930s, but it was only a brief gasp for air in what was an otherwise extended suffocation of adult cycling in the United States. For the most part, during this period the bicycle thrilled children, but nearly everyone out of high school seemed too bored, embarrassed, or afraid to ride a bicycle on public roads. Largely forgotten as a sport, bicycle racing continued in the United States but only on the margins. Perhaps the one thing keeping the sport of cycling holding on was the fact that it was an Olympic sport. It is one of the few perennial sports that has appeared in all of the modern Olympic Games since their resurrection in 1896. The fact that U.S. Olympians fared poorly in cycling events in the first half of the twentieth century, however, did not bode well for an Olympic committee that would rather invest money in the sports with the highest probability of netting medals. Still, it was in the pursuit of an Olympic medal that the first Black cyclist to gain notoriety in more than forty years would emerge.

The Black cyclists to rise out of the Civil Rights Era and in the shadow of the Vietnam War were not the descendants of "Major" Taylor, Woody Hedspeth, William Ivy or any other notable Black cyclist from the early

182   *Epilogue*

1900s. In fact, other than Taylor, they may not have heard of these men. One of those young cyclists, Alex Harsley, says that he and other Black cyclists he knew in New York City during the 1950s had in fact heard of Taylor, and they thought, "if he can do it, we can do it too." This sort of inspiration was a major goal in Taylor's decision to publish his autobiography. Harsley discovered the bicycle for himself around 1943, when he was just four or five years old. He and his friends found a rusty old model in a barn in rural South Carolina. Even though he did not know how to ride a bicycle and had never been on one, he dared to be the first to "slide" down the hill on it. He was immediately enthralled with the machine. After his family moved to New York in 1948, Harsley began to ride more seriously. This was especially true when he endeavored to ride a borrowed bicycle from Harlem to Orange, New Jersey—a round trip of around fifty miles. From there he decided he wanted a lighter bicycle for racing, and so he worked and saved his money until he was able to buy his first racing machine—a Freju model from Tom Avenia at his shop on 119th Street between Park and Madison Avenues.[1] More important perhaps than selling Harsley his first race bike, Avenia introduced Harsley to another Black cyclist named Herbie Francis. They quickly found they shared a lot of interests and started doing long training rides together around 1958. Francis was young, around eighteen at the time, but he was already determined to compete in the Olympics. Harsley and Francis were not the only ambitious Black cyclists in New York at the time.

Another young Black cyclist in New York making a name for himself was sixteen-year-old Perry Metzler. Metzler would become the first Black cyclist to win a national championship since "Major" Taylor.[2] He, and his twin brother Jerry Metzler, as well as several other Black youngsters from Brooklyn, rode together as a part of the Crusaders Club. It was Jerry who was the first from the club to secure a victory, however, winning the twenty-five-mile time trial for the junior division in 1954, but Perry got second place and his perseverance in the sport would outlast his brother's. Both were mentored by yet another Black cyclist named Amos Ottley from Queens who was in his early thirties. Many of their early achievements occurred at the local velodrome in Flushing Meadows. It was not uncommon for the Metzlers to ride their bikes to the races there, traveling from their family's apartment in the public housing high-rises located in Bedford-Stuyvesant.[3] While the Crusaders Club, in its short-lived tenure, and New York in general

Epilogue   183

seemed to offer the Black cyclist some opportunities in the 1950s, the rest of the United States could prove entirely less welcoming.

The Metzler brothers learned this the hard way in 1956, after winning first and second in the New York State Amateur Bicycle League of America Championship. This qualified them for nationals, which were to be held in Orlando, Florida. Even though their mentor, Amos Ottley, discouraged them from making the trip, the twins went anyway. Ottley, recognizing the fact that even in Brooklyn, there were places he could not go in the 1950s, believed Florida would prove much more restrictive. The twins, having lived in Mississippi before their family moved to Brooklyn, hoped that he was wrong but soon discovered otherwise. After disembarking the bus they had taken from New York to Florida, they found that no hotels or restaurants near the venue for the championships would accommodate them. The two were devastated and forced to make their way back to New York without competing. The disappointment was enough to drive Jerry Metzler from the sport completely.[4] Perry would not give up as easily. He went on to accomplish even bigger things on his bicycle.

If Metzler heard stories of "Major" Taylor's victories and sought to emulate his success, it is also true that he was inspired by a Barbadian immigrant who imported a renewed vigor for bicycle racing. At least that seemed to be the case in New York City, the temporary hub of the rebirth of the Black cyclist. His name was Ken Farnum and he competed as a cyclist for his native country of Barbados in the 1952 Olympics in Helsinki. It was just after those games that he established residency in Manhattan. Perry Metzler, along with his coach Ottley, Herbie Francis, and another Black cyclist named Jeff Wood would occasionally get together with Farnum for training rides.[5] Metzler, Wood, and Francis all experienced significant success on the bike but it was Metzler and Francis who would make the biggest waves—with Metzler going on to become the first Black cyclist to win an Amateur Bicycle League of America national title and medal.[6]

As the 1960 Olympics of Rome drew near, Perry Metzler was poised to compete for the United States, especially since the Rome Olympics would allow the US to send two match race sprinters. Jeff Wood had quit the sport by that time and Metzler was still training daily, between shifts in the garment district of New York. His talents had caught the eye of the Century Road Club of New York, which sought to recruit him, but it was soon pointed out that they still had a statute in place that effectively barred Black cyclists

184 *Epilogue*

from membership. Seemingly unfazed, Metzler claimed to be Mexican in his application materials and was granted membership. That was not enough to save him from Uncle Sam, however. In 1960, Perry Metzler was drafted into the army and that seemed to dash his shot at the Olympics. Even with a United States Olympic Cycling Committee member, Al Toefield, petitioning the army on Metzler's behalf to be assigned to the special services so that he could continue to train, it was a Colonel from the South who blocked his transfer.[7] Metzler would end up dying in Vietnam.

The closing of the Olympic door for Metzler, due to being drafted into military service, opened the door for another Black cyclist—the 20-year-old man from Harlem with a much more muscular physique than the average competitive cyclist, Herbie Francis. While he seemed a little too muscular and therefore too heavy to be a threat, Francis had a powerful sprint that made him well-suited for short fast efforts.[8] Francis had an early breakthrough when he was invited to compete in the 1959 Six-Day Bicycle Race held at Madison Square Garden. It was around this time that Alex Harsley had taken a step back from cycling to pursue his passion for photography. At the same time, he became a more dedicated student of cycling tactics, doing so from the sidelines enabled him to help Herbie Francis hone his strategy in local races, such as those at Willets Point, which was the location of a makeshift velodrome that incorporated a parking lot as part of the track.[9] It was also the location where Francis made a name for himself by beating one of the strongest riders in the United States at the time, Jack Simes III, a White cyclist. Simes and Francis would wind up teaming together to compete for the United States in the Rome Olympics. This made Francis the first Black cyclist to compete in the Olympics on behalf of the United States. Both Simes and Francis, however, were eliminated from the competition fairly quickly.[10] The experience in Rome seemed to crush Francis's aspirations. He told Harsley that the new experience of riding on a track with steeply banked turns had been alien to him and Simes, and he blamed the lack of experience in that sort of environment for their quick exit from the competition.[11] Regardless of the failure to medal, Francis seemed to have broken through an important barrier. As a representative for the United States in the 1960 Olympics, he made considerable progress over the Black cyclists of the early 1900s who struggled to even be considered true American citizens. Even though he and Metzler both probably fell short of the goals they had set for themselves, their efforts and achievements would

Epilogue

inspire other Black cyclists to press onward. While Francis may have given up on his own cycling aspirations, he recognized the importance of developing other riders in the United States and began a bicycle racing program on Morningside Avenue in Harlem near Columbia University.[12]

The most immediate and successful Black cyclist to rise out of Francis's and Metzler's wake was Oliver "Butch" Martin of Harlem. Martin's rise in the sport was meteoric. Making his way into the pages of *Ebony* by the age of 21, readers were told: "Not many youngsters become sports stars at 20. Even fewer turn out to be headliners in minor sports and hardly ever does a young Negro athlete go places outside the big spectators' sports. That's what makes Oliver (Butch) Martin Jr. so amazing. He's only 21 and is already a big leaguer in a sport most Americans ignore and where you would least expect to find a Negro—bicycling."[13] The article recounts his entrance into the sport after seeing a group of cyclists riding down the street in Harlem when he was fifteen. He immediately asked his parents' permission and financial assistance in buying a bike. That first bike cost his parents $119. His mother was floored by the price saying, "that's more than our rent."[14] Somewhat begrudgingly, they bought him the bike anyway and Martin quickly put it to good use, riding it as much as he could. He joined the Unione Sportiva Italiana cycling team one year later. The difficulties for Black cyclists in an otherwise White sport was not lost on *Ebony*, which added that Unione Sportiva was "one of the few U.S. clubs which admits Negroes. A close friend [Jerry Metzler] dropped out of a club three years ago because of anti-Negro bias."[15] Martin also experienced his own fair share of inequities. He admits that one of the things that changed him at an early age was winning a junior's race by a wheel's length but then finding that the judges' placed him second and gave first to the other rider, who happened to be White, like the judges. In Martin's words they did it "because they knew I was Black." On another occasion, Martin was given second place in a time-trial event due to the fact that all five judges recorded a different time for him. Since they could not agree on his time, they argued that they could not confidently say he won. When Martin complained to his father and seemed to want to quit the sport, his father said, "next time, go out there and win by such a wide margin, they'll have no choice but declare you the winner."[16]

Brushing episodes like that aside and using them to fuel his fire, Martin quickly made his way through the ranks winning a junior title as a rookie in

186   *Epilogue*

a 50-mile road race and from there he continued on his upward trajectory moving into the top five among professional rankings and qualifying for the U.S. Olympic cycling team in 1964. He excelled in the longer distance races, with the ability to race over 87 miles at an average speed of 28.5 miles per hour.[17] Falling short of medaling in the 4000-meter pursuit at the 1964 Olympics, Martin showed that he was not satisfied with merely being a part of the Olympics by moving to Italy to learn from and race against some of the world's best in 1965–66. The trip abroad proved worthwhile as he won four races, finished second in eleven others, and made it to the top 5 in twenty-six other races. He qualified for the 1968 Olympic cycling team and the 1971 Pan American Team. All told, Martin won more than fifty races in his career.[18]

Like Perry Metzler, Butch Martin was unable to afford a large enough course load at the City College of New York to warrant a deferment and he too was drafted into the army. Unlike Metzler, however, Martin was able to make his way into the special service as a member of the U.S. Army cycling team.[19] He attributes this to his father, who had some political pull in New York.[20] As a special service member, Martin was able to train for the 1968 Olympics in Mexico City. While being a two-time Olympian and competing in the Pan American games is impressive enough, Martin arguably made an even bigger impact on cycling in the United States when he retired from professional racing and began an extensive coaching career. Beginning in 1974, he coached the U.S. men's 100K Team Time Trial to a ninth place finish, and then he served as the U.S. national road coach from 1975 to 1977, including the 1976 Olympics in Montreal where American George Mount took sixth and the 1977 Venezuela World Championships where one of his female athletes, Connie Carpenter, took second in the women's road race.[21] After taking a decade or two off from coaching to start a family and pursue a career in business, Martin came back to the sport in the 2000s. He not only raised the bar for American cycling, coaching athletes to impressive finishes at a time in which American cyclists generally finished at the back of the pack, or not at all, but he also brought long-standing and visible diversity to the sport.

Butch Martin's impact on the homogeneity of cycling was apparent in his connection to the most prominent Black cyclist of the 1980s, Nelson Vails. In the late 1970s, Butch Martin worked with people connected to Muhammad Ali due to Ali's efforts to start a bicycle club and racing team.

Epilogue 187

The turnout for their club was little under-whelming, however, with only 10–12 kids showing up. Ultimately, the club was short-lived and the money quickly ran out. It was at one of these club meetings that Nelson's older brother Ronnie first introduced him to competitive cycling.[22] Vails was also from Harlem, where he was the youngest of ten brothers and sisters. He quickly announced his arrival on the scene at local races in Central Park while still young. Outside the racing world, he worked as a bicycle messenger to help support his family. He trained and raced locally during his time off from work.[23] All that work helped to build powerful legs and lungs. He soon became more serious about the sporting aspects of cycling after joining the Toga Bike Shop cycling team. This led to him being invited to a U.S. Cycling Federation development camp in Colorado in 1981. It was there that he earned a spot on the 1983 Pan American Games team. He would go on to win a gold medal at those games. He also succeeded in becoming the U.S. sprint champion in 1984 as well as the tandem champion in 1984, 1985, and 1986. More importantly, Vails competed in the 1984 Olympics and won the silver medal, coming in second to his American compatriot, Mark Gorski. Marking another momentous occasion, this was the first time a Black cyclist had won a medal for the United States. Vails did not make it onto a Wheaties box, nor did he gain any huge endorsements, but he did make his way into a cameo for the movie *Quicksilver* starring Kevin Bacon. Released in 1986, Bacon's character worked for a bicycle messenger service and playing the role as a fellow messenger was easy for Vails since he had actual experience. After the 1984 Olympics, Vails turned professional and specialized in 6-day races throughout Europe and then the Keirin Circuit in Japan—a very popular and lucrative variety of racing there.[24] Vails was ultimately inducted into the United States Bicycling Hall of Fame in 2009. His 1984 Olympic compatriot, Mark Gorski, however, was given the same honor fourteen years earlier in 1995. Another 1984 silver medalist in cycling from the United States, Leonard Nitz, was inducted in 1996.[25] The fact that it took thirteen more years for Vails' induction than his peers is just further evidence that, historically, the Black cyclist has not been given the same support and treatment as their White competitors, even in the recent past.

It would take nearly two decades before there would be another Black cyclist to assume the mantle of Vails and all those who had come before. He did not know Vails when he got his start and he lived on the other side of the continent, but there was a connection. It would be on the campus of

188 *Epilogue*

California State, at that that very same cycling track where Nelson Vails won his silver medal, where the young Black cyclist from Compton, California would get his introduction to competitive cycling. It was almost accidental, the way Rahsaan Bahati came to the sport. After getting in trouble at school, he was given the option of either spending time after school in detention or going to the velodrome used for the 1984 Olympics to learn about riding and racing "bikes." When Bahati was first presented with the two options, he mistakenly thought he would get to ride dirt bikes (motorcycles) and so it was an easy choice for him. After finding out it would be bicycles with skinny tires on an indoor track, he was less excited but stuck with it. Still, he kept it low-key at first, hiding his lycra spandex gear from his friends at school because he was sure they would make fun of him.[26] By the time he was 18, Bahati was already the United States Junior criterium champion and road champion (two separate categories and styles of racing). He also became the United States Cycling Federation amateur national champion for the criterium in the same year. He would go on to have some success at the collegiate level, racing, in part, for Team Major Taylor at Indiana University's Little 500. In the early 2000s Bahati had several significant wins in the professional ranks but it was in 2008 that he really made a statement by winning the United States National Criterium Championships. He won many other prestigious races that year but as National Champion, he would wear a stars and stripes designation on his jersey for the entire season of 2009.

Bahati continued racing, often winning, as a professional through 2013, at which point he retired. More recently, the ten-time U.S. National Champion has spent time working on the Bahati Foundation, which he created. In part, this is his own team, which works on developing diversity in the sport through mentoring young riders who are at a disadvantage in competitive cycling because they lack the resources and support network of many of those whom they compete against. As he works with inner-city youth, whom he reminds people can also be White, the diversity that he is bringing to the sport is socioeconomic first. In this manner, locally, he is helping to level the playing field. Bahati also serves as a brand ambassador for the aptly named Giant bicycle company—Giant because they are such a major player in bicycle production worldwide. On top of that, he is the social impact manager for Zwift, an online cycling app that allows cyclists to compete against each other using "smart" trainers (home trainers with the ability to communicate with pcs, tablets, and phones) all around the world.[27]

With more than twenty years of experience in the sport, Rahsaan Bahati has a lot of insights into cycling and its apparent challenges to becoming a more inclusive sport. Bahati told *Velonews* magazine, "I've dealt with so much racism, injustice, being marginalized for what I listen to, what I look like, how I dress, how I move around. And I mean, in the bike industry. I'm not gonna say, I've become used to it, but I figured out how to maneuver. . . . What sucks is that I've had to conform to get my foot in the door just a little. As long as I'm getting the job done I should be treated like others, but that's not reality."[28] He certainly faced some rejection while racing, recounting instances like the time he was at the Tour of America's Dairyland (a race that was formerly run by Oliver "Butch" Martin) and a White cyclist told him, "no one wants your Black ass out here."[29] He can give many other similar examples and has said that when he went to Europe, to race and train, it was "the same level of ignorance and racism" as he recounts how he was held to a higher standard than some of his White American compatriots who had also made the trip abroad.[30] Bahati's experiences seem to reflect the experiences of so many Black athletes over the years—simply being as good as their peers was not good enough. To thrive in sport, they had to be better, clearly superior, or they were quickly written off just as Bahati was when he overheard someone with team management say, "he's no good."[31]

When asked if he believes the racism he has experienced in cycling is systemic Bahati spoke about his 2006 season. "My experience," he said, "on TIAA-CREF in 2006 was like being in a predominantly white fraternity, and I didn't fit in. That's what it felt like. And what it feels like today." He then spoke of other retired racers who are still involved with the sport but have done nothing to make the sport more inclusive making the point that their cliques have consisted of the same core group for years. He said, "They're not bringing new people to help develop a new formula. . . . It's this frat and once you're in, you're in, and that's it." Bahati argues that "there are a lot of people in the industry who aren't doing enough to include people of color" and they are "part of a system" that has done very little "to help the Black community."[32]

In 2020 it seemed that the United States Cycling Organization was coming to terms with the lack of diversity in the sport by making an announcement that it would work toward diversity and inclusion. Bahati's reaction was, "OK, you already knew you were part of the problem, why did it take you so long to say something? Alright, next time there's a big round of hiring, how many Black people will you interview? How many will be on your board? Black people work. They're in R&D and science and accounting. I work for Zwift. There's probably five Black people that work for Zwift. That's where you can start making a difference. How do you have this diversity and inclusion program, when the person running it has no idea what it feels like to be Black and excluded? It's like saying you work for Ferrari but have never driven one. Change can start there."[33] When asked about cycling media outlets and their role in excluding people of color he said, "Now there's so much content out there. For a while it was just ones or twos, like Gideon [Massie] and Nelson [Vails], and then it was me. . . . Now the community is bigger. There's more Black kids and women racing bikes, and our story is still not always told." He also made a point about brands using Black people in their ads and attempts to use diversity in their campaigns, but he does not really believe that is evidence of a sincere push for change. 'There are more Black people buying bikes than ever, we better put them in ads,' he said.[34]

While Rahsaan Bahati has been working to improve the sport for more than a decade, there are newer faces in the effort to make cycling more diverse and inclusive such as Ayesha McGowan from Atlanta, Georgia and Justin Williams from Los Angeles. McGowan set her sights on becoming the first female Black cyclist from the United States to race as a professional several years ago. She ultimately accomplished that goal, with an announcement in February 2021 that she would ride as a professional for the Liv Racing WorldTour Team.[35] Simply racing as a professional, however, is not enough for McGowan as she has taken a lead as an activist cyclist who works to make cycling more inclusive, especially for women of color. She does this through public speaking engagements, interviews, her own published writing and podcast, as well as her work to spearhead initiatives to raise money to support young cyclists of color. She has helped create a mini-grant where five to seven women of color will receive entry and support to race the Tour of America's Dairyland. This includes race entries, travel, accommodations, food, race kits, transportation during the race week, and mechanical support at the race. The aim is to get young women the experience and points that can come through racing the Tour of America's Dairyland that will allow them to move up in rank.[36] It is surprising that McGowan is the first Black woman to attain the status of a professional cyclist but maybe it should not be. After all, the situation for Black men in the modern peloton is barely better. In 2020, less than 1 percent of the 743 cyclists riding at the World Tour (elite) level were Black. The number was smaller with USA Cycling, where zero of the 113 professional riders were Black. In the 2020 edition of the Tour de France, of the 176 riders to take the start, only one was Black, French cyclist Kèvin Reza.[37] McGowan and Williams, however, both of whom turned professional in 2021, are clearly trying to change those statistics.

As an eleven-time U.S. National Champion, Justin Williams has certainly been cause for some excitement around the issue of diversity in cycling and the direction of the sport in general. Williams, from South Central Los Angeles, like Rahsaan Bahati, says that he has also had to "tone down" who he was in the past to fit into the sport. He argues that making the sport more accessible could serve to deepen the pool of talent.[38] Williams began cycling at an early age after realizing it could be a way for him to bond with his father, who is from Belize and very passionate about cycling—like many people from the country. Like Martin, Bahati, and many other promising young riders, Williams made the trip to Europe where the learning curve is much steeper. While the adjustment to European racing and living in Europe, away from one's family, is difficult for most young riders, Williams found it doubly hard as a young Black man. He believes the trip may have been more successful if he had a deeper network of support. With experiences that seemed to mirror that of Bahati, while in Europe for just the one season in 2009, Williams said he was called "difficult" and "a charity case" as he was "stereotyped . . . as an angry Black man." He explained, "I was written off faster than other riders and watched a lot of guys get on teams that never won a race. As a Black man from the 'hood, I was typecast before managers even got to know me."[39] The next year he came back to the United States, put cycling on the back burner and pursued a degree in graphic design. He would return to cycling in 2016, however. His motivation really started to rise after seeing his younger brother Cory go through many of the same things he experienced in cycling.[40] Together, he and Cory have built the Legion Cycling of Los Angeles, a professional team "determined to make a difference in the sport." They do that through their representation of diverse racial and ethnic backgrounds, but also through their work "to provide a pathway into the sport for young athletes from

192   *Epilogue*

all backgrounds. . . . In 2020 . . . the team managed to raise $50,000 to help increase diversity and inclusion within cycling." In their own words, "Legion is about more than becoming a better cyclist, it's about becoming a better person and redressing some of the imbalances that continue to characterize our sport."[41] Justin Williams says, "we are the change we want to see . . . we are on a mission to become the only Black owned professional cycling team in America in 2021."[42] The fact that his team is Black owned is what really stands out. For the first time, control is in the hands of a Black cyclist. A higher percentage of any money the team earns will go to the Black cyclist—a deviation from the long history of White owners and managers profiting from the labor of Black bodies.

While Black ownership in cycling is certainly an admirable endeavor, Legion of Los Angeles and Ayesha McGowan, on a more fundamental level, are adamant in showing that representation matters. Justin Williams says, "if you give kids something they can look at . . . a person they can . . . aspire to be or that they admire, that's the first step in getting people into a sport. If no one looks like you when you go out to a bike race or if you see a bike race on t.v. . . . it's not something you will believe you can do and that's something that we want to focus on. Us being a team that promotes diversity is great, but us getting on the podium and standing on the top step from time to time is even better. . . . If we can be this face that is winning races and showing younger kids from different demographics that this is possible, you can do it . . . that's a really big step in the right direction for getting them to maybe consider bike racing as a viable option for the future."[43] Williams has designed the team so that he can use his own image and results to get the resources that will help level the field for other young riders who do not come from the traditional White middle class backgrounds. He feels it is important to create something that more people than just himself can benefit from. That is what the team he has created is about; making it so that the riders who enter the sport after him can have the opportunity he does not feel he fully had.[44]

In the throes of the #BlackLivesMatter movement, some of the powerbrokers in the cycling industry, such as Dennis Kim, the global vice president for marketing at Cannondale, proclaims the company took "a hard look in the mirror and asked ourselves what type of role we would play in making change."[45] On January 25, 2021 the virtual cycling and running app Zwift, for which Rahsaan Bahati works, announced the "Black Celebration

Epilogue 193

Series." This series would run throughout the year with various activities and events to "celebrate the Black experience in cycling and running as it shines a light on the accomplishments of Black athletes and lays the foundation for future advancement."[46] The company felt it was necessary that while the initiative was launched during Black History Month, it was "committed to the continual recognition and support of Black athletes." The company also established a team for Diversity, Equity, Inclusion, and Belonging at the end of 2020 with a Black woman (Lisa Bourne) leading the effort and guests from the Black Cyclists Network as well as the Level Up Movement and individual Black cyclists like Cory Williams, Ama Nsek (both from Legion of Los Angeles), Nelson Vails, and Rahsaan Bahati. The company also announced it would be participating in a partnership where it would donate $25,000 to the Los Angeles Bicycle Academy, "a nonprofit on a mission to empower, educate, and develop leadership skills in boys and girls from communities where access to the sport of cycling is limited." It does this through a youth education program, a community bike shop, and a youth cycling team.[47]

The United States Cycling Association (USAC), a modern version of the League of American Wheelmen which serves as a sanctioning body for most of the domestic races in the United States, also seems to be willing to do more than simply pay lip-service to efforts to increase diversity and inclusion in the sport. They began by conducting a demographic study in 2020 to get a better idea of what the percentages look like. The study was a survey made available to members of USAC asking questions about racial, ethnic, and gender identity as well as other basic demographic information. A little more than 7,000 members responded and of those, 86% identified as White or Caucasian, 6% Hispanic or Latino, 4% Asian or Asian American, 3% Black or African American, 1% American Indian or Alaskan Native, and 1% Native Hawaiian or other Pacific Islander; 2% of the respondents chose not to disclose and 3% said they were "something else."[48] While the results are not surprising, perhaps they can serve to validate the need for deliberate action. To that end, USAC plans to launch a collegiate cycling team seed program and cycling industry mentorship program at Historically Black Colleges and Universities and Tribal Colleges and Universities. It also has plans for "Let's Ride Camps" which will teach kids about bike safety and "provide access to bikes for kids who would not otherwise have such an opportunity."[49] It is not clear whether the "access to bikes" the children will

194 *Epilogue*

receive is temporary and only during the camp or if there is some kind of long-term or permanent donation plan. The program sounds very similar to the type of thing the Cycle Trades of America planned in the 1940s and '50s, not in attempts to diversify cycling but more so as a means of selling more bicycles. Since children represent a dwindling number of cyclists in the United States, the "Let's Ride Camps" seem more about building interest in bicycles for the future among the general population, not necessarily an effort to make the sport more diverse and inclusive, but USAC may hope it is a side effect. USAC has also created a task force on diversity and inclusion in the sport, which includes Ayesha McGowan and Rahsaan Bahati among its ten members. Even the League of American Bicyclists, the most direct descendant of the League of American Wheelmen, has presented its first annual Kittie Knox award for championing equity, diversity, and inclusion to McGowan. This seems to represent a significant move toward diversity in the sport considering the fact that the League of American Wheelmen still had the racially exclusive language adopted under William Watts' leadership on their books up until 1999.[50] All of these developments over the course of 2020 and 2021 seem to suggest that key players in the U.S. cycling industry are beginning to wake up. Of course, some entities are more daring than others.

Rivendell Bicycle Works, a boutique manufacturer of bicycle frames in the San Francisco Bay Area went a few steps beyond others in the industry by announcing plans for "Black Reparations Pricing" in late 2020. The program would give a 45% discount to Black customers. Their CEO, Grant Petersen, posted the announcement saying:

> The American bicycle industry has been racist, often overtly racist, since 1878, and Rivendell has been obliviously—not 'obviously'—racist ever since 1994. We say this not to scold the industry, not to scold other bicycle businesses, and not to be on trend. . . . Racism doesn't respond to inaction or self-proclamation. In other words, it doesn't go away when you know, even in your bones, that all people are created equal. It responds to anti-racist action. Reparations are an example. Not because Reparations are "a nice thing to do," but because they're owed. Reparations acknowledges that, in this country, white wealth—recent or inherited/generational, has been 'earned' by the labor of Black people, who, even after slavery, were never given a leg up. Your non-Black tycoon great-grandpa may have been born poor, may have been a sharp and clever go-getter at the top of his class, but he wasn't born Black.[51]

Epilogue 195

This was perhaps the boldest initiative to emerge from industry leaders and as such, it was met with a considerable amount of controversy. There were "nasty emails, phone calls, threats to [individuals at the company] and threats of lawsuits, a flurry of one-star ratings on assorted Yelp-Google type sites, and a painful legal bill."[52] Rivendell felt they were, "from a legal perspective . . . handcuffed" and announced the termination of the Black Reparations Pricing and a change for the Black Reparations fund. It would become instead, the Bicycles R Fun (fund) and all proceeds from the sales of BRF stickers, buttons, patches, hats, mugs, et cetera, "will be used legally and appropriately to help more under-represented people ride bikes—regardless of brand. . . . All of it will help put more people, of assorted colors, genders, and whatever, onto bicycles."[53] This brought up an important point—one that some critics of the Black Reparations Pricing program also noted. Cycling has not only effectively excluded Black people in the United States, but all people of color.

As the reaction to the Black Reparations Pricing program suggests, there were outspoken opponents, with those who were even willing to resort to violence and intimidation to dissuade Rivendell. Some of those reactions were born out of alarmist feelings that Whiteness was under threat. The idea for this policy came amid the #BlackLivesMatter movement and at a time when discussions of governmental reparations for Black people were on the rise. In fact, House Resolution 40 was introduced in January 2021. It would establish a "Commission to Study and Develop Reparation Proposals for African Americans Act."[54]

Barely more than a week after Rivendell announced its program, "Harmeet Dhillon, a lawyer, former Republican Party official, frequent Fox News guest, and founder of the Center for American Liberty" went to work in attempts to stop the program.[55] Citing federal and state laws prohibiting businesses from racial discrimination, Dhillon issued a press release saying the program was illegal. She explained, "Every customer is entitled to pricing on non-discriminatory terms. We demand you discontinue this policy immediately, or legal action may ensue."[56] Grant Petersen of Rivendell likely realized this was no empty threat. Dhillon is known for being quite litigious, especially in the face of progressive initiatives. She has been connected to fights against shelter-in-place orders in California during the COVID-19 pandemic; against a bill requiring former President Donald Trump to publish his tax information; and in defense of Ann Coulter after the University of California Berkeley canceled one of her speaking engagements on its campus, citing security reasons.[57] Given this high-profile challenge to Rivendell's program and the individual, physically threatening, responses, which had Rivendell employees in fear for their own personal safety, it seemed prudent to think of an alternative way to try to diversify cycling. A more inclusive program like the Bicycles R Fun fund will undoubtedly be better received than one that is solely for Black people, as was the Black Reparations Pricing. That is not to say Rivendell's first initiative was wrongheaded, but it was so mired in controversy that it would have been stifled and ineffective. Helping to make cycling more accessible to people of all colors and genders is a little more difficult to target as an unfairly biased program.

There are few minorities of any type among U.S. elite professionals. There are some notable exceptions to this, however. For example, there is the pro tour rider and possible future Tour de France hopeful Nielson Powless. He is of Oneida descent and the first Native American (from the United States) to compete in the Tour de France. There is also Coryn Labecki (née Rivera), an American woman of Filipino descent. Rivera is in league of her own, winning seventy-three national titles and counting, as well as some of the most prestigious women's professional races in the world. The fact that both are extraordinary examples of non-White cyclists from the United States to achieve considerable success only serves to reiterate the monochromatic appearance of U.S. cycling, particularly when it comes to competitive cycling.

These examples also show that the often-claimed economic barrier to cycling is not the only obstacle and perhaps not even the biggest hurdle to overcome. Most of the cyclists mentioned above did not come from affluent backgrounds. They, or their parents, struggled to scrape together enough money to buy their first bikes, but if you are as good as they were, you can ride that budget level bicycle to good results, which may lead to a team membership or sponsorship that affords one better equipment and more support. That is, if you manage to overcome the tendency for team managers and sponsors to write you off as "no good," "a charity case," "uncoachable," or some other coded excuse for denying you the same treatment as other riders. Becoming a professional cyclist takes a lot of talent, discipline, and hard work. For the Black cyclist or any non-White cyclist, it takes even more. Rahsaan Bahati made an important and apropos point on social media in response to comments from people like, "I wish someone would give me a bike like that." Bahati responded, "nothing has been given to me in this sport. I have had to earn everything I have." For him, the Williams brothers, Nelson Vails, Ayesha McGowan, Oliver Martin, and all the riders discussed above, this statement rings true. Unlike the children of former professional riders or wealthy amateurs who can pull strings to get their kids on a development team before they have proven themselves, the door does not swing open as freely for cyclists of color. It never has.

Whether the scant amount of diversity and representation at the higher levels of competitive cycling today will make a difference in the future is difficult to predict. As Justin Williams points out, the sport has an image problem because it just is not cool. Until kids see someone like him and say to themselves, "man, that guy is dope" it will be hard to generate enough excitement about cycling to see the rush to the sport that could bring the level of diversity many desire. That is a bigger problem than simply making the sport more inclusive, however. It also means making bicycle racing more visible through increased media coverage. Legion of Los Angeles and Rahsaan Bahati have made steps in that direction by posting their own race footage to YouTube and their various social media accounts, but those videos are mostly seen by cyclists and/or people who already know about them, so reaching all those who may not even know professional bicycle racing exists (outside the Tour de France) is perhaps the bigger hurdle to cross.

Still, it does seem that in the United States, the sport is on the precipice of significant change, especially in terms of diversity and inclusivity. The fact that there are several Black cyclists involved in the sport at the highest levels who are making a concerted effort to create change is not entirely unprecedented, but it feels different this time. Even at the turn of the century, when there were also many Black cyclists racing at the highest levels of the sport, in most cases they could not be as vocal about their hopes and dreams for greater equality. There were few independent and unbiased media outlets for them to turn to. They could not start their own YouTube channel, or go to Twitter, Instagram, et cetera, to document their journey. Additionally, the Black cyclists of the present era are not only more intentional in their push to diversify the sport, it also seems that some of the major players in the sport, such as Zwift, Velonews, USA Cycling, Cannondale, Specialized, and Giant, are actually listening. Outside the professional ranks, there are thousands of amateur cyclists in the United States who take to the roads and trails on a daily basis—often doing group rides together with twenty or more people. Seeing more diversity on those rides, which are usually more than an hour, means people will be forced out of their racial and ethnic bubbles. They will have little choice but to talk to each other, when the pace is not too high, of course. More prominent and visible Black cyclists, such as Justin Williams and Ayesha McGowan, could also show Black teenagers that there are more options open to them if they like sports and are tired of the constant attempts to "funnel" them onto the track, basketball courts, or football fields. A sport that is more representative of American demographics will inevitably lead it to become an even more popular sport and thus deepen the pool of talented American cyclists. From there, it could swell into something huge.

Notes

Introduction

1. David Herlihy, *Bicycle: The History* (New Haven: Yale University Press, 2004), 106.

2. Herlihy, *Bicycle: The History*, 108.

3. Herlihy, *Bicycle: The History*, 114.

4. Margaret Guroff, *The Mechanical Horse: How the Bicycle Reshaped American Life* (Austin: University of Texas Press, 2016), 23.

5. I go into much more depth about trends and marketing in an earlier book: Robert Turpin, *First Taste of Freedom: A Cultural History of Bicycle Marketing in the United States* (Syracuse: Syracuse University Press, 2018), 55–56.

6. Price Collier, "Sport's Place in the Nation's Well-Being," *Outing, an Illustrated Monthly Magazine of Recreation* 32, no. 4, (July 1898): 386.

7. Charles E. Pratt, *The American Bicycler: A Manual for the Observer, the Learner, and the Expert* (Boston: Osgood and Company, 1879), 30.

8. Throughout this work I have capitalized both Black and White in reference to race. When considering this choice, an article by Kwame Anthony Appiah in *The Atlantic* resonated with me on several points. As he points out, capitalizing all "races," as I have done, "highlights the artificiality of race." I worried that capitalizing Black but not White, as is common at the moment, may make it seem that Whiteness is natural and thereby make it somewhat invisible. Not calling out Whiteness is problematic because much of its power comes through its invisibility. There is also the argument that Black should be capitalized but not White because Black people have a shared culture. Accordingly, White people,

on the other hand, have many different cultures. That is a troubling premise. As Appiah asks, "is Africa less culturally varied than Europe?" For his full argument, see: Kwame Anthony Appiah, "The Case for Capitalizing the B in Black," *The Atlantic*, June 18, 2020. https://www.theatlantic.com/ideas/archive/2020/06/time-to-capitalize-blackand-white/613159/.

9. Elizabeth Stordeur Pryor, *Colored Travelers: Mobility and the Fight for Citizenship before the Civil War* (Chapel Hill: University of North Carolina Press, 2016), 80–81. Pryor argues that if Black people were doing it, it was not considered progress.

Chapter 1. From the Outset

1. *New York Herald*, April 10, 1869, 7; *The Home Journal*, April 15, 1869; "Southern News," *Courier-Journal*, March 29, 1869.

2. Quoted in David Herlihy, *Bicycle: The History* (New Haven: Yale University Press, 2004), 103.

3. Edith Abbott, "The Wages of Unskilled Labor in the United States, 1850–1900," *The Journal of Political Economy* 13, (June 1905): 363.

4. *Charleston Daily News*, March 8, 1869.

5. Herlihy, *Bicycle: The History*, 108, 112–14.

6. Herlihy, *Bicycle: The History*, 114.

7. Quoted in Herlihy, *Bicycle: The History*, 115.

8. Herlihy, *Bicycle: The History*, 121; *Indianapolis Journal*, April 1, 1869.

9. "The Steel Horse," *People's Advocate*, May 14, 1881. The story originated in the pages of the *New York Herald*.

10. Robert J. Turpin, *First Taste of Freedom: A Cultural History of Bicycle Marketing in the United States* (Syracuse: Syracuse University Press, 2018), 18–21.

11. "The Steel Horse," *People's Advocate*, May 14, 1881.

12. Herlihy, *Bicycle: The History*, 15–155.

13. *The Bicycling World and L.A.W. Bulletin*, October 11, 1889, 642.

14. *The Bicycling World and L.A.W. Bulletin*, October 11, 1889, 642.

15. "A Bicycle Built Out of Old Iron Scraps," *The Bicycling World and L.A.W. Bulletin*, September 22, 1893, 40.

16. "Auburn Notes," *New York Globe*, July 26, 1884.

17. Herlihy, *Bicycle: The History*, 206–15. Much of this general history of the high wheeler, tricycle, and safety bicycle can be found in Herlihy's *Bicycle: The History*, 75–200.

18. *Springfield Republican*, May 2, 1904.

19. *Outing*, V. VII, no. 1 (October, 1885): 99; *The Bicycling World*, Jan. 29, 1886, 225–26.

20. "The Meet of the Wheelmen," *Harper's Weekly*, June 5, 1886, 363.

21. http://Brookeline.com/corey-hill, accessed March 13, 2020.

22. "The Meet of the Wheelmen," *Harper's Weekly*, June 5, 1886, 363.

Notes to Chapters 1 and 2

23. Lorenz Finnison, *Boston's Cycling Craze* (University of Massachusetts Press, 2014), 270, no. 14.

24. *The Bicycling World*, October 23, 1885, 577.

Chapter 2. The Mode of Liberation

1. J. Gordon Street, "The Conference at Boston: A strong Protest Against Discrimination," *New York Freeman*, September 25, 1886.

2. Street, "The Conference at Boston."

3. Charles W. Puttkammer and Ruth Worthy, "William Monroe Trotter, 1872–1934," *The Journal of Negro History* 43, no. 4 (October 1958): 299.

4. William Harrison, "Phylon Profile IX: William Monroe Trotter-Fighter," *Phylon* 7, no. 3 (1946): 239.

5. Street, "The Conference at Boston."

6. J. Gordon Street, "Honoring the Recorder: Banquet to Mr. Trotter," *New York Freeman*, August 27, 1887.

7. Kerri K. Greenidge, *Black Radical: The Life and Times of William Monroe Trotter* (New York: Liveright Publishing Corporation, 2020), xvii.

8. Greenidge, *Black Radical*, xi.

9. Herlihy, *Bicycle: The History*, 189.

10. *The Bicycling World and L.A.W. Bulletin*, December 4, 1885, 85.

11. Andrew Ritchie, *Major Taylor: The Extraordinary Career of a Champion Bicycle Racer* (Baltimore: Johns Hopkins University Press, 1988), 23.

12. Bruce Epperson, *Peddling Bicycles to America: The Rise of an Industry* (Jefferson: McFarland, 2010), 91.

13. *The Bicycling World*, November 20, 1885, 46.

14. *The Bicycling World*, October 8, 1886, 555.

15. "Interesting Muscular Contests on the Field," *Boston Daily Advertiser*, July 5, 1887.

16. "Street's Boston Budget," *New York Freeman*, July 9, 1887.

17. *The Bicycling World*, July 6, 1888, 202.

18. *The Bicycling World*, Aug. 27, 1886, 420.

19. J. Gordon Street, "Queen Victoria's Jubilee: How It Was Observed in Boston," *New York Freeman*, June 25, 1887.

20. David K. Wiggins, *Glory Bound: Black Athletes in a White America* (Syracuse: Syracuse University Press, 1997), 21.

21. Louis Moore, *I Fight for a Living: Boxing and the Battle for Black Manhood, 1880–1915* (Urbana: University of Illinois Press, 2017), 127.

22. "The Bicycle Races," *Boston Daily Journal*, July 5, 1888.

23. "The Bicycle Races," *Boston Daily Journal*, July 5, 1888.

24. "Boston Notes," *The Bicycling World and L.A.W. Bulletin*, Aug. 9, 1889, 403.

25. "Boston Notes," *The Bicycling World and L.A.W. Bulletin*, May 9, 1890, 40.

26. Herlihy, *Bicycle: The History*, 246.

202 *Notes to Chapter 2*

27. "Boston Notes," *The Bicycling World and L.A.W. Bulletin,* Aug. 9, 1889, 403; "Amateur Sports: The Bicycle Tournament," *Worcester Daily Spy*, May 25, 1890.

28. Herlihy, *Bicycle: The History*, 241.

29. Bruce Epperson, "How Many Bikes: An Investigation into the Quantification of Bicycling, 1878–1914," in *Cycle History 11: Proceedings of the 11th International Cycling History Conference*, eds. Andrew Ritchie and Rob Van der Plas (San Francisco, Van der Plas Publications, 2001), 49.

30. Robert A. Smith, *A Social History of the Bicycle: Its Early Life and Times in America* (New York: American Heritage Press, 1972), 115.

31. Smith, *A Social History of the Bicycle*, 115.

32. Epperson, "How Many Bikes," 44.

33. "Leading Measures," *The Bearings*, February 23, 1893.

34. Evan Friss, *The Cycling City: Bicycles & Urban America in the 1890s* (Chicago: University of Chicago Press, 2015), 37.

35. Carlton Reid, *Roads Were not Built for Cars: How Cyclists were the First to push for Good Roads and Became the Pioneers of Motoring* (Washington, DC: Island Press, 2015), 175.

36. "Boston Notes," *The Bicycling World and L.A.W. Bulletin*, May 9, 1890, 40.

37. Herlihy, *Bicycle: The History*, 232–33.

38. Smith, *A Social History of the Bicycle*, 115.

39. *The Cycle*, July 2, 1886, 255.

40. Reid, *Roads Were Not Built for Cars*, 248. This could have been an issue of access to cameras, however, or a lack of the feelings of vanity that would prompt one to feel the need to document the moment and see to it that the photo was saved for posterity.

41. Quoted in Evan Friss, *The Cycling City: Bicycles & Urban America in the 1890s* (Chicago: University of Chicago Press, 2015), 36.

42. Smith, *A Social History of the Bicycle*, 119.

43. "Milwaukee, Wis," *Cleveland Gazette*, June 5, 1886.

44. *Cleveland Gazette*, August 18, 1888.

45. National Bureau of Economic Research, ed. Clarence D. Long, *Wages and Earnings in the United States, 1860–1890* (Princeton University Press, 1960), 98.

46. Herlihy, *Bicycle: The History*, 261.

47. "Garrison in Bronze," *New York Freeman*, May 22, 1886.

48. Carroll D. Wright and Oren W. Weaver, eds., *Bulletin of the Department of Labor: Condition of the Negro in Various Cities* (Washington: Government Printing Office, 1897), 319.

49. J. Gordon Street, "A New Memorial Movement," *New York Freeman*, July 16, 1887.

50. J. Gordon Street, "Street's Boston Budget," *New York Freeman*, July 9, 1887.

51. J. Gordon Street, "Queen Victoria's Jubilee: How it was Observed in Boston," *New York Freeman*, June 25, 1887.

Notes to Chapters 2 and 3 203

52. Greenidge, *Black Radical*, 40.

53. "Flotsam and Jetsam," *Indianapolis Freeman*, September 15, 1888.

54. Charles Pratt, *The American Bicycler: A Manual for the Observer, the Learner, and the Expert* (Boston: Osgood and Company, 1879), 31–32.

55. Reid, *Roads Were Not Built for Cars*, 175.

Chapter 3. Drawing the Color Line

1. "Leading Measures," *The Bearings*, February 23, 1893.

2. *Indianapolis Journal*, February 21, 1894.

3. "The National Assembly," *The Bearings*, February 23, 1894.

4. "The National Assembly," *The Bearings*, February 23, 1894.

5. "The National Assembly," *The Bearings*, February 23, 1894.

6. "Turn of the Wheel," *Jersey City News*, February 19, 1894.

7. *Indianapolis Journal*, February 21, 1894.

8. *Indianapolis Journal*, February 21, 1894.

9. "Meeting of Cyclists," *Courier-Journal*, February 19, 1894.

10. *The Bicycling World and L.A.W. Bulletin*, March 2, 1894, 433.

11. *Indianapolis Journal*, February 21, 1894. For the number of members per delegate see: "Amateur Cyclists," *Courier-Journal*, February 25, 1893. He said by two in the coming year. Two more delegates would have equaled around 400 new members total.

12. *The Editor & Publisher and the Journalist*, August 14, 1915.

13. *Courier-Journal*, June 22, 1921.

14. Daniel Decatur Moore, *Men of the South: A Work for the Newspaper Reference Library* (New Orleans: Southern Biographical Association, 1922); "Klan Views A Vowed by Confederates: I am a Ku Klux' Shouts Carr, Veterans' Commander—Sons' New Chief Klansman," *New York Times*, April 13, 1923; John Breckinridge Castelman, *Active Service* (Louisville: Courier-Journal Job Printing Co., 1917), 260.

15. *Courier-Journal*, June 23, 1921.

16. W. H. Perrin, J. H. Battle, and G. C. Kniffin, *Kentucky: A History of the State*, 7th ed. (Louisville: F.A. Battey and Company, 1887), 713.

17. Chandra Manning, *What This Cruel War Was Over: Soldiers, Slavery, and the Civil War* (New York: Alfred A. Knopf, 2007), 190–91. John English is quoted in Manning's text.

18. "Turn of the Wheel," *Jersey City News*, February 19, 1894.

19. "The Constitutional Convention," *The Referee & Cycle Trade Journal*, February 24, 1893.

20. The Constitutional Convention," *The Referee & Cycle Trade Journal*, February 24, 1893.

21. "Leading Measures," *The Bearings*, February 24, 1893.

22. "Leading Measures," *The Bearings*, February 24, 1893.

204 Notes to Chapter 3

23. The Constitutional Convention," *The Referee & Cycle Trade Journal*, February 24, 1893.

24. "Leading Measures," *The Bearings*, February 24, 1893.

25. "Leading Measures," *The Bearings*, February 24, 1893.

26. Quoted in Andrew Ritchie, "The League of American Wheelmen, Major Taylor and the 'Color Question' in the United States in the 1890s," in *Ethnicity, Sport, Identity: Struggles for Status*, eds. J.A. Mangan and Andrew Ritchie (London: Routledge, 2004), 14, footnote 12.

27. "The Constitutional Convention," *The Referee & Cycle Trade Journal*, February 24, 1893.

28. "Leading Measures," *The Bearings*, February 24, 1893.

29. "The Constitutional Convention," *The Referee & Cycle Trade Journal*, February 24, 1893.

30. "'Sterling' Elliott, 'Our Colored Brother,'" *The Bicycling World and L.A.W. Bulletin*, June 3, 1892, 1065.

31. "'Sterling' Elliott, 'Our Colored Brother,'" *The Bicycling World and L.A.W. Bulletin*, June 3, 1892, 1065.

32. "The Constitutional Convention," *The Referee & Cycle Trade Journal*, February 24, 1893.

33. "An Open Letter," *The Bearings*, March 10, 1893.

34. "Leading Measures," *The Bearings*, February 24, 1893.

35. "Leading Measures," *The Bearings*, February 24, 1893.

36. "Amateur Cyclists," *Courier-Journal*, February 25, 1893.

37. "Amateur Cyclists," *Courier-Journal*, February 25, 1893.

38. "Leading Measures," *The Bearings*, February 24, 1893.

39. "Amateur Cyclists," *Courier-Journal*, February 25, 1893.

40. A. S. Hardin, "The Negro Question," *The Bearings*, August 5, 1892.

41. A. S. Hardin, "The Negro Question," *The Bearings*, August 5, 1892.

42. "Amateur Cyclists," *Courier-Journal*, February 25, 1893.

43. A. S. Hardin, "The Negro Question," *The Bearings*, August 5, 1892.

44. "Amateur Cyclists," *Courier-Journal*, February 25, 1893.

45. George C. Wright, *Racial Violence in Kentucky: Lynchings, Mob Rule, and 'Legal Lynchings'* (Baton Rouge: Louisiana State University Press, 1990), 51.

46. Wright, *Racial Violence in Kentucky*, 54.

47. "Will they Succeed," *The Referee & Cycle Trade Journal*, February 4, 1893.

48. Wright, *Racial Violence in Kentucky*, 48.

49. *The Bearings*, May 12, 1893.

50. "Stray Shots," *The Bearings*, April 21, 1893.

51. "Barring the Negro at Denver," *The Bearings*, April 21, 1893.

52. "Colored Cycler's Cut," Detroit *Plaindealer*, September 16, 1892.

53. *Cleveland Gazette*, May 13, 1893.

54. "Color Line Drawn," *The Bearings*, April 21, 1893.

Notes to Chapter 3

55. "Elevating Cycling Journalism," *The Bearings*, April 28, 1893.

56. "Tennesseans Wrought up on the Negro Question," *The Bearings*, March 24, 1893.

57. "Turn of the Wheel," *Jersey City News*, February 20, 1894.

58. "Will the South Secede?" *The Bearings*, February 17, 1893.

59. "Chief Consul Holm's Denial," *The Bearings*, March 3, 1893.

60. "Ready for a Strike," *The Referee & Cycle Trade Journal*, April 14, 1893.

61. "Secesh! Secesh!" *The Bearings*, May 19, 1893.

62. "The Negro Question Again," *The Bearings*, September 22, 1893.

63. "The Negro Question Again," *The Bearings*, September 22, 1893.

64. "The Negro Question Again," *The Bearings*, September 22, 1893.

65. "Who is 'Dock'?" *The Bearings*, December 8, 1893.

66. "Who is 'Dock'?" *The Bearings*, December 8, 1893.

67. "Who is 'Dock'?" *The Bearings*, December 8, 1893.

68. "Who is 'Dock'?" *The Bearings*, December 8, 1893.

69. "Who is 'Dock'?" *The Bearings*, December 8, 1893.

70. "Stray Shots: The Southern Negro," *The Bearings*, December 22, 1893.

71. "Stray Shots: The Southern Negro," *The Bearings*, December 22, 1893.

72. "Southrons on the Rampage," *The Bearings*, April 14, 1893.

73. *The Bicycling World*, October 6, 1893. The experiences of Black female cyclist Kittie Knox seem to verify this point. Attempts to exclude her from League social meets were based largely on the jealousy of White female cyclists.

74. For a more thorough discussion of the classed implications in bicycle marketing see: Robert J. Turpin, *First Taste of Freedom: A Cultural History of Bicycle Marketing in the United States* (Syracuse: Syracuse University Press, 2018).

75. "Missouri Will Support Watts," *The Bearings*, February 10, 1893; "Missourians Objected to Negro," *The Bearings*, October 13, 1893.

76. "Missourians Objected to Negro," *The Bearings*, October 13, 1893.

77. *Evening World*, February 3, 1894.

78. "The Negro Question Again," *The Bearings*, December 29, 1893.

79. "The Negro Question Again," *The Bearings*, December 29, 1893.

80. "The Negro Question Again," *The Bearings*, December 29, 1893.

81. "The Negro Question Again," *The Bearings*, December 29, 1893.

82. "The Negro Question Again," *The Bearings*, December 29, 1893.

83. "Anent the Negro Question," *The Bearings*, February 16, 1894.

84. "Ephraham Jones' Prediction," *The Bearings*, February 16, 1894.

85. "'The Idler's' Warning," *The Bearings*, February 9, 1894.

86. "Chief Consul Harris Has no Love for Negroes," *The Bearings*, January 12, 1894.

87. "Gerould for the Negro," *The Bearings*, January 5, 1894.

88. "Chief Consul Harris Has no Love for Negroes," *The Bearings*, January 12, 1894.

Chapter 4. In Response to the Color Line

1. *New York Daily Tribune*, Sunday, February 25, 1894.
2. *New York Daily Tribune*, Sunday, February 25, 1894.
3. *New York Daily Tribune*, Sunday, February 25, 1894.
4. "The League Situation," *The Bearings*, February 23, 1894.
5. "Colored L.A.W. Members," *The Bearings*, April 6, 1894.
6. "The Negro Question," *The Bearings*, March 2, 1894.
7. "The Negro Question," *The Bearings*, March 2, 1894.
8. "What the Colored Brother Says," *The Bearings*, March 3, 1893.
9. "What the Colored Brother Says," *The Bearings*, March 3, 1893.
10. "What the Colored Brother Says," *The Bearings*, March 3, 1893.
11. "What the Colored Brother Says," *The Bearings*, March 3, 1893.
12. "The Other Side," *The Bearings*, February 2, 1894.
13. "The Other Side," *The Bearings*, February 2, 1894.
14. "The Other Side," *The Bearings*, February 2, 1894.
15. "The Other Side," *The Bearings*, February 2, 1894.
16. "Mr. Scott, Colored, Replies" *The Bearings*, March 30, 1894.
17. "Mr. Scott, Colored, Replies," *The Bearings*, March 30, 1894.
18. "Mr. Scott, Colored, Replies," *The Bearings*, March 30, 1894.
19. "But They're Not," *The Referee & Cycle Trade Journal*, April 13, 1894.
20. *Jamestown Weekly Alert*, August 28, 1890.
21. "First of His Race," *Courier-Journal*, December 11, 1892.
22. "Laws for the Wheelmen," *New York Times*, February 18, 1895.
23. "Negroes are Indignant," *The Bearings*, March 9, 1894.
24. "Negroes are Indignant," *The Bearings*, March 9, 1894.
25. "Negroes are Indignant," *The Bearings*, March 9, 1894.
26. "Among the Wheelmen," *New York Times*, March 8, 1894.
27. "Negroes are Indignant," *The Bearings*, March 9, 1894.
28. "Negroes are Indignant," *The Bearings*, March 9, 1894.
29. "Negroes are Indignant," *The Bearings*, March 9, 1894.
30. "Negroes are Indignant," *The Bearings*, March 9, 1894.
31. "Spring Meet Will Be Held in Boston," *The Bearings*, March 16, 1894.
32. "Spring Meet Will Be Held in Boston," *The Bearings*, March 16, 1894.
33. "That Resolution of Mr. Teamoh's," *The Bearings*, March 30, 1894.
34. "Boston's News Budget," *The Referee & Cycle Trade Journal*, April 2, 1894.
35. "Boston's News Budget," *The Referee & Cycle Trade Journal*, April 2, 1894.
36. "Boston's News Budget," *The Referee & Cycle Trade Journal*, April 2, 1894.
37. "Boston's News Budget," *The Referee & Cycle Trade Journal*, April 2, 1894.
38. "Mr. Teamoh Again," *The Bearings*, April 6, 1894.
39. "Mr. Teamoh Again," *The Bearings*, April 6, 1894.
40. Arthur K. Peck, "Uncolored Facts," *Boston Sunday Post*, April 1, 1894.
41. Arthur K. Peck, "Uncolored Facts," *Boston Sunday Post*, April 1, 1894.

Notes to Chapters 4 and 5　207

42. "The National Assembly," *The Referee & Cycle Trade Journal*, February 23, 1894.

43. "The National Assembly," *The Referee & Cycle Trade Journal*, February 23, 1894.

44. "Two Little Ballroom Scenes the Cause," *The Bearings*, February 2, 1894.

45. "Public Opinion," *The Referee & Cycle Trade*, March 23, 1894.

46. "The National Assembly," *The Referee & Cycle Trade Journal*, February 23, 1894. It appears Boston did not actually get that meet and it wound up going to Asbury Park instead.

47. "Seen and Heard," *The Bicycling World and L.A.W. Bulletin*, February 23, 1894, 403.

48. "Aftermath of the Assembly" and "Watts and the Chief," *The Bearings*, March 2, 1894.

49. "The Passing Hour," *The Bicycling World and L.A.W. Bulletin*, March 2, 1894, 431.

50. "The National Assembly," *The Referee & Cycle Trade Journal*, February 23, 1894.

51. "The National Assembly," *The Referee & Cycle Trade Journal*, February 23, 1894.

52. "Two Little Ballroom Scenes the Cause," *The Bearings*, February 2, 1894.

53. "Two Little Ballroom Scenes the Cause," *The Bearings*, February 2, 1894.

54. "Two Little Ballroom Scenes the Cause," *The Bearings*, February 2, 1894.

55. "Two Little Ballroom Scenes the Cause," *The Bearings*, February 2, 1894.

56. "Colored Wheelmen Indignant," *Richmond Planet*, March 10, 1894.

57. "A Kite-Shaped Track in Jersey," *The Bearings*, March 30, 1894.

58. "The 'Dark Secret' and the Monkeys," *The Referee & Cycle Trade Journal*, March 9, 1894. For other descriptions of Backus see: "Afraid of Zim's Swift Kick," *The Referee & Cycle Trade Journal*, August 18, 1893; "Zimmy's Mascot," *The Referee & Cycle Trade Journal*, January 6, 1893.

59. "Welcome! Farewell!" *The Referee & Cycle Trade Journal*, April 21, 1893.

60. "Zimmerman's Defeat," *The Bearings*, July 6, 1894; "The 'Dark Secret' Arrives," *The Bearings*, July 20, 1894.

61. "A Kite-Shaped Track in Jersey," *The Bearings*, March 30, 1894.

62. Andrew Ritchie, "The League of American Wheelmen, Major Taylor and the 'Color Question' in the United States in the 1890s," in *Ethnicity, Sport, Identity: Struggles for Status*, eds. J.A. Mangan and Andrew Ritchie (London: Routledge, 2004), 19.

63. "Laws for the Wheelmen," *New York Times*, February 18, 1895.

64. Andrew Ritchie, "The League of American Wheelmen," 11.

Chapter 5. The New Woman

1. "Two Dark a Brunette for Some at the Ball," *The Referee & Cycle Trade Journal*, July 18, 1895; "The L.A.W. Ball" *The Bearings*, July 18, 1895; and "Fine Racing by

208 *Notes to Chapter 5*

Cyclers," *New York Times*, July 12, 1895, 2; "Meet-y Notes," *The Wheel and Cycling Trade Review*, July 19, 1895, 35.

2. Nathan Cardon, "Cycling on the Color Line: Race, Technology, and Bicycle Mobilities in the Early Jim Crow South, 1887–1905," *Technology and Culture* 64, no. 4 (October 2021): 985.

3. Patricia Marks, *Bicycles, Bangs, and Bloomers: The New Woman in the Popular Press* (Lexington: University Press of Kentucky, 1990), 175.

4. Robert J. Turpin, *First Taste of Freedom*, 33.

5. "Bloomers in Jail," *Enterprise Omaha*, Aug. 28, 1895.

6. "The Darktown Bicycle Club—On Parade" and "The Darktown Bicycle Club—Knocked Out," *Currier and Ives*, 1892, Library of Congress Prints and photographs division, pga 06613 and pga06612//hdl/loc/gov/loc/pnp/pga.06612.

7. "The Darktown Bicycle Race—The Start: 'Now for de Fastest record eber known'" and "The Darktown Bicycle Race—A sudden Halt," *Currier and Ives*, 1895, Library of Congress Prints and Photographs Division, https://lccn.loc.gov/91724154 and https://lccn.loc.gov/91724148.

8. "Darktown Bicycling—A Tender Pear," *Currier and Ives*, 1987, Library of Congress Prints and Photographs Division) 1897, Digital ID: pga 06616//hdl.loc.gov/loc.pnp/pga.06616.

9. "Darktown Bicycling—Scooped de Pear," *Currier and Ives*, 1897, Library of Congress Prints and Photographs Division, Digital ID: pga 06617 //hdl.loc.gov/loc.pnp/pga.06617.

10. Nathan Cardon, "Cycling on the Color Line: Race, Technology, and Bicycle Mobilities in the Early Jim Crow South, 1887–1905," *Technology and Culture* 64, no. 4 (October 2021): 987; and Evan Friss, *The Cycling City: Bicycles & Urban American in the 1890s* (Chicago: Chicago University Press, 2015), 60–61.

11. "Negro Cyclist Kills Woman," *The Sun*, April 21, 1913.

12. See: Friss, *The Cycling City*, 60–61; and Cardon, "Cycling on the Color Line," 987.

13. Lorenz Finnison, *Boston's Cycling Craze* (University of Massachusetts Press, 2014), 5. Finnison provides more detail about Knox's life in his book about cycling in Boston.

14. Finnison, *Boston's Cycling Craze*, 15–16.

15. Finnison, *Boston's Cycling Craze*, 38.

16. "Invaded by Bicyclists," *New York Times*, July 9, 1895; "At Asbury Park," *The Wheel and Cycling Trade Review*, July 12, 1895, 25. The *New York Times* claimed six years but other sources like *The Wheel* said it was five.

17. *The Bicycling World & L.A.W. Bulletin*, May 11, 1888, 34.

18. Finnison, *Boston's Cycling Craze*, 164.

19. "The Asbury Park Meet," *The Bearings*, July 11, 1895, 4.

20. "Invaded by Bicyclists," *New York Times*, July 9, 1895.

21. "Invaded by Bicyclists," *New York Times*, July 9, 1895; *Red Lodge Picket*, September 7, 1895.

Notes to Chapter 5

22. *New Haven Journal Courier*, Wednesday, July 10, 1895; *San Francisco Call*, July 10, 1895.

23. *The Wheel and Cycling Trade Review*, July 12, 1895, 25.

24. "Kittie a Quaker Favorite," *The Referee & Cycle Trade Journal*, July 25, 1895.

25. Here, I am referring specifically to John Backus mentioned in a previous chapter.

26. "Flashes of Cycling Life," *The Bearings*, December 29, 1893.

27. "Bloomers Won the Race," *Washington Times*, July 5, 1895; "Bloomers Have It," *Wichita Daily Eagle*, July 5, 1895; "The Bloomers Win," *Seattle Post-Intelligence*, July 5, 1895; "Athletic Carnival" *Roanoke Daily Times*, July 5, 1895.

28. "Johnson Sets Up a New Mark," *The Bearings*, July 11, 1895, 6.

29. "Bloomers Won the Race," *Washington Times*, July 5, 1895.

30. "Bloomers Won the Race," *Washington Times*, July 5, 1895.

31. "May Be Racing Today," *New York Times*, July 10, 1895.

32. "Two Little Ballroom Scenes the Cause," *The Bearings*, February 2, 1894.

33. "Two Little Ballroom Scenes the Cause," *The Bearings*, February 2, 1894.

34. Finnison, *Boston's Cycling Craze*, 15–16.

35. Finnison, *Boston's Cycling Craze*, 12–13.

36. Finnison, *Boston's Cycling Craze*, 14.

37. "Summer Girl," *Indianapolis Freeman*, June 17, 1893; "Summer Girl," *Indianapolis Freeman*, August 5, 1893.

38. "The L.A.W. Ball," *The Bearings*, July 18, 1895.

39. "Fine Racing by Cyclers," *New York Times*, July 12, 1895.

40. "Two Dark a Brunette for Some at the Ball," *The Referee & Cycle Trade Journal*, July 18, 1895.

41. "Fine Racing by Cyclers," *New York Times*, July 12, 1895.

42. "Meet-y Notes," *The Wheel and Cycling Trade Review*, July 19, 1895, 35. This source also talks about the meeting as mediocre and maybe pursued solely for the $10,000 that should have been awarded to help differ the costs of planning and hosting.

43. "Color Line Among Wheelmen," *New York Herald-Tribune*, July 12, 1895. Quoted in Finnison, *Boston's Cycling Craze*, 42.

44. "Color Line Among Wheelmen," *New York Herald-Tribune*, July 12, 1895. Quoted in Finnison, *Boston's Cycling Craze*, 42.

45. "The National Meet of the L.A.W. at Asbury Park," *Wheelwoman*, July 1895. Quoted in Finnison, *Boston's Cycling Craze*, 42–43.

46. "Excluded from a Century Run, They Sue," *The Wheel*, November 15, 1895, 48.

47. "Miss Knox Entertained," *The Bearings*, July 25, 1895.

48. Finnison, *Boston's Cycling Craze*, 5.

49. "Colored War in Boston," *The Bearings*, November 14, 1895.

50. "Colored War in Boston," *The Bearings*, November 14, 1895.

51. "Excluded from a Century Run, They Sue," *The Wheel*, November 15, 1895, 48.

52. "Colored War in Boston," *The Bearings*, November 14, 1895.

210   *Notes to Chapters 5 and 6*

53. "Elliott's Proposed Amendments," *The Bearings*, January 4, 1895, 9.

54. "Pen Punctures," *Wheeling and Cycling Trade Review*, April 12, 1895, 42.

55. "Meet of the Bicyclists," *The Morning News*, July 10, 1895, 5.

56. "Rescued from Thieves," *The Referee & Cycle Trade Journal*, July 11, 1895.

57. "The Asbury Park Meet," *The Bearings*, July 11, 1895, 4.

58. Quoted in Finnison, *Boston's Cycling Craze*, 35.

59. "Color Line Drawn," *San Francisco Call*, July 10, 1895, 2; "At Asbury Park," *The Wheel and Cycling Trade Review*, July 12, 1895, 25.

60. "The Asbury Park Meet," *The Bearings*, July 11, 1895, 4.

61. "Two Dark a Brunette for Some at the Ball," *The Referee & Cycle Trade Journal*, July 18, 1895.

62. "Kittie a Quaker Favorite," *The Referee & Cycle Trade Journal*, July 25, 1895.

63. "Kittie a Quaker Favorite," *The Referee & Cycle Trade Journal*, July 25, 1895.

Chapter 6. Six Days in a Row

1. "Long Cycle Race Starts," *New York Times*, December 8, 1902, 7; "The Man in the Clock Tower," *Forest and Stream: A Journal of Outdoor Life, Travel, Nature Study, Shooting, Fishing, Yachting* (Dec. 18, 1897): 489.

2. "Ready for Six-Day Grind," *The Bicycling World and Motorcycle Review*, December 2, 1905, 200a.

3. "Walthour's Cyclone Finish," *The Bicycling World and Motorcycle Review*, December 19, 1903, 318.

4. "Six-Day Bicycle Races," *Medical News* 71 no. 25 (Dec. 18, 1897): 801.

5. "Six-Day Bicycle Races," *Medical News* 71, no. 25 (Dec. 18, 1897): 801.

6. "Long Cycle Race Starts," *New York Times*, December 8, 1902, 7; "Ready for Six-Day Grind" *The Bicycling World and Motorcycle Review*, December 2, 1905, 200a.

7. "Types at a Six-Day Race," *The National Police Gazette* 87, no. 1481 (December 30, 1905): 10.

8. Peter Joffre Nye, Jeff Groman, and Mark Tyson, *The Six-Day Bicycle Races: America's Jazz-Age Sport* (San Francisco: Van der Plas Publications, 2006), 55, 149.

9. "Riders' Clothes Stolen," *New York Times*, December 14, 1902, 8.

10. "Six Day's Extraordinary," *The Bicycling World and Motorcycle Review*, December 12, 1903, 289.

11. "The Man in the Clock Tower," *Forest and Stream: A Journal of Outdoor Life, Travel, Nature Study, Shooting, Fishing, Yachting* (Dec. 18, 1897): 489.

12. "The Man in the Clock Tower," *Forest and Stream: A Journal of Outdoor Life, Travel, Nature Study, Shooting, Fishing, Yachting* (Dec. 18, 1897): 489.

13. "The Man in the Clock Tower," *Forest and Stream: A Journal of Outdoor Life, Travel, Nature Study, Shooting, Fishing, Yachting* (Dec. 18, 1897): 489.

14. "The Man in the Clock Tower," *Forest and Stream: A Journal of Outdoor Life, Travel, Nature Study, Shooting, Fishing, Yachting* (Dec. 18, 1897): 489.

15. Louis Moore, *I Fight for a Living: Boxing and the Battle for Black Manhood, 1880–1915* (Urbana: University of Illinois Press, 2017), 12.

Notes to Chapter 6

16. Moore, *I Fight for a Living*, 12.

17. Nye, *The Six-Day Bicycle Races*, 127.

18. Nye, *The Six-Day Bicycle Races*, 165–66.

19. "Walthour's Cyclone Finish," *The Bicycling World and Motorcycle Review*, Dec. 19, 1903, 317.

20. "Riders Likely to Try all Kinds of Tricks to Win Big Six-Day Race at the Garden," *The World*, December 1, 1903, 10; "Six Day Riders Behind the Record," *Brooklyn Daily Eagle*, December 8, 1902. Hedspeth rode with Alex Peterson in 1902 on a team referred to as the "white and black team." After Hedspeth was forced to resign due to the accident, Peterson was combined with a White rider who had also lost his teammate. The two had never met. The *Brooklyn Daily Eagle* reported that Hedspeth broke his collar bone in a sudden crash that happened in one of the turns as the riders "were all bunched together."

21. "Long Race Starts," *New York Times*, December 8, 1902.

22. "Walthour's Cyclone Finish," *The Bicycling World and Motorcycle Review*, Dec. 19, 1903, 318.

23. "Six-Day Bicycle Races," *Medical News* 71, no. 25 (Dec. 18, 1897): 801.

24. "Six-Day Bicycle Races," *Medical News* 71, no. 25 (Dec. 18, 1897): 801.

25. "The New Crop of Professionals," *The Bicycling World and Motorcycle Review*, March 12, 1904, 685.

26. "Racing Notes," *The Bicycling World and Motorcycle Review*, Apr. 16, 1904, 113.

27. "Exodus to Europe Likely," *The Bicycling World and Motorcycle Review*, Dec. 26, 1903, 351.

28. "Black Dove to go Abroad," *The Bicycling World and Motorcycle Review*, February 4, 1905, 450.

29. "The Prostitution of Amateurism," *The Bicycling World and Motorcycle Review*, May 14, 1904, 233.

30. "The Prostitution of Amateurism," *The Bicycling World and Motorcycle Review*, May 14, 1904, 233.

31. "The Prostitution of Amateurism," *The Bicycling World and Motorcycle Review*, May 14, 1904, 233.

32. "The Prostitution of Amateurism," *The Bicycling World and Motorcycle Review*, May 14, 1904, 233.

33. "The Prostitution of Amateurism," *The Bicycling World and Motorcycle Review*, May 14, 1904, 233. It was likely Betts since he went on to become a Governor of the Amateur Athletic Union.

34. The Prostitution of Amateurism," *The Bicycling World and Motorcycle Review*, May 14, 1904, 233.

35. "A.A.U. Disagrees with N.C.A.," *The Bicycling World and Motorcycle Review*, May 21, 1904, 267.

36. "A.A.U. Disagrees with N.C.A.," *The Bicycling World and Motorcycle Review*, May 21, 1904, 267.

Notes to Chapter 6

37. "Ritchie Betts Dies, Retired Publisher," *New York Times*, August 21, 1951, 26; Lacar Muscrove, "Astride Lofty Wheels: Ritchie Betts," https://www.vianolavie.org/2019/01/22/astride-lofty-wheels-ritchie-betts/.

38. "Ritchie Betts Dies, Retired Publisher," *New York Times*, August 21, 1951, 26.

39. "Irvington-Millburn Gossip," *The Bearings*, May 25, 1894, 3.

40. "The Irvington-Millburn," *The Bearings*, June 1, 1894, 15.

41. "Race Committee Resigned," *New York Times*, June 16, 1894, 3.

42. "A.A.U. Disagrees with N.C.A.," *The* Bicycling *World and Motorcycle Review*, May 21, 1904, 267.

43. This is discussed further in the chapter titled "Going Abroad" which focuses on the European travels of the Black cyclist.

44. "Ready for Six-Day Grind," *The Bicycling World and Motorcycle Review*, December 2, 1905, 200c.

45. "Cyclists Forced to Quit," *New York Times*, December 10, 1903, 7.

46. "Cyclists Start off in Six Days' Race," *New York Times*, December 4, 1905, 4; "Ready for Six-Day Grind," *The Bicycling World and Motorcycle Review*, December 2, 1905, 200c.

47. "Ready for Six-Day Grind," *The Bicycling World and Motorcycle Review*, December 2, 1905, 200c.

48. "Packed House all Week," *The Bicycling World and Motorcycle Review*, December 9, 1905, 223–24; "Some Six-Day Statistics," *The Bicycling World and Motorcycle Review*, December 23, 1905, 270.

49. "Packed House all Week," *The Bicycling World and Motorcycle Review*, December 9, 1905, 223–24; "Some Six-Day Statistics," *The Bicycling World and Motorcycle Review*, December 23, 1905, 270.

50. David K. Wiggins, *Glory Bound: Black Athletes in a White America* (Syracuse: Syracuse University Press, 1997), 177–79.

51. "Excitement at Vailsburg," *The Bicycling World and Motorcycle Review*, October 1, 1904, 15.

52. "Excitement at Vailsburg," *The Bicycling World and Motorcycle Review*, October 1, 1904, 15.

53. Deborah Willis, *Black Venus 2010: They Called Her 'Hottentot'* (Philadelphia: Temple University Press, 2010), 4–5.

54. "Excitement at Vailsburg," *The Bicycling World and Motorcycle Review*, October 1, 1904, 15.

55. "Rupprecht and Dove Suspended," *The Bicycling World and Motorcycle Review*, October 1, 1904, 16; "Dove Fined and Lectured," *The Bicycling World and Motorcycle Review*, October 1, 1904, 16.

56. "Rows at Vailsburg," *The Bicycling World and Motorcycling Review*, July 9, 1904, 464.

57. "Police Arrest Cyclists," *New York Times*, July 5, 1904, 16.

58. "Rows at Vailsburg," *The Bicycling World and Motorcycle and Motorcycle Review*, July 9, 1904, 464.

Notes to Chapters 6 and 7

59. "McFarland Whips Hadfield," *The Bicycling World and Motorcycle Review*, July 9, 1904, 464.

60. This was particularly true when it came to fears that cyclists posed a danger to horse-drawn vehicles and pedestrians. See: Evan Friss, *On Bicycles: A 200-Year History of Cycling in New York City* (New York: Columbia University Press, 2019), 3, 55–57.

Chapter 7. Going Abroad

1. "Les Velodromes Parisiens," *La Nature*, September 19, 1903, 251; La Societe d'histoire du Vesinet, "The Buffalo Velodrome," http://histoire-vesinet.org/extras/duncan/velodrome-buffalo.htm.

2. "The Game of 'Black and White'," *The Bicycling World and Motorcycle Review*, August 29, 1903, 649.

3. Marshall W. "Major" Taylor, *The Fastest Bicycle Rider in the World: The Autobiography of Major Taylor* (Battleboro: S. Greene Press, 1972), 61. He did not necessarily see all Black people as equal to White people. In his autobiography, he described himself as being as White as the Whitest men he raced against. In a poem, he wrote, "As white as you are, and black as I be still I'd rather be me. For black as I be and white as you are I may be whiter inside by far. As white as you are, and black as I be still it was nature's decree for black as I be, and white as you are I can be white though blacker than tar."

4. "Spokes from a Wheel," *Indianapolis Recorder*, October 21, 1899.

5. Tiffany Benedict Browne, "Newby Oval: the Track Before the Track," *Indianapolis Monthly*, May 19, 2016, https://www.indianapolismonthly.com/news-opinion/newby-oval/.

6. Advertisement for the opening of the Newby Oval, *Indianapolis News*, July 2, 1898.

7. "Spokes from a Wheel," *Indianapolis Recorder*, October 21, 1899.

8. "Music, Speed and Fire," *Indianapolis Journal*, July 5, 1899.

9. "Music, Speed and Fire," *Indianapolis Journal*, July 5, 1899.

10. His full name was Germain Ibron and he was French. He was also often referred to as Germain "le negre."

11. "General Sporting Notes," *New York Press*, Sunday Morning, November 30, 1902.

12. "Building the Record Table," *The Bicycling World and Motorcycle Review*, October 30, 1902, 1.

13. "Exodus to Europe Likely," *The Bicycling World and Motorcycle Review*, December 26, 1903.

14. "Six Day Riders Behind the Record," *The Brooklyn Daily Eagle*, December 8, 1902, 2.

15. "Les Americains sur nos Velodromes," *La Vie Au Grand Air*, June 5, 1903, 363.

214 *Notes to Chapter 7*

16. *Patterson Evening News*, June 16, 1903.

17. "Three Americans Score," *The Bicycling World*, September 10, 1904, 684.

18. "Negro Question Crops Up Abroad," *The Bicycling World*, August 5, 1905, 464.

19. Theresa Rundstedtler, *Jack Johnson, Rebel Sojourner: Boxing in the Shadow of the Global Color Line* (Berkely: University of California Press, 2013), 142, 145.

20. "Hedspeth Wins a Race at Last," *The Bicycling World*, May 12, 1906, 207.

21. "Walthour Suffers Defeat Abroad," *The Bicycling World*, August 4, 1906, 545.

22. "Walthour Suffers Defeat Abroad," *The Bicycling World*, August 4, 1906, 545.

23. "American Negro in the Money," *The Bicycling World*, June 9, 1906, 311.

24. *Western Appeal*, May 4, 1889. Quoted in Louis Moore, *I Fight for a Living: Boxing and the Battle for Black Manhood, 1880–1915* (Urbana: University of Illinois Press, 2017), 38.

25. "American Negro Wins in German," *The Bicycling World*, September 22, 1906, 740.

26. "What the Americans are Doing Abroad," *The Bicycling World*, June 9, 1906, 308.

27. "More Foreign Candidates for Six-Days," *The Bicycling World*, October 20, 1906, 98.

28. Elizabeth Stordeur Pryor, *Colored Travelers: Mobility and the Fight for Citizenship before the Civil War* (Chapel Hill: University of North Carolina Press, 2016), 7.

29. "Paris as a 'Nigger Heaven,'" *The Bicycling World*, May 18, 1907, 272.

30. "Paris as a 'Nigger Heaven,'" *The Bicycling World*, May 18, 1907, 272. It was a little odd that Germain Ibron and Vendredi were included since neither were from America. Vendredi's real name was Hippolyte Figaro.

31. The historian Theresa Rundstedtler discusses similar circumstances for Black boxers in Paris and London since Black men were allegedly "permitted to mix with white women on social equality." See: Rundstedtler, *Jack Johnson*, 145, 156.

32. Jason Farago, "Courtesans and Street Walkers: Prostitutes in Art," September 10, 2015, http://www.bbc.com/culture/story/20150910-courtesans-and -street-walkers-prostitutes-in-art.

33. Miranda Gill, *Eccentricity and the Cultural Imagination in Nineteenth-Century Paris* (New York: Oxford University Press, 2009), 126.

34. Gill, *Eccentricity and the Cultural Imagination*, 103–4.

35. Gill, *Eccentricity and the Cultural Imagination*, 107. Gill briefly mentions the zoological descriptions of French women in those terms.

36. Moore, *I Fight for a Living*, 124.

37. "Taylor Will Stay Abroad," *Cleveland Gazette*, June 29, 1901.

38. "Taylor Will Stay Abroad," *Cleveland Gazette*, June 29, 1901.

39. "Taylor Will Stay Abroad," *Cleveland Gazette*, June 29, 1901.

40. Pryor, *Colored Travelers*, 4, 8.

41. Moore, *I Fight for a Living*, 3–4.

Notes to Chapters 7 and 8

42. Pryor, *Colored Travelers*, 4.

43. "Same Old Major," *Cleveland Gazette*, March 30, 1901.

44. "America's Crack Cyclist is Given Tea Parties in Paris, France—Refined Parisian Women in Attendance," *Topeka Plaindealer*, April 19, 1901.

45. Rundstedtler, *Jack Johnson*, 141.

46. "'Major' Taylor: The Little Afro-American Cyclist Who is Champion of America," *Cleveland Gazette*, May 11, 1901.

47. "France at his Feet," *Cleveland Gazette*, July 13, 1901.

48. "France at his Feet," *Cleveland Gazette*, July 13, 1901.

49. "America's Crack Cyclist is given Tea Parties in Paris, France—Refined Parisian Women in Attendance," *Topeka Plaindealer*, April 19, 1901.

50. "Walthour's Merry Christmas," *The Bicycling World*, December 29, 1906, 387.

51. "Next Year's Racing Prospects," *The Bicycling World*, December 29, 1906, 387.

52. *Worcester Telegram*, July 6, 1904. Quoted in Ritchie, *Major Taylor*, 203. See also pp. 199–203; Ritchie documents the factors weighing on Taylor's decision to take a break from racing.

53. "La Resurrection Du Negre," *L'Auto*, March 7, 1907.

54. Paul G. Halpern, *A Naval History of World War I* (Annapolis: Naval Institute Press, 2012), 386.

55. Rebecca Jo Plant and Frances M. Clarke, "'The Crowning Insult': Federal Segregation and the Gold Star Mother and Widow Pilgrimages of the Early 1930s," *Journal of American History* 102, no. 2 (2015): 407, 410, 429, 431. Drs. Plant and Clarke describe the stories about the conditions on the segregated ships as "rumor" that served Democratic operatives in trying to lure Black voters away from the Republican Party in the early 1930s. Plant and Clarke also highlight many of the fine accommodations provided for the Black mothers once they were in Europe.

56. "Major Taylor Floating Toward France," *The Bicycling World and Motorcycle Review*, May 9, 1908, 296.

57. *Worcester Telegram*, July 6, 1904; Reproduced in Andrew Ritchie, *Major Taylor: The Extraordinary Career of Champion Bicycle Racer* (Baltimore: Johns Hopkins University Press, 1988), 203.

58. "Le Roman Du Negre," *L'Auto*, April 21, 1907, 5.

59. *L'Auto*, April 23, 1907.

60. "Riders Coy Towards Salt Lake," *The Bicycling World and Motorcycle Review*, April 18, 1908, 126.

Chapter 8. Home Trainers and Vaudeville

1. Michelle R. Scott, *Blues Empress in Black Chattanooga: Bessie Smith and the Emerging Urban South* (Urbana: University of Illinois Press, 2008), 116.

2. Details about the Florida Blossoms act come from: *Ocala Evening Star*, January 29, 1907; *Franklin's Paper, The Statesman*, August 26, 1911; and *The Covington Leader*, July 18, 1917.

3. Scott, *Blues Empress in Black Chattanooga*, 117.

216   *Notes to Chapter 8*

4. Nicholas Gebhardt, *Vaudeville Melodies: Popular Musicians and Mass Entertainment in American Culture, 1870–1929* (Chicago: University of Chicago Press, 2017), 135.

5. Scott, *Blues Empress in Black Chattanooga*, 129.

6. Rick Altman, *Silent Film Sound* (New York: Columbia University Press, 2004), 96.

7. Sharon Ammen, *May Irwin: Singing, Shouting, and the Shadow of Minstrelsy* (Urbana: University of Illinois Press, 2016), 14.

8. Scott, *Blues Empress in Black Chattanooga*, 127.

9. *The Covington Leader*, July 18, 1917.

10. Allison Keyes, "The East St. Louis Race Riot Left Dozens Dead, Devastating a Community on the Rise," *Smithsonian Magazine*, June 30, 2017.

11. Altman, *Silent Film Sound*, 96.

12. "Notes from Florida Blossom's Company," *Indianapolis Freeman*, January 1, 1916.

13. "The Circle Theater, Philadelphia, PA," *Indianapolis Freeman*, July 19, 1913.

14. Elizabeth Stordeur Pryor, *Colored Travelers: Mobility and the Fight for Citizenship before the Civil War* (Chapel Hill: University of North Carolina Press, 2016), 92.

15. "May Race 100 Miles on Home Trainers," *The Bicycling World and Motorcycle Review*, March 28, 1909, 15.

16. "Stageology at Capital City," *New York Age*, November 2, 1911.

17. Obituary for William Ivy, *Moline Daily Dispatch*, February 25, 1956; Stockton State Hospital Record of William F. Ivy Case no. 23191. In author's possession.

18. *The Bicycling World and Motorcycle Review*, March 7, 1908, 815.

19. *The Bicycling World and Motorcycle Review*, March 7, 1908, 815. He did actually go to Europe to race and had some impressive results.

20. "Charges Follow Roller Racers," *The Bicycling World and Motorcycle Review*, March 14, 1908, 848.

21. "Charges Follow Roller Racers," *The Bicycling World and Motorcycle Review*, March 14, 1908, 848.

22. "Charges Follow Roller Racers," *The Bicycling World and Motorcycle Review*, March 14, 1908, 848.

23. Joseph Boskin, *Sambo: The Rise and Demise of an American Jester* (New York: Oxford University Press, 1988), 13.

24. Boskin, *Sambo*, 14.

25. Bruce Epperson, "How Many Bikes: An Investigation into the Quantification of Bicycling, 1878–1914," in *Cycle History 11: Proceedings of the 11th International Cycling History Conference*, eds. Andrew Ritchie and Rob Van Der Plas (San Francisco: Van Der Plas Publications, 2001), 49. Epperson studied census reports of "apparent bicycle consumption" and compared numbers there to those reported by members of the bicycle industry. Finding neither completely trustworthy, he estimates bicycle production at 109,300 in 1894; 437,200 in 1896; and 928,000 in 1898.

Notes to Chapter 8

26. I explore this topic fully in another book. See: Robert Turpin, *First Taste of Freedom: A Cultural History of Bicycle Marketing in the United States* (Syracuse: Syracuse University Press, 2018).

27. *The Bicycling World and Motorcycle Review*, January 23, 1909, 696. The 1910 census lists him as being married to Bertha Jackson.

28. *The Bicycling World and Motorcycle Review*, February 6, 1909, 781.

29. *The Bicycling World and Motorcycle Review*, November 26, 1904, 209.

30. "Theater and Stageology at the Capital City," *Indianapolis Freeman*, January 13, 1912.

31. Hardy A. Jackson, inmate #17994, Inmate Case Files, Charlestown State Prison, HS9.01/ series 305, Massachusetts Archives, Boston, Massachusetts.

32. "Record Races at Vailsburg," *New York Times*, July 14, 1902.

33. "Cyclists Ran into Women," *New York Times*, September 1, 1906.

34. "Pursued by Puncture Fiend," *The Bicycling World and Motorcycle Review*, August 28, 1909, 853.

35. "Amateurs Stir Garden Crowds," *The Bicycling World and Motorcycle Review*, September 19, 1908, 964.

36. "Five Teams Bunched," *New York Times*, September 19, 1908.

37. "Whites and Blacks on the Rollers," *The Bicycling World and Motorcycle Review*, March 30, 1907, 21.

38. "Whites and Blacks on the Rollers," *The Bicycling World and Motorcycle Review*, March 30, 1907, 21

39. Boskin, *Sambo*, 65. Boskin quotes the Bishop Henry Benjamin Whipple on this point. Whipple wrote in his diary, "Some of the funniest beings I have ever seen are of the negro dandy species—so much gas and wind and smoke with a little charcoal is seldom seen."

40. "Hardy Jackson Winner at Last," *The Bicycling World and Motorcycle Review*, August 31, 1907, 703.

41. "Hardy Jackson Winner at Last," *The Bicycling World and Motorcycle Review*, August 31, 1907, 703.

42. "Hardy Jackson Winner at Last," *The Bicycling World and Motorcycle Review*, August 31, 1907, 703.

43. *The Bicycling World and Motorcycle Review*, Sept. 21, 1907, 790.

44. There were fewer independent countries in Africa at the time than there are now, but the "partition of Africa" was well established by 1907.

45. The Great Adams may have also been a former competitive cyclist but that is not clear. He may have been the Black cyclist Earl Adams from Montclair, New Jersey, but then again, his real name may not have been Adams at all.

46. Hardy A. Jackson, inmate #17994, Inmate Case Files, Charlestown State Prison, HS9.01/ series 305, Massachusetts Archives, Boston, Massachusetts.

47. Erin Blakemore, "Explore the Flickering, Forgotten Past of African-Americans in Silent Film," *Smithsonian Magazine*, November 8, 2016.

Chapter 9. Once Was Lost

1. Andrew Ritchie, *Major Taylor: The Extraordinary Career of a Champion Bicycle Racer* (Baltimore: Johns Hopkins University Press, 1988), 220. Ritchie says that one account claims he had $75,000 in cash reserves while another puts that figure at $35,000.

2. Ritchie, *Major Taylor*, 221. Ritchie was able to interview Sydney before her death.

3. Ritchie, *Major Taylor*, 223–25.

4. Ritchie, *Major Taylor*, 227.

5. Ritchie, *Major Taylor*, 235.

6. Ritchie, *Major Taylor*, 235.

7. Ritchie, *Major Taylor*, 236.

8. Ritchie, *Major Taylor*, 237–38.

9. Ritchie, *Major Taylor*, 247–48.

10. Ritchie, *Major Taylor*, 248–49.

11. Ritchie, *Major Taylor*, 252–53.

12. Marshall W. "Major" Taylor, *The Fastest Bicycle Rider in the World; The Autobiography of Major Taylor* (Brattleboro: S. Greene Press, 1972), 417.

13. Joint Committee on Printing, "Memorial Services for James Bernard Bowler: Eighty-Fifth Congress First Session" (Washington: U.S. Printing Office, 1957), 5, 10; Ritchie, *Major Taylor*, 253.

14. Joint Committee on Printing, "Memorial Services for James Bernard Bowler: Eighty-Fifth Congress First Session" (Washington: U.S. Printing Office, 1957), 10–13.

15. Ritchie, *Major Taylor*, 255.

16. F. Robert Hunter, "Tourism and Empire: The Thomas Cook & Son Enterprise on the Nile, 1868–1914," *Middle Eastern Studies* 40, no. 5 (Sep. 2004): 30.

17. He may have even left a wife behind, but it does not look like they had much of a relationship. There is a marriage license listing the name of Winnie Partee, whom he married in Marion County, Indiana, in 1899. Of course, the auspices of that marriage are slightly suspicious since some of the details are off. The marriage license lists him as Woody Hedgepath, son of Frank Hedgepath, born in Kentucky in 1880. A few other sources list his year of birth as 1884 or 1881. The 1900 census lists Woody as single and a "roomer" in the home of Frank Harris.

18. http://www.lepetitbraquet.fr/chron103_Hedspeth-woody.html

19. "Mac Lean and Hedspeth Get Licenses," *The Bicycling World and Motorcycle Review*, July 20, 1907, 530.

20. http://www.lepetitbraquet.fr/chron103_Hedspeth-woody.html

21. "Report of the Death of an American Citizen," American Foreign Service, May 8, 1941, Serial number 1221.

22. "Report of the Death of an American Citizen," American Foreign Service, May 8, 1941, Serial number 1221.

Notes to Chapter 9 219

23. Le Petit Braquet, "Woody Hedspath: D'Indianapolis à Paris, l'étrange histoire du négre no. 2," https://www.lepetitbraquet.fr/chron103_hedspath-woody.html.

24. Finnison, *Boston's Cycling Craze*, 16, 214.

25. Finnison, *Boston's Cycling Craze*, 214.

26. Emily K. Abel, "Taking the Cure to the Poor: Patient's Responses to New York City's Tuberculosis Program, 1894–1918," *American Journal of Public Health* 87, no. 11 (November 1997): 1808.

27. "Secrecy about Imported Teams," *The Bicycling World and Motorcycle Review*, November 13, 1909, 259.

28. "Recorder Trotter," *Boston Daily Advertiser*, August 18, 1887.

29. "Many Diseases Carried by House Flies," *Trenton Evening Times*, June 13, 1911.

30. "Insane Tortured, Dragged by Hair, Nurses Charge," *Boston Journal*, October 22, 1913.

31. "More Nurses Tell of Torture: Councilman saw Women 'Kneed,'" *Boston Journal*, October 23, 1913.

32. "Insanity Board to Probe Charges of Brutality Tuesday," *Boston Journal*, October 25, 1913.

33. "Insanity Board to Probe Charges of Brutality Tuesday," *Boston Journal*, October 25, 1913.

34. "Insanity Board at Odds Over Torture Probe," *Boston Journal*, October 30, 1913.

35. "Drunkards Guard Bay State Insane, Attendant Says," *Boston Journal*, November 4, 1913.

36. "Drunkards Guard Bay State Insane, Attendant Says," *Boston Journal*, November 4, 1913; "Insane Wards were 'Doped,' Probers Hear," *Boston Journal*, November 8, 1913.

37. "Doctor Admits Sane People Are Held in Asylum," *Boston Journal*, November 20, 1913.

38. "His Ribs Fatally Brittle," *Washington Bee*, February 14, 1914.

39. "Says Hot Water Caused Death," *Boston Journal*, April 21, 1915.

40. "Clarke and Mac Are Beaten in First Races," *Patterson Morning Call*, February 2, 1909. In his hospital records, while interviewed Ivy claimed he won the Luxemburg twenty-four-hour race in 1909, the twenty-four-hour race at Marseilles, but was cheated in the end, and the Bal-Der. Twenty-four-hour race in Paris.

41. "Racing Fast but Standing Still," *The Bicycling World and Motorcycle Review*, February 29, 1908, 814.

42. World War II Draft Card, Sept. 12, 1918, included in his hospital records.

43. Dr. Young, "Clinical Commitence," March 29, 1917.

44. Dr. Y. Alameda, "Commitment Paper," March 7, 1917.

45. Stockton State Hospital, Patient record for William F. Ivy, Case No. 23191, 1917, p.4. In author's possession.

46. Stockton State Hospital, record for William F. Ivy, 4–8.

Notes to Chapter 9

47. Stockton State Hospital, record for William F. Ivy, 5.

48. Stockton State Hospital, record for William F. Ivy, 19.

49. Stockton State Hospital, record for William F. Ivy, 5.

50. Dr. Y. Alameda, "Commitment Paper," March 7, 1917. Included in the Stockton State Hospital patient record for William F. Ivy.

51. "The Official or Detailed Report of the Visit of Julius F. Taylor to the Prince Hall Masonic and Order of Eastern Star Home at Rock Island, Illinois, July 4 and 5," *Chicago Broad Axe*, July 12, 1924.

52. Stockton State Hospital, record for William F. Ivy, 19; D.S.S. Form 1, Selective Service Registration Card, 1942.

53. "Cyclists Ran into Women," *New York Times*, September 1, 1906.

54. JoAnne Sweeny, "Undead Statutes: The Rise, Fall, and Continuing Uses of Adultery and Fornication Criminal Laws," *Loyola University Chicago Law Journal* 46, no. 1 (Fall 2014): 158, 160.

55. Sweeny, "Undead Statuses," 162.

56. Sweeny, "Undead Statuses," 165.

57. Massachusetts Civic League, Inc., "The Children's Commission," 3 Joy Street, Boston (January 1930), 18, https://harvardartmuseums.org/collections/object/3.2002.1874.31.

58. Carolyn Cocca, *Jailbait: The Politics of Statutory Rape Laws in the United States* (Albany: State University of New York Press, 2004), 11.

59. Cocca, *Jailbait*, 12.

60. Cocca, *Jailbait*, 13.

61. Cocca, *Jailbait*, 14.

62. Cocca, *Jailbait*, 14.

63. Cocca, *Jailbait*, 16.

64. W.F. O'Brien, Hardy A. Jackson History, March 14, 1930, in Hardy A. Jackson, inmate #17994, Inmate Case Files, Charlestown State Prison, HS9.01/ series 305, Massachusetts Archives, Boston, Massachusetts.

65. William T. Hanson, M.D. Medical Director of State Farm Massachusetts report to Francis Lanagan, Warden of Charlestown State Prison. October 16, 1936. Hardy A. Jackson, inmate #17994, Inmate Case Files, Charlestown State Prison, HS9.01/ series 305, Massachusetts Archives, Boston, Massachusetts.

66. Hardy A. Jackson, inmate #17994, Inmate Case Files, Charlestown State Prison, HS9.01/ series 305, Massachusetts Archives, Boston, Massachusetts; Joanne Schumpert (granddaughter of Hardy Jackson), interview by author, August 4, 2019.

67. Robert J. Turpin, *First Taste of Freedom: A Cultural History of Bicycle Marketing in the United States* (Syracuse: Syracuse University Press, 2018), 74–94.

68. Katherine C. Mooney, *Race Horse Men: How Slavery and Freedom were Made at the Racetrack* (Cambridge: Harvard University Press, 2014), 212, 237–38.

69. Mooney, *Race Horse Men*, 234–35.

Notes to Chapter 9 and Epilogue

70. Louis Moore, *I Fight for a Living: Boxing and the Battle for Black Manhood, 1880–1915* (Urbana: University of Illinois Press, 2017), 166–70.

Epilogue

1. Alex Harsley, interview by author, April 28, 2021.
2. Peter Joffre Nye, *Hearts of Lions: The History of American Bicycle Racing* (Omaha: University of Nebraska Press, 2020), 203.
3. Nye, *Hearts of Lions*, 203.
4. Nye, *Hearts of Lions*, 204.
5. Nye, *Hearts of Lions*, 204–5.
6. Nye, *Hearts of Lions*, 206.
7. Nye, *Hearts of Lions*, 216–17.
8. Nye, *Hearts of Lions*, 216.
9. Alex Harsley, interview by author.
10. Nye, *Hearts of Lions*, 216, 218.
11. Alex Harsley, interview by author.
12. Alex Harsley, interview by author.
13. "Champion on Wheels," *Ebony*, September, 1967, 108.
14. Oliver Martin, interview by author, May 4, 2021.
15. "Champion on Wheels," 108; Oliver Martin, interview by author, May 4, 2021.
16. Oliver Martin, interview by author; Joe Fitzgibbon, "Renowned Cycling Coach Lights Fire Under Riders," *The Oregonian*, October 18, 2007, https://www.oregonlive.com/oregonoutdoors/2007/10/renowned_cycling_coach_lights.html.
17. "Champion on Wheels," 113.
18. "Oliver 'Butch' Martin," U.S. Bicycling Hall of Fame, https://usbhof.org/inductee/oliver-butch-martin/.
19. "Champion on Wheels," 110.
20. Oliver Martin, interview by author.
21. "Oliver 'Butch' Martin," U.S. Bicycling Hall of Fame, https://usbhof.org/inductee/oliver-butch-martin/.
22. Oliver Martin, interview by author; "Anything but Idle," *Kids of Bike*, May 17, 2011, http://kidsofbike.blogspot.com/2011/05/.
23. "Nelson Vails Biography," United States Bicycle Hall of Fame, https://usbhof.org/inductee/nelson-vails/.
24. "Hall of Fame," Valley Preferred Cycling Center, https://thevelodrome.com/hall-of-fame/.
25. "Inductees," United States Bicycle Hall of Fame, https://usbhof.org/inductees/.
26. Rahsaan Bahati, interview by author, March 5, 2008.
27. Betsy Welch, "Rahsaan Bahati: 'I've had to conform to get my foot in the door,'" *Velonews*, June 4, 2020, https://www.velonews.com/news/rahsaan-bahati-ive-had-to-conform-to-get-my-foot-in-door/.

28. Welch, "Rahsaan Bahati."

29. Rahsaan Bahati, interview by author.

30. Welch, "Rahsaan Bahati."

31. Welch, "Rahsaan Bahati."

32. Welch, "Rahsaan Bahati."

33. Welch, "Rahsaan Bahati."

34. Welch, "Rahsaan Bahati." Giddeon Massie is a former American professional track cyclist and multi-time national champion in the United States. He competed in the 2003 Pan American Games and the 2004 and 2008 Olympic games.

35. Jessica Coulon, "Ayesha McGowan Joins the Liv Racing Women's WorldTour Team," *Bicycling*, February 17, 2021, https://www.bicycling.com/news/a35537117/ayesha-mcgowan-joins-womens-world-tour-liv-racing/.

36. Ayesha McGowan, "A Quick Brown Fox," aquickbrownfox.com.

37. Andy Cochrane, "This Los Angeles Team Wants to Diversify Cycling. They're Starting with its Podiums," *New York Times*, December 1, 2020.

38. InCycle, "Promoting Diversity in Cycling," interview of Justin Williams, https://www.youtube.com/watch?v=oQpU2lRACHs.

39. Andy Cochrane, "This Los Angeles Team Wants to Diversify Cycling. They're Starting with its Podiums," *New York Times*, December 1, 2020.

40. Global Cycling Network, "Making the Coolest Team in Pro Cycling: L39ion of LA and Justin Williams," February 15, 2020, https://www.youtube.com/watch?v=WzB2oOftfiI.

41. "Legion of Los Angeles," https://www.rapha.cc/us/en_US/stories/legion-of-los-angeles.

42. "Legion of Los Angeles," https://www.rapha.cc/us/en_US/stories/legion-of-los-angeles.

43. InCycle, "Promoting Diversity in Cycling."

44. Global Cycling Network, "Making the Coolest Team in Pro Cycling: L39ion of LA and Justin Williams."

45. Andy Cochrane, "This Los Angeles Team Wants to Diversify Cycling."

46. Zwift, "Zwift News: Zwift's Diversity Initiatives Update," January 25, 2021, https://www.zwift.com/news/24792-diversity-initiatives-2021.

47. Zwift, "Zwift News."

48. USA Cycling, "USA Cycling Demographics Survey 2020 Results," https://s3.amazonaws.com/usac-craft-uploads-production/documents/Demographics-Report-2020.pdf.

49. USA Cycling, "Getting Kids on Bikes: Let's Ride Camps," https://usacycling.org/lets-ride-camps.

50. Lorenz Finison, "The Outer Line: The Kittie Knox Award—for equity, diversity and inclusion in cycling," *Velonews*, July 29, 2020, https://www.velonews.com/culture/the-outer-line-the-kittie-knox-award-for-equity-diversity-and-inclusion-in-cycling/.

Notes to Epilogue

51. Logan Watts, "Rivendell Bicycle Works offers Black Reparations Pricing (BRP) Press Release," BikePacking.com, October 1, 2020, https://bikepacking.com/news/rivendell-bicycle-Black-reparations-pricing/.

52. Rivendell Bicycle Works, "BRF Update Feb 24, 2021," https://www.rivbike.com/pages/Black-reparations-pricing.

53. Rivendell Bicycle Works, "BRF Update Feb 24, 2021."

54. "Commission to Study and Develop Reparation Proposals for African Americans Act," 117th Congress, Congress.gov/bill/117th-congress/house-bill/40.

55. Haden Coplen, "This Bike Company Launched a Black Reparations Program. Then the Lawyers Called," *Outside*, August 4, 2022, https://www.outsideonline.com/outdoor-gear/bikes-and-biking/rivendell-black-reparations/.

56. Coplen, "This Bike Company Launched a Black Reparations Program."

57. Ben Christopher, "Churches, Gunshops and Irate Brides: All the Shutdown Lawsuits Against Newsome, Explained," *ABC*, https://www.abc10.com/article/news/health/coronavirus/all-the-shutdown-lawsuits-against-newsom-explained/103–4f6f7b14–0015–4831-b09b-b094527a8e65.

Index

Adams, Earl, 151, 217n45
adultery: as crime, 171–73
Alabama division of LAW, 58
Ali, Muhammad, 186
Alvorado, Ceylin del Carmin, 9
Amateur Athletic Union, 109–10
amateurism, 44, 60, 107–10; class B, 44, 60
American Racing Cyclists Union, 106
Anthony, Susan B., 36, 80
Armstrong, Henry, 178
Asbury Park, 40–41, 70–71, 77–78, 86–87, 92–96, 207n46
Associated Cycling Clubs of Chicago, 51
Atlanta, 58, 126, 133, 190
Atlantic City, 144
Avenia, Tom, 182

B&O Railroad, 61
Backus, John, 73–74, 207n58, 209n25
Bacon, Kevin, 187
Bader (German cyclist), 126–27
Bahati, Rahsaan, 8, 188–94, 196–97
Bardgett, Walter, 106, 124
Barrett, George K., 53–54, 57, 61
Bartley, Johnson & Company, 42. *See also* Belle of Nelson Whisky

Bassett, Abbot, 40, 67–68
Batchelder, A. G., 109–11, 116–17
battle royal, 118
Bearings, The: on Black LAW, 73–74, 91; and the color line, 56–57, 61–64, 88, 91, 95; and Kittie Knox, 93–96; and LAW Assembly, 44, 47–48, 71; and LAW debauchery, 70–71; and the MACC, 110–11; relaying threats, 58; response to British press, 50; on secession from LAW, 52–56; and Robert Teamoh, 65–68, 73
Bedford-Stuyvesant, 182
Belle of Nelson Whisky, 41–42, 71
Benfica Cemetery, 163
Berlin, 126–28, 132
Berlo, P. J., 28–29
Betts, Ritchie G., 108, 110–11, 211n33
bicycle: boom 4, 18, 30–31; production, 30–31, 76, 79, 147, 188, 216n25
Bicycling World and LAW Bulletin, The, 17–18, 20, 26, 29–30, 46, 70; bias, 28
Bicycling World and Motorcycle Review, The: bias against professionalism, 110, 123–24; treatment of Black cyclists, 106–11, 113–17, 126, 128, 133–36, 145, 148–53, 171

226 Index

Bicycles R Fun, 195–96
Black codes, 24
BlackCycling, 8
Black cycling club, 11, 62, 75, 97; of Louisville, 66. *See also* League of Colored Wheelmen of America
Black cyclists: combination against, 112; as dangerous, 81–85
BlackLivesMatter movement, 192, 195
Black manhood, 6, 21, 36–37, 45, 103, 118, 137, 146
Black prizefighters, 28, 114, 126, 130, 178, 214n31
Black Reparations Pricing program, 194–96
Blackstone Bicycle Works, 8
Bleuzat, Ernest, 153
Blizzard, William S., 116–17
"bloody shirt," 53–54
bloomers, 4, 80–81, 84, 89–90, 92
boneshaker, 3. *See also* velocipede
Boskin, Joseph, 146, 217n39
Boston, 65–68, 75, 85, 87, 94, 124, 165–66, 207n46; cycling renaissance, 19–20, 26–27, 29; cycling scene, 35; as host city, 40, 70–71; politics, 66; as racially progressive, 23–24
Boston Daily Journal, 27
Boston Globe, 65
Boston Post, 68
Boston Wheelmen, 94
Bourne, Lisa, 193
Bourotte (French cyclist), 120–21
Bowler, James Bernard, 160–61
Braggs, Andrew, 33–34
Brandenburg, Germany, 127
Brandes, Otto, 145–46
Brewer, John, 151
Breyer, Victor, 131, 133
Brooklyn, NY, 182–83
Bruce, Blanche K., 23
Brunswick, GA, 55, 80, 97
Buffalo Velodrome, 120, 122
Burdette, Charles L., 43

Caldwell, H. L., Jr., 28–29
Calumet Cycling Club, 62

Cambridge, MA, 25–26, 28, 34–36, 165
Cambridgeport Bicycle Club, 28, 36
Cannondale, 192, 197
Cape Town, 164
Capital Cycling Club of Nashville, 52–53
Capone, Al, 101
Cardon, Nathan, 84
Carpenter, Connie, 186
Cave Hill Cemetery, 42
Centennial International Exhibit of 1876 in Philadelphia, 14
Center for American Liberty, 195
Central Park, 187
Century Road Club of New York, 183
Chandler, Ida May, 171–73, 176
Chaplin, Charlie, 155
Charlestown State Prison, 174, 176–77
Chicago, 31–32, 50–51, 55, 73; colored bicycle club, 37; and Thomas Sheridan, 43–44; and "Major" Taylor, 1, 160–61
Chicago Broad Axe, 170
Chicago Tribune, 31
citizenship, 27, 126–28, 131, 137
Civil War, 5, 11, 14, 22, 24–25, 42; memory of, 53–54
Clayton, Lonnie, 178
Cleburne, TX, 54
Cleveland, 33, 73, 91, 170
Cleveland, Grover, 23
Cleveland Gazette, 33, 51, 91, 131, 133
Cocca, Carolyn, 174
cock fighting, 69–71, 105
Cody, "Buffalo" Bill, 120
"colored flyer," 19
Company A of the 25th Infantry, 168
Confederate monuments, 42
Conference of the Colored Men of New England, 22–23
Cook County Hospital, 160
Coquelle, Robert, 133
Corbett, Jim, 102, 104
Corey, Timothy, 20
Corey Hill, 19–20
costumes, 84, 89–92, 97
Cottage City, 72, 91–92
Coubertin, Pierre de, 109
Courier-Journal, 11, 41–42, 47, 49–51

Index

227

crashes, 113, 116–17, 124, 211n20
Crusaders Club, 182
Crutcher, Robert, 18
cycling: boom, 4, 18, 30–31; clubs, 3–4,
11–13, 28–29, 31–33, 37, 51, 61–63, 80,
119, 147, 186; as dangerous, 15, 19, 29,
78, 213n60; as democratic, 7, 33; development in the U.S., 2–4, 20, 30; fashion,
4, 80–81, 84, 89–92, 97; paramilitary
training, 4; popularity, 2–5, 7, 11–12,
15, 18–19, 30–31, 76, 79–80, 85, 147; as
a social statement, 4, 17, 21, 34, 37, 80,
98, 117, 137

dandy-horse (draisine), 2, 12
Darktown Comics, Darktown Bicycle Club
series, 81–84
Davis, A. C., 50
Davis, Alphonso, 152
Dayton, OH, 123
Denver, 40–41, 50, 69–71, 94; wheelmen,
50–51
Desgrange, Henri, 162
Detroit Plaindealer, 51
Deupree, T. J., 52,
Dhillon, Harmeet, 195
Diggs, J. C., 111, 115
Dinnel and Jackson Velodrome, 148–49
"Dock" (editorial pseudonym), 53–54
Dorsey (of Milwaukee), 33
Dorsey, Thomas, 40
Douglass, Frederick, 22–23
Dove, Melvin T., 99–100, 104–9, 111–19,
123–24, 164–65
draisine, 2, 12
drug use, 103
Drummond, David, 23–31, 34–37, 144,
165–68, 171, 176

East Moline State Hospital, 170
East St. Louis race riot, 140
Ebony, 185
Ellinger, Robert, 37
Elliott, Sterling, 46–48, 51
Elrey people, 169
English, John, 43
Epperson, Bruce, 216n25

Eureka Wheel Club, 73
Excello Manufacturing Co., 158
exoticism, 130, 146

Farnum, Ken, 183
Faucheux, Lucien, 161, 163–64
feminisim, 6, 36–37, 80–81, 88, 174. *See
also* womanhood
Fenn, W. S., 116
fetishization, 130
Figaro, Hippolyte, 214n30. *See also* Ven-
dredi
Finnison, Lorenz, 94, 208n13
Fleming Home Trainers, 169
Florida Blossoms, 138–40
Flushing Meadows Velodrome, 182
fornication: as crime, 172–73
Foss, Eugene Noble, 166
Fourth of July races on Boston Common,
27–29
Fox News, 195
Francis, Herbie, 182–85
Freju, 182
Friss, Evan, 33, 84

Galt House, 39, 41
Galvin, J. Frank, 101–2, 116
Gene, Yohann, 9
Gerould, F. W., 58,
Gervex, Henri, 129
Giant Bicycle Company, 188, 197
Gill, Miranda, 129–30
Godfrey, George, 131
gold star mothers, 134
good roads, 38, 45–46, 67
Gorski, Mark, 187
Gougoltz, Jean, 112–13
Gray (lesser-known black cyclist), 103
Great Adams, The (trick cyclist), 138, 140,
147, 154, 217n45
Greenidge, Kerri, 24,

Hadfield (cyclist), 116–17
Haldeman, William Birch, 42
Hall, Charles H., 94
Hamilton, William, 91, 164
Handy, W. C., 139

228   *Index*

Handy, William B., 94
Hanlon Brothers, 12
Hannibal Athletic Club, 62, 75
Hardin, A. S., 48, 56
Harlem, 182, 184–85, 187
Harris (Chief Consul of Alabama LAW), 58
Harris, George, 144
Harris, James, 85
Harrison, Michael, 176
Harrison, William Henry, 38
Harsley, Alex, 182, 184
Harvard University Cycling Club, 29
Hawley, Fred, 110–11
Hedspeth, Woody, 118–19, 176–77, 181;
    comparison to Taylor, 132; death, 163–
    64; early life, 121–23, 218n17; at the end
    of his career, 161–63; in Europe, 106–7,
    120–21, 123–30, 135–37; six-day racing,
    99, 104–5, 108, 112–14, 211n20
Hemingway, Ernest, 101
Hendricks, H. V., 167
Herlihy, David, 3, 26–27
high wheeler, 3–4, 14–21, 29–30, 78–80
Hintze, Herman, 143
hobbyhorse, 2, 12
Holm (Chief Consul of St. Louis), 52
home trainer, 141–42, 145, 148, 152–54,
    168–69, 171, 188. *See also* rollers
Hotel Scribe, 132
hottentot, 115
House Resolution 40, 195
Howard Theater, 143
Hunter, Robert, 114–15
Hurley, Marcus L., 108

Ibron, Germain, 123, 129, 213n10, 214n30
Illinois Central Railroad, 110
Illinois Cycle Company, 52
Illinois division of LAW, 43, 45, 51, 58
Indianapolis, 1, 14, 21, 63, 122, 162
Indianapolis Freeman, 37, 92, 140, 149
Indianapolis Journal, 40
Indianapolis Journal Recorder, 122–23
Indiana University Little 500, 188
Indo-American Exhibit 1889, 120
Instagram, 197

International Cycle Association, 148,
    151–52
International Cycle Works, 148
International Cyclists' Union, 125–26
International Six-Day Bicycle Race, 99–
    100, 102, 104, 112, 118, 163
Irvington-Milburn Road Race, 110–11,
    118, 148
Isom, Albert, 178
Iver Johnson Company, 158,
Ivy, Alice, 170
Ivy, William Fleming, 154–55, 165, 176–77,
    181; early life, 144–45; in Europe, 129,
    137, 170, 219n40; home-trainer racing,
    145–46; life after racing, 168–71; 24-
    hour record, 170

Jackson, Bertha, 172, 217n27
Jackson, Hardy K., 141–44, 148–56, 165,
    171–77
Jackson, Peter, 127, 178
Jacquish, Louis, 78
Jeffries, Howard, 42
Jersey City, 148
Jim Crow, 8, 76, 132, 134–35, 141, 161, 165,
    179
Johns, Alphonso, 152
Johnson, Colonel G. Edward, 40, 42, 47, 50
Johnson, Fred, 158
Johnson, Jack, 126, 141, 178
Johnson, John S., 132
John Street Baptist Church, 158
Jones, Ephraham, 57
Jue (French cyclist), 120–21

Kapchovsky, Annie, 80
Kay Jewelry Store, 174–75
Keaton, Buster, 155
Keirin Circuit, 187
Kentucky, 17, 39–40, 42, 70–71, 178; divi-
    sion of LAW, 47; lynchings 49–50; Little
    Hickman, 69–70; and Hedspeth, 121–22,
    162
Kentucky Derby, 178
Khoikhoi, 115
Kim, Dennis, 192

Index

Kimble, Owen, 128
King Williams, 138
Kipling, Rudyard, 46
Kirkpatrick, Thomas J., 46–47
knickerbockers, 80, 90
Knights of Pythias, 35, 165
Knox, Katherine Towel "Kittie," 94, 97–98, 176–77, 194, 208n13; activism, 78, 94; death, 164–65; early life, 85; fashion, 77, 90; jealousy of, 88, 91–93, 95–96, 205n73; as member of LAW, 78, 85–87, 89; and womanhood, 7
Kramer, Frank, 124, 133–34, 150
Ku Klux Klan, 24

LA Sweat, 8
L'Auto, 134
La Vie Au Grand Air, 124–25
Labecki, Coryn (née Rivera), 196
Lafayette Theater, 148
Lallement, Pierre, 2
laufmaschine, 2
Lawrence, Mace, 140
Lawson, Iver, 124
League of American Bicyclists, 194
League of American Wheelmen, 19, 145, 193–94; and the color line, 37–98 *passim*, 110, 119, 156; debauchery 70–71; membership, 31, 76
League of Colored Wheelmen of America, 73–75
Lebanon, KY, 121
Legion of Los Angeles, 191–93, 197
Le Havre, 134
Le Maitre, Rosalie, 162–63
Let's Ride Camps, 193–94
Le Velo, 131–32
Level Up Cycling Movement, 8, 193
lewd and lascivious cohabitation, 171–74
Lewis, George, 92
Lewis, Jackson, 14
Lindsay, Ike, 129
Lisbon, Portugal, 163
Little Rock, AR, 81, 90
London, 125, 161, 163, 214n31
Los Angeles Bicycle Academy, 193

Louis, Joe, 178
Louisville, KY, 40, 42, 50, 58–59, 61, 64–66, 70
Louisville Times, 42, 64
Luscomb, Charles H., 43, 45–46, 69, 71
lynching, 49–50, 85, 139
Lynn, MA, 26, 173–75

Madison Square Garden, 100, 102, 148, 184; crowds, 104, 113, 151; and home-trainer races, 145
Major's Tire Shop, 158
Malcolm X, 174
Manet, Edouard, 129
Manhattan, 113, 148, 150, 183
Manhattan Beach, 116
manhood, 5, 28, 36, 45, 102–3, 104, 118, 137. *See also* Black manhood
Mann Act, 178
Manning, Chandra, 42
Marks, Patricia, 80
Martello, Mary, 174–75
Martin, Oliver "Butch" Jr., 185–86, 189, 191, 197
mascot, 73–74, 88, 101
masculinity. *See* manhood
Massachusetts Bicycle Club, 32, 34, 95
Massie, Gideon, 190, 222n34
Mastadon Minstrels, 140
McCurdy, A. A., 26–27
McDaniels, Lester, 140–41
McFarland, Floyd, 116–17, 124, 128, 136
McGowan, Ayesha, 8, 190–92, 194, 197–98
McMillan, Frank, 153
Medical News, 100, 105, 118
medical/moral debate around female cyclists, 81
Memphis, TN, 50, 52
mental delusions, 105, 169, 175–76
Meriden Wheel Club, 32
Metal Taylor Tire, 158
Meteor Wheelmen, 97
Metropolitan Association of Cycling Clubs, 110–11, 119
Metzler, Jerry, 182–83
Metzler, Perry, 182–86

230   *Index*

Middle Passage, 137
Miller, Charlie, 123
Miller, Chas "Mush Mouth," 138
minstrel, 138, 140–41
Missouri, 41, 52, 55–56, 139
mobility, 5, 14, 21, 107, 131, 137, 141; social, 34, 37, 97, 103, 107, 137, 155, 177
Montmartre, 162
Moore, Louis, 103, 130, 178
Morrison, Anna, 79, 97
Moulin Rouge, 129
Mount Glenwood Cemetery, 161
Mount, George, 186
Munger, Louis "Birdie," 26–27, 157
Murphy, Isaac, 141, 178
Musee d'Orsay, 129

NAACP, 49, 118, 135
National Assembly of LAW, 44, 72; of 1894, 39, 41, 43, 53, 57, 68–69, 71; of 1895, 67, 92, 94–96
National Bicycle Club of Washington, 62. *See also* Hannibal Athletic Club
National Cycling Association, 117, 119, 123, 145–46; and amateurism, 106–9; criticized by Europeans, 126; and Hedspeth as professional, 162; suspension of Dove, 115; suspension of Taylor, 133
Navarre Wheelmen, 148–49
Nazi occupation of Paris, 163
neurasthenia, 5
Newark, NJ, 111; velodrome, 150
Newby Oval, 122–23
New Haven Journal Courier, 88
New Orleans, 110, 160
New York, 110, 112–13, 133–34, 160; Auburn, 18; legislature, 100; and Charles Luscomb, 43, 45–46; State Amateur Bicycle League, 183
New York Age, 143
New York City, 12, 31, 149, 151–53, 163–64, 182–83, 186
New York City College, 186
New York Daily Tribune, 60
New York Freeman, 27–28, 36
New York Herald, 11, 15, 31, 93
New York Sun, 85

New York Times, 88, 116–17
Nitz, Leonard, 187
Normandy, France, 134–35
Nsek, Ama, 193
Nye, Peter, 104

Ocean House, 93
Old Park Cycling Club of Chicago, 32
Olympic Games, 8, 109, 118, 182–84, 186–88
Orange, NJ, 182
ordinary, 3, 14, 30, 90. *See also* high wheeler
Orlando, FL, 183
Ottley, Amos, 182–83
Overstreet, J. W., 69

Pan American Games, 186–87
Paris, 120, 122, 125, 168, 170; and Hedspeth, 162–64; as paradise for Black people, 128–32
Pash, John, 17, 18
Peck, Arthur K., 68
Pedal2thePeople, 8
Penn, William A., 151, 154–55
penny farthing, 14. *See also* high wheeler
Perkins, George A., 68–69, 71, 96
Perkins, James, 178
Petersen, Grant, 194–95
Peterson, Alexander, 105, 123, 211n20
Philadelphia, 73, 85, 96–97; First Chinese Bicycling Club, 33; LAW Assembly, 39–40, 43, 50–52, 62
Pickett, James, 140, 144, 154
Plessy v. Ferguson, 49, 75
pneumatic tires, 3, 30, 79, 81, 84
pocketing, 104, 117
Pontius, W. H., 46
Pope, Colonel Albert, 14, 34
Potter, Isaac, 46
Powers, Patrick T., 112, 128
Powless, Nielson, 196
Pratt, Charles, 5, 37
Premier Cycle Company, 55–56
prizefights, 102–3
professionalism, 26, 62, 111–13, 161, 181, 186–88, 190–92, 196–97; class implica-

tions, 95; and the color line, 119, 124, 128, 130, 154, 156; and Melvin Dove, 105–9; and Woody Hedspeth, 162; William Ivy, 168; and Hardy Jackson, 150; and Marshall "Major" Taylor, 1, 159. *See also* amateurism

Progressive Era, 1, 6–7, 179

prostitution, 129–30; as analogous to professional racing, 107

Provence, 134

Provident Hospital, 160–61

Pryor, Elizabeth, 128, 131, 141, 200n9

Pullman: porter, 61–63; road race, 51

Quicksilver, 187

racial uplift, 8, 46, 133

racism: abroad, 121, 135–36, 164; Black bodies, 115, 130, 192 (*see also* exoticism; fetishization); Black people as backward, 6; Black people as childlike, 81–85, 118; Black physiology, 28; descendant of Ham, 127; epithets, 57, 63, 69–71, 130, 138–39; general stereotypes, 21, 114, 129, 152, 154, 191; hypersexuality, 174; LAW voucher system, 45, 49; sambo, 146

Ravenswood Track, 122

Razoux, Charles L., 94

Red Cross, 163

Red Lodge Picket, 88

Reese, Benzina, 85–86, 91–92, 95, 97

Referee & Cycle Trade Journal, The, 44, 64, 67, 69, 71, 73–74, 86, 88, 96

Reid, Carlton, 33, 38

resolution of censure, 65–67, 75, 78

Revere Track, 148, 150, 155, 171

Richmond Planet, 73

Ritchie, Andrew, 6, 157–58, 160, 218n1

Rivendell Bicycle Works, 194–96

Riverside Cycle Club, 64, 78, 85, 91–92

Robinson (LAW representative from Massachusetts), 68

Robinson, Sugar Ray, 178

Rock Island, IL, 170–71

rollers, 141–46, 148, 152. *See also* home trainer

Root, Eddie, 101–2, 124

Rousseau, M., 125

Rundstedtler, Theresa, 132, 214n31

Rupprecht, Edward, 114–15

Sacco and Vanzetti, 174

safety bicycle, 20, 29–30, 165, 200n17; rover style, 30; and women, 78–80

sambo, 88, 146

Samuels, Grand Master, 170

sanctions, 44, 145

San Francisco Call, 88

Savannah, GA, 11–12, 136

Savannah Morning News, 95–96

Schwab, Oscar, 127

Schwalbach, Alex, 111

Scofield Barracks Hospital, 169

Scott, Frederick J., 40, 61, 64–65, 113–14

Scott, Michelle, 139

Scott, Ulysses Grant, 104, 113–14, 119

Seattle Post-Intelligence, 90

secession from LAW, 52–53, 55

Second Industrial Revolution, 4

Seldney, A. J., 153

Seneca Falls Convention, 80

Shaw and Hilton Rink, 13

Shelby City, 64

Sheridan, Thomas F., 43–45, 51, 69

Simes, Jack, III, 184

Simmons, David, 110–11, 118

Simmons, W. S., 148

Simms, Willie, 178

six-day bicycle racing, 99–119 *passim*, 128, 134, 141, 147, 154–55, 181, 184; atmosphere, 101; health effects, 100, 102, 105, 119; and masculinity, 118. *See also* International Six-Day Bicycle Race

Smith, Bessie, 139

Smith, Henry Worcester, 159

social mobility, 34, 37, 97, 103, 107, 137, 155, 177

Society for the Prevention of Cruelty to Children, 175

society women, 4, 19, 56

South Boston Flyer, 29

southern cyclists, 53–54

Southern Knights of the Wheel, 53–54

232   *Index*

Southern Wheelmen, 39

Spain, A. C., 129, 137

Specialized Bicycle Components, 197

Spencer, Freddie, 103, 105

Springfield, MA, 71, 91

S.S. Baradine, 161

Stanton, Elizabeth Cady, 36, 80

Star Bicycle, 26

statutory rape, 174

Steiglitz track, 126

St. Louis, 50, 52, 56, 140; Exposition, 106, 124

Stockton State Hospital, 168–70

Stoddard Lovering & Co., 35

Street, J. Gordon, 22–23, 36, 65

strenuous life, 15, 81

Suffolk County House of Corrections, 172

Sullivan, James, 109

Sunny Dixie Minstrels, 140

Sweeny, Joanne, 171, 173

Sydney, Australia, 134

Sylvester, Nigel, 8

syphilis, 169–70

Taylor, Daisy, 159–60

Taylor, Marshall "Major," 6–8, 25–26, 75–76, 112–13, 117; autobiography, 6, 21, 121, 159–60, 182; comparisons to, 122, 151, 153; in early career, 2; feelings about race, 61–65, 121; impact on diversity in cycling, 178, 182–83; nickname, 147; as only professional in U.S., 108–9, 119, 130, 150, 154; as race hero, 133; racing in Europe, 120–21, 123–25, 128–36; in retirement and death, 134, 155, 157–62, 164, 177; and six-day racing, 103–6; as world champion, 1, 122

Taylor, Sydney, 134, 157–60

Taylor and Quick, 158

Team Major Taylor, 188

Teamoh, Robert, 61, 65–69, 72–73, 75–76, 78; attacks against, 67–68

Technological Revolution, 4, 25

Temple, William, 94

Tennessee, 11, 50, 52, 55, 139–40

Texas, 54, 139–40

Thacker, Charles, 54

Thomas Cook and Son, 161–62

Tioga, 97

Toefield, Al, 184

Toga Bike Shop, 187

Topeka Plaindealer, 132–33

Toulouse-Lautrec, Henri de, 129

Tour de France, 9, 162, 191, 196–97

Tour of America's Dairyland, 189–90

Trenton Evening Times, 166

trick riding, 138, 140–41, 143, 146–47

tricycle, 19–21, 29, 78–80

Tri-Mountain Athletic Club, 29, 31–32, 34

Trotter, James Monroe, 22–24, 36, 63, 165

Trotter, William Monroe, 36

Twitter, 197

Tyler, Rose Ivy, 171

Union Army, 42–43

Union Cycle Club, 40

Unione Sportiva Italiana, 185

United Confederate Veterans, 42

United States Bicycling Hall of Fame, 187

United States Cycling Federation, 187–88

USA Cycling, 191, 197

Vails, Nelson, 8, 186–88, 190, 193, 197

Vails, Ronnie, 187

Vailsburg track, 106, 108, 114–17, 148, 150, 168

Van Deever, Charles, 17–19

Van den Dries, William, 153

Van Dendries, Mourice, 153

Vaudeville, 138–56 *passim*, 164, 171

Veblen, Thorstein, 4

Veldrome d'Hiver, 162

velocipede, 2–3, 11–15, 21; rinks, 12; clubs, 11

Velonews, 189, 197

Vendredi, 129, 214n30

Védrines, Ernest, 161, 164

Vichy France, 163

Vietnam War, 181, 184

Vogel, John W., 140

Waltham, MA, 89–90

Walthour, Robert J. "Bobby," 106, 124, 126–28, 133

Index

Washington, Booker T., 36
Washington Times, 90
Watertown State Hospital, 170
Watterson, Henry, 42, 50
Watts, William O., 42
Watts, William Wagner, 39–44, 47, 49–50, 58, 66, 70–72, 75, 194; Watts Amendment, 45, 52, 55–56, 60–62, 66–67, 69, 71–72, 75, 78, 94
Wells, Ida B., 50
Wheaties, 187
Wheaton, Viola, 85–86, 91–92, 95, 97, 164
Wheel and Cycling Trade Review, The, 88, 92–93, 110
Wheelman's Gazette, 45
Whipple, Henry Benjamin, 217n39
Whiteness, 6, 195; and class, 46, 57, 107; and gentility, 88, 91, 95, 97; supremacy, 46; and womanhood, 56, 77, 88, 93, 150, 171, 174
Wichita Daily Eagle, 90
Willard, Frances, 36, 80
Willets Point, 184
Williams, Cory, 8, 193, 197
Williams, John, 19–20

Williams, Justin, 8, 190–92, 197–98
Winchester, TN, 11
Winn, H. J., 52
wire spoke, 14
womanhood, 4, 7, 19, 80, 97. *See also* Whiteness, and womanhood
Women's Christian Temperance Union, 174
Wood, Jeff, 183
Worcester, MA, 1, 78, 133, 135–36, 157–60
Worcester Daily Spy, 30
Worcester Polytechnic Institute, 157
Worcester State Hospital, 165; conditions, 166–67
Worcester Telegram, 135
Worthey, Frank and Pete, 139
Wright, George C., 49

Yale-Harvard assembly, 71
YMCA, 32, 34, 160
YouTube, 197

Zimmerman, Arthur Augustus, 41, 53, 73–74, 132
Zulu, 111, 115
Zwift, 8, 188, 190, 192, 197

ROBERT J. TURPIN is an associate professor of history and the assistant director of the honors program at Lees-McRae College. He is the author of *First Taste of Freedom: A Cultural History of Bicycle Marketing in the United States*.

The University of Illinois Press
is a founding member of the
Association of University Presses.

University of Illinois Press
1325 South Oak Street
Champaign, IL 61820–6903
www.press.uillinois.edu